Lift Every Voice and Sing

St. Louis African Americans in the Twentieth Century

Narratives Collected by Doris A. Wesley

Photographs by Wiley Price

Edited with an Introduction by Ann Morris

University of Missouri Press   Columbia and London

Library of Congress Cataloging–in–Publication Data

Lift every voice and sing : St. Louis African Americans in the
    twentieth century : narratives collected by Doris A. Wesley ;
    photographs by Wiley Price ; edited with an introduction by Ann
    Morris.
        p.   cm.
    Includes index.
    ISBN 0–8262–1253–0 (alk. paper)
    1. Afro-Americans—Missouri—Saint Louis Interviews. 2. Afro-
Americans—Missouri—Saint Louis Biography Anecdotes. 3. Afro-
Americans—Civil rights—Missouri—Saint Louis—History—20th
century Anecdotes. 4. Saint Louis (Mo.) Biography Anecdotes.
5. Saint Louis (Mo.)—Race relations Anecdotes. 6. Oral history.
I. Wesley, Doris A., 1952–   . II. Morris, Ann, 1944–   .
F474.S29N4   1999
977.8' 6600496073' 00922—dc21
[B]
                                                                99-36471
                                                                CIP

Designer: Kristie Lee
Typesetter: Crane Composition, Inc.
Printer and binder: Dai-Nippon
Typefaces: Minion and Utopia

The University of Missouri Press offers its grateful acknowledgment to the Trustees of
the Gertrude and William A. Bernoudy Foundation, to Anheuser-Busch Companies,
Inc., and to the State Historical Society of Missouri for their generous contributions in
support of the publication of this volume.

This book is dedicated to our parents and to all those who have gone before us, with gratitude for their hard work.

This book is also dedicated to our children and to all those who will come after, with a challenge to try to live up to these inspiring examples.

Lift Every Voice and Sing

Lift every voice and sing, till earth and heaven ring,
Ring with the harmonies of liberty,
Let our rejoicing rise, high as the listening skies,
Let it resound loud as the rolling sea.

Sing a song full of the faith that the dark past has taught us;
Sing a song full of the hope that the present has brought us;
Facing the rising sun, of our new day begun,
Let us march on till victory is won.

Stony the road we trod, bitter the chastening rod,
Felt in the days when hope unborn had died;
Yet with a steady beat, have not our weary feet
Come to the place for which our fathers sighed?

We have come over a way that with tears has been watered;
We have come, treading our path thro' the blood of the slaughtered,
Out from the gloomy past, till now we stand at last,
Where the white gleam of our bright star is cast.

God of our weary years, God of our silent tears,
Thou who hast brought us thus far on the way;
Thou who hast by Thy might, led us into the light,
Keep us forever in the path, we pray.

Lest our feet stray from the places, our God, where we met Thee,
Lest our hearts, drunk with the wine of the world, we forget Thee;
Shadowed beneath Thy hand, may we forever stand,
True to our God, true to our native land.

James Weldon Johnson

Contents

Alphabetical Listing of Narratives

Foreword

I am pleased that the Urban League of Metropolitan St. Louis was able to help the Western Historical Manuscript Collection at the University of Missouri–St. Louis produce the Lift Every Voice and Sing project. The Urban League's Vaughn Cultural Center proudly presented the three original exhibits of visually rich photographs and histories that lie at the heart of our culture.

The Urban League of Metropolitan St. Louis is a civil rights agency with a history that spans more than eighty years. Our goal is to equalize life's chances. We strive to teach, to train, to expand opportunities, to help people become less dependent, to make people whole. We raise people up, through education, scholarships, and job placement. We strive to equalize life's chances.

And so I found it a pleasure to read about the lives of the one hundred individuals who participated in the Lift Every Voice and Sing project. Their lives have paralleled the history of the Urban League. Their stories exemplify the hard work and the realized potential that the Urban League hopes to impart to all who use our services.

I am especially pleased that Lift Every Voice and Sing includes both the stories of St. Louis's obvious leaders and the stories of our unsung heroes. The stories of the contributions of our well-known leaders give an authenticity to the history that is presented here. But the true history of the past century, the struggle for civil rights, is best revealed in the stories of the common man and woman. It has been the goal of the Urban League to make small people whole, for small people provide the backbone of our history.

As the fifth president of the Urban League of Metropolitan St. Louis, I am proud to share these voices of humanity and these noble portraits with future generations. I hope this important historical resource will find its way into every household and school in Missouri, passing on these inspiring stories to the twenty-first century.

James H. Buford

About the Lift Every Voice and Sing Project

In 1990, Doris Wesley, reference specialist at the Western Historical Manuscript Collection at the University of Missouri–St. Louis, began tape-recording oral history interviews with St. Louis African Americans. She wanted to save their stories of growing up in a segregated city, stories that are difficult to find because so many people want to forget those times.

Wesley interviewed men and women who had grown up in the Ville, a black neighborhood that produced many great business leaders and educators. She interviewed African American pioneers in broadcasting and journalism. Finally she interviewed those recommended by others, people from all walks of life who had interesting stories and who could tell about the changes brought about by integration and the civil rights movement.

As Wesley collected these unique historical perspectives, an idea for an exhibit evolved. Wiley Price, an award-winning photojournalist at the *St. Louis American* newspaper, visited Wesley's interview subjects with her and made a black-and-white portrait of each of them. Ann Morris, associate director of the Western Historical Manuscript Collection, edited the interviews, distilling the most interesting stories and insights to capture the essence of each person and of the past. In preparing the stories for publication, she added some uniformity to the grammar and arranged the narratives in a loosely chronological order, so that the stories of earliest times come first. The full unedited transcripts and original recordings are available at the Western Historical Manuscript Collection at the University of Missouri–St. Louis.

The Vaughn Cultural Center at the Urban League of Metropolitan St. Louis has held three exhibits of Price's portraits and Wesley's narratives. Each exhibit offered an opportunity for old friends to meet again, to marvel at the ability of the photographer to capture personalities as art, and to be grateful that Wesley has saved these stories so that they may inform future generations about St. Louis and its past.

A Note from the Chancellor

The University of Missouri–St. Louis is most proud to have played a role in this historic publication. Doris Wesley and Ann Morris of the Western Historical Manuscript Collection on our campus have woven together St. Louis's rich history with the contributions and personal recollections of one hundred African American citizens. The one hundred narratives and photographs of African American men and women are a poignant legacy of courage.

The University of Missouri–St. Louis's campus reflects the rich heritage of our region. We celebrate differences through art, music, and history. Our traditional and not-so-traditional pursuits of knowledge help us to understand those differences. *Lift Every Voice and Sing* will hold a proud place in that continuing celebration.

Blanche M. Touhill

Acknowledgments

We wish to thank the following individuals and groups for their financial support, their help, and their encouragement during the collection of these stories and the preparation of the Lift Every Voice and Sing exhibits: the Missouri Arts Council; the Regional Arts Commission; Jacqueline Cecil; the *St. Louis American;* Stephen M. Coleman of Daedalus Capital LLC; the Missouri Lottery; O. J. Photo Supply, Inc.; the Richard S. Brownlee Fund of the State Historical Society of Missouri; E. Terrence Jones; and, at the University of Missouri–St. Louis, the Office of Continuing Education and Outreach, the Public Policy Research Centers, the Office of Equal Opportunity, the Center for the Humanities, the School of Education, the Department of Anthropology, the Center for Human Origin and Cultural Diversity, the Gerontology Program, and the Public Policy Administration Master's Program.

Special thanks are due to our mentors: Bennie Rodgers, John Bass, Melba Sweets, Vivian Dreer, and Norman Seay.

And last but not least, we wish to thank our partners at the Urban League of Metropolitan St. Louis, Almetta Jordan and Marsha Leonatti Boeck, and our co-conspirators in saving history at the Western Historical Manuscript Collection and the University Archives, Kenn Thomas, Zelli Fischetti, and Linda Belford.

Doris A. Wesley, Wiley Price, Ann Morris

Lift Every Voice **and Sing**

Introduction

In 1900 James Weldon Johnson wrote "Lift Every Voice and Sing," and his brother, John Rosamond Johnson, set it to music. They taught the song to a chorus of five hundred schoolchildren in their hometown of Jacksonville, Florida, and the children performed it for a celebration of Abraham Lincoln's birthday. "Lift Every Voice and Sing" touched a chord in many souls, for long after the Johnsons had forgotten about it, the children continued to sing it and pass it on. It is now known throughout the country as the "Negro National Anthem."[1]

Inspired by the words of James Weldon Johnson's song, this collection of memories uses the voices of one hundred St. Louis African Americans to tell a history of St. Louis that has not been told before, the story of a segregated city in the twentieth century and the changes brought about by integration and the civil rights movement.

The battle to end segregation in St. Louis was waged with meetings, with lawsuits, with sit-ins, with picket lines, with politics, with education, and with everyday acts of integrity and heroism. The stories gathered here record the struggles, the heartbreak, the anger, the strategies, and the accomplishments associated with that battle.

In 1900 St. Louis bustled with more than half a million people. It ranked as the fourth largest city in the country, and almost 7 percent of its population was African American. Within that 7 percent lay the whole panorama of Negro America: musicians, educators, Pullman porters, steelworkers, postal workers, businessmen, laborers, domestics, politicians, doctors, lawyers, preachers, and the inspiration for ragtime, jazz, gospel, and the blues.

St. Louis spread west from the levee, where stevedores unloaded wholesale commercial goods from riverboats on the Mississippi. In 1901, civic booster H. B. Wandell described the mercantile glory of St. Louis in his *500 Facts about St. Louis: The Story of a Great City in a Nutshell.* He said St. Louis was the largest hardwood lumber market, the largest horse and mule market, and the greatest distribution center for agricultural implements in the world; it was the largest millinery market, the largest inland coffee distributing center, and the largest receiving and shipping market for fruits in America. He claimed St. Louis led the United States in the manufacturing of boots, shoes, hats, caps, gloves, blue jeans, saddles, harnesses, trunks, bags, chairs, coffins, chemicals, tobacco, and crackers; St. Louis possessed the largest brewery, the largest brickworks, the largest leadworks, the largest iron-rail factory, the largest sewer-pipe factory, the largest terra-cotta factory, the largest stove factory, the largest tinware-stamping plant, the largest streetcar factory, the largest boot and shoe factory, the two largest tobacco factories, the largest hardware company, the largest woodenware company, the largest drug company, and the largest electric plant in the United States. And he ranked St. Louis as the second city in the production of wheat flour, the third largest grocery market, the

1. James Weldon Johnson, *Along This Way: The Autobiography of James Weldon Johnson* (1933; rpt. New York: Viking Press, 1968), 154–55.

third largest dry-goods market, and the third largest furniture manufacturing center in America.[2]

In 1901 twenty-four railroads terminated in St. Louis. Railways from the east crossed the Mississippi on Eads Bridge, a bridge owned by the Terminal Railroad Association, whose high tariffs were causing more and more rail traffic to cross the river at Chicago. Railways from the east and those from the west met at St. Louis's Union Station, and their tracks streamed west through Mill Creek Valley. Wholesale houses and heavy industries spread north and south along the riverfront and west along the railroad tracks.

Directly west of the levee, ten-, twelve-, and sixteen-story buildings pierced the sky in the center of the city. Brick, stone, and shingle-style mansions of the wealthy surrounded Forest Park and Tower Grove Park at the west end of the city. A large German population occupied well-kept brick row houses in the southern half of the city. Italians lived on the Hill south of Forest Park. Immigrants from Eastern Europe filled the central corridor and the area around the breweries and Soulard Market where South Broadway overlooked the Mississippi River. The Irish lived on the north side of the city, where they had created a Democratic political machine. African Americans lived in the remaining residential areas, including the tenements in the central part of the city and Mill Creek Valley and in the neighborhood called Elleardsville, or the "Ville," just north of the Central West End.[3]

For most of its residents at the turn of the century, St. Louis was filled with opportunity. But for the 7 percent of the population who were African American, St. Louis remained very much like the South. Missouri had been a slave state before the Civil War but stayed in the Union during the rebellion. After the war, St. Louis and Missouri continued to observe many of the customs and practices of the South. All public schools in Missouri were segregated by law, and most public facilities, including restaurants, hotels, department stores, theaters, and hospitals, were segregated in practice.[4]

The long fight to end segregation in Missouri began during the last half of the nineteenth century. Two great African American leaders, James Milton Turner and Charleton Tandy, rose to prominence in the Union Army and continued the battle for equality after the Civil War ended. As secretary of the Missouri Equal Rights League, the first black political organization in Missouri, Turner traveled throughout the state advocating education for blacks and the right to vote for black men. He knew that blacks needed to vote to protect their freedom.[5] At the same time, Charleton Tandy fought to enforce an 1868 court injunction that ended segregation on St. Louis streetcars. Sometimes he even went so far as to grab a trolley horse's reins so the driver could not pass up a black passenger. His vigilance through the turn of the century kept public transportation integrated in St. Louis, while segregated trains, streetcars, and, later, buses operated throughout the rest of the South.[6]

The 1904 World's Fair

In 1904 many blacks traveled from the South for the first time to visit the St. Louis World's Fair. They came to see the excitement, the electric lights, and the exhibits from all over the world. And they came because they heard there were jobs available at the fair. The organizers planned for the fair to be open to all. A black committee prepared to celebrate Emancipation Day at the World's Fair on August 1, 1904. However, concessionaires and military regiments from the South refused to participate at the fair unless dining facilities and campgrounds were segregated. Rather than lose the participation of the South, fair organizers established an Afro-American Bureau, which provided water, rest rooms, and a place to meet for blacks attending the fair. The adverse publicity surrounding these changes caused the black committee to cancel the Emancipation Day celebration.[7]

However, blacks attending the 1904 World's Fair found that press reports of discrimination had been exaggerated. The excitement of the fair and the opportunities available in the city

2. H. B. Wandell, *500 Facts about St. Louis: The Story of a Great City in a Nutshell* (St. Louis: H. B. Wandell, 1901).

3. Lawrence O. Christensen, "Black St. Louis: A Study in Race Relations, 1865–1916" (Ph.D. diss., University of Missouri, 1972), 97.

4. Ibid., 189; Herman Dreer, "Negro Leadership in St. Louis: A Study in Race Relations" (Ph.D. diss., University of Chicago, 1955), 8–10.

5. Lorenzo J. Greene, Gary R. Kremer, and Antonio F. Holland, *Missouri's Black Heritage: Revised Edition* (Columbia: University of Missouri Press, 1993), 97; Christensen, "Black St. Louis," 181.

6. John A. Wright, *Discovering African American St. Louis: A Guide to Historic Sites* (St. Louis: Missouri Historical Society Press, 1994), 65; Christensen, "Black St. Louis," 195.

7. Christensen, "Black St. Louis," 199–203.

attracted many African Americans to move to St. Louis. They secured jobs as laborers, servants, draymen, teamsters, porters, hod carriers, barbers, laundresses, teachers, boardinghouse keepers, and seamstresses. Blacks worked for the Pullman Company, the U.S. Post Office, the Liggett and Myers Tobacco Company, and Scullin Steel. It was a time of great migration.[8]

African Americans moved into the neighborhoods that whites were leaving. During the last decade of the nineteenth century, the extension of street railways into the suburbs, in addition to the existing commuter trains, led real estate developers to build many moderately priced houses in the suburbs. Middle-class and upper-middle-class white families escaped the noise and pollution of ever expanding industries in the city by commuting to work from the suburbs.[9]

The Neighborhoods

Real estate developer Elezy Meacham created two suburban subdivisions for African Americans: Meacham Park near Kirkwood in 1892, and Elmwood Park near Overland in 1893.[10] In addition, there were small black communities in suburbs such as Kirkwood, Webster Groves, Clayton, Richmond Heights, Kinloch, Black Jack, Ballwin, and Chesterfield. But most African Americans lived in the central corridor of St. Louis, on both sides of Market Street, and in Mill Creek Valley. The central corridor, about twelve blocks wide, began at the riverfront and extended westward, with tenements crowded between the ironworks, the tobacco factories, hotels, businesses, public buildings, restaurants, taverns, dance halls, breweries, railroad yards, and smoke-belching factories.[11]

At the same time, tenements intermingled with fine old houses in Mill Creek Valley, from Eighteenth Street to Grand Avenue and from the railroad tracks to Olive Street. Rich and poor, black and white, lived in Mill Creek Valley at the turn of the century, but whites were moving west. The poorest tenants of Mill Creek used outdoor privies and got their water from hydrants between the two- and three-story brick buildings. Black businesses lined Market Street across from City Hall,

including the first black hardware store and C. K. Robinson's Printing Company.[12]

When the nights hung hot and humid, down the streets, across the tracks, through the open doors of nightclubs and honky-tonk taverns came the sound of Mill Creek music: ragtime, jazz, the blues. At Tom Turpin's Rosebud Bar on Market, at Jim McMinn's Club Four Roses farther west, at the Gilt Edge Bar, the Hurrah Sporting Club, and the Four Deuces Saloon, Scott Joplin, Tom Turpin, Blind Boone, Joe Jordan, Louis Chauvin, Charlie Warfield, Roosevelt Sykes, Henry Townsend, and others played the piano; and W. C. Handy wrote the "St. Louis Blues." Pool halls, crap games, prostitutes, smoke and whiskey, saxophones, fiddles, and barrelhouse banjos blended with the kerosene lamps and the red lights on Chestnut Street. Frankie killed Johnnie in a lodging house on Targee Street, and the next night Bill Dooley wrote a song about it. Josephine Baker grew up in Mill Creek Valley and sang and danced at the Booker T. Washington Theater, before she became famous in Paris, in 1925, at the age of nineteen. Charles Turpin owned the Booker T. Washington Theater at 2100 Market Street, where great performers such as Eubie Blake, Ethel Waters, and Bessie Smith entertained black St. Louis.[13]

Just south of Mill Creek Valley, black families moved into the Compton Hill neighborhood as railroad car shops, the Liggett and Myers Tobacco Company, the Independent Packing Company, the Funston Nut Company, and other industries moved west along Chouteau Avenue and the railroad tracks, and as white families moved to the suburbs. The Compton Hill neighborhood stretched from Jefferson Avenue west to Grand Avenue and from Papin Avenue south to Park Avenue. The two-story brick town houses, built in the late nineteenth century, had tall windows, stone foundations, and small front yards with wrought-iron fences. Here and there, one-story brick houses with flat roofs interrupted the skyline. Mom-and-pop grocery stores, confectioneries, and churches were sprinkled through the neighborhood. Dr. E. T. Taylor owned the pharmacy at Compton and Chouteau. Men walked to work at industries along the railroad, women shelled nuts for the Funston Nut Company, and, when the 9:00 P.M. whistle blew at the Liggett and Myers Tobacco Company, children knew it was

8. Ibid., 167, 175; Dreer, "Negro Leadership in St. Louis," 7.
9. Dreer, "Negro Leadership in St. Louis," 8; Christensen, "Black St. Louis," 133.
10. St. Louis County Recorder of Deeds Plat Book 3, pp. 33, 41.
11. Christensen, "Black St. Louis," 124–25.

12. Wright, *Discovering African American St. Louis,* 23; conversation with Bennie Rodgers, 1997.
13. Wright, *Discovering African American St. Louis,* 23–27.

time to go home. Henry Armstrong, the boxing champion, grew up in Compton Hill, Josephine Baker's mother moved to Compton Hill, and Quincy Troupe and his brothers played amateur baseball for the Compton Hill Cubs on the ball field at Compton and Chouteau.[14]

North of what is now called the Central West End, a prosperous black community developed in Elleardsville, a neighborhood named for Charles Elleard, who owned a large nursery there after the Civil War. African Americans settled among German and Irish immigrants on the quiet, rural, tree-lined streets. Successful teachers, steelworkers, postal workers, and professionals bought or built modest one-story frame cottages, brick bungalows, and flat-roofed houses with manicured lawns and beautiful flower and vegetable gardens. They called the area the "Ville," and by the 1920s a self-contained community for blacks had blossomed there, with grocery stores on most corners, drugstores, ice cream parlors, bakeries, barbershops, a dry-goods store, a furniture store, a tailor, a cleaners, restaurants, a filling station, and craftsman-style duplexes and apartments.[15]

Sumner High School

By 1906 the St. Louis Board of Education was providing twelve elementary schools and one high school for blacks.[16] African American students came from all over St. Louis and from other towns and suburbs to attend Sumner High School, at Fifteenth and Walnut, an educational oasis amid the train yards, industries, pool halls, and other "demoralizing establishments" east of Mill Creek Valley. The Board of Education planned to enlarge Sumner, but the Reverend George Stevens of Central Baptist Church and other black ministers and lawyers petitioned the board to relocate Sumner to the more wholesome atmosphere of the Ville. In 1910, Sumner High School moved into a beautiful Georgian revival brick building, designed by William B. Ittner, on Cottage Avenue in the Ville.[17]

14. Conversation with Bennie Rodgers, 1997.

15. Carolyn Hewes Toft, *The Ville: The Ethnic Heritage of an Urban Neighborhood* (St. Louis: Landmarks Association of St. Louis, 1975), 15.

16. Fifty-second Annual Report of the Board of Education, St. Louis Public Schools, 1906.

17. Toft, *The Ville*, 9–10; George Stevens, *The History of Central Baptist Church* (St. Louis: King Publishing Co., 1927), 16–17 (Collection 28, Western Historical Manuscript Collection, University of Missouri–St. Louis.)

When the St. Louis Board of Education established Sumner High School in 1875, it was the first high school for blacks established by a public school district west of the Mississippi. A few years earlier, in 1868, veterans of the Sixty-second U.S. Colored Infantry had established Lincoln Institute in Jefferson City as a private high school and teacher-training institute for blacks. The Missouri Legislature began funding Lincoln Institute in 1870, but it still required a small tuition.

In the North schools were integrated. But in the South schools were segregated, and most school boards did not provide an education for black children beyond the eighth grade. Sumner remained the only public high school for blacks in the St. Louis area until 1928, and it became a paragon of education. African American scientists and intellectuals with advanced degrees from great universities, including Harvard and Yale, could not teach at most universities. So they taught at black colleges in the South or at Sumner. Many of the faculty at Sumner had master's degrees, and some had doctorates. Black families from the South sometimes arranged for their children to live with relatives in St. Louis during their high school years, so that they could benefit from the outstanding education provided by Sumner High School.[18]

Segregation

As St. Louis's African American population increased, and as blacks moved into the western residential neighborhoods of the city, white property owners created restrictive covenants in their real estate deeds forbidding the sale or rental of the property to blacks. These covenants were especially prevalent in the neighborhoods surrounding the Ville. For several years whites, led by members of the Real Estate Exchange, lobbied the St. Louis Board of Aldermen to pass an ordinance prohibiting the sale or rental of property to blacks anywhere in the city unless blacks already occupied 75 percent of the property in the same block. The Board of Aldermen would not pass the ordinance, so the segregationists petitioned for a referendum election. In that election in 1916, voters passed the segregation ordinance by an overwhelming majority. The St.

18. Vashon High School was established in St. Louis in 1928, and Douglass High School was established the same year in Webster Groves. Ann Morris and Henrietta Ambrose, *North Webster: A Photographic History of a Black Community* (Bloomington: Indiana University Press, 1993), 10, 20.

Louis building commissioner did not enforce the ordinance, and in 1917 the U.S. Supreme Court ruled that a residential segregation ordinance is unconstitutional.[19]

Meanwhile, other factors were straining race relations in St. Louis. The federal Immigration Act of 1917 limited immigration for the first time, by barring some immigrants, including those who could not read. The decrease in the number of new immigrants increased the demand for skilled and semiskilled Negro labor in big cities.[20] World War I took men from their jobs to fight in Europe, and many African Americans migrated north to St. Louis during the war to fill those jobs. Blacks left the South to escape lynchings, the Ku Klux Klan, injustice in the courts, poor wages, a prejudiced credit system, poor schools, and the failure of cotton crops due to the boll weevil.[21]

On July 2, 1917, racial tension exploded in the bloody, fiery East St. Louis Race Riot. Throughout the United States, interracial violence flared up eighteen times during the World War I era, from 1915 to 1919, as the influx of Negro migrants from the South competing for low-wage jobs and housing sparked anger among white residents. In 1917 riots also broke out in Chester and Philadelphia, Pennsylvania, and Houston, Texas. But the riot in East St. Louis, Illinois, remains the most serious race riot of the century.[22]

East St. Louis was an unpleasant place to begin with. Railroads, low taxes, and cheap fuel turned East St. Louis into an ugly industrial offshoot of St. Louis, across the river. Thousands of low-wage workers labored in the stockyards, the meatpacking plants, and the manufacturing industries: Swift, Armour, Morris Meat Packing Company, the Aluminum Ore Company, the Missouri Malleable Iron Company. The companies filled the air with dirt, soot, noise, and horrid odors. Workers and their families crowded together in small wooden shacks close to the factories.[23]

In 1916 and 1917, when workers tried to organize labor unions to address their low wages, the companies recruited and imported large numbers of African Americans from the South to replace union agitators. Rumors and exaggerations in the local press inflamed racial tension. Beginning in May 1917, the mobs of angry union men and the incidents of interracial beatings, shootings, and vandalism escalated to such a point that Mayor Fred Mollman called in the National Guard.[24]

On July 1, a drive-by shooting in a Negro neighborhood caused the black residents to retaliate with gunfire when a second car drove through the troubled area. Those shots killed two police officers who were riding in the car. The next day, newspaper accounts of the incident and the bullet-riddled car, parked in front of City Hall, incited a growing mob to fury. Blacks were pulled from streetcars and beaten. Gangs set black homes on fire and shot entire families as they ran from their burning houses. Fires lit the night sky with a terrible glow as thousands fled across the bridges to St. Louis, where city officials and the Red Cross provided help. Beatings continued, and fires flared for several weeks. Rioters killed more than 100 people and destroyed 312 buildings.

Later that summer black leaders in Harlem sponsored a silent parade through New York City to draw attention to the East St. Louis holocaust and President Wilson's lack of response. In October and November, a congressional investigation determined that the riot had been caused by the actions of employers, labor organizers, politicians, and public officials who turned their backs instead of preventing or stopping the violence. As a result of the riot, many African Americans left East St. Louis forever, moving to St. Louis and Kinloch, a small suburb northwest of St. Louis.[25]

By 1920 African Americans made up 9 percent of the population of St. Louis.[26] As the population grew, another example of racial discrimination developed. Although St. Louis's Protestant churches had always been segregated, until 1917 the Catholic churches had welcomed black parishioners. However, between 1917 and 1920, Archbishop John Glennon directed Catholic priests to send all African Americans to St. Elizabeth's Catholic Church on Pine Street. For nearly thirty years, Catholic schools

19. Toft, *The Ville*, 7; Christensen, "Black St. Louis," 228, 262, 266.

20. Ivan Chermayeff, Fred Wasserman, and Mary J. Shapiro, *Ellis Island: An Illustrated History of the Immigrant Experience* (New York: Macmillan, 1991), 104.

21. Dreer, "Negro Leadership in St. Louis," 7; Stevens, *History of Central Baptist Church.*

22. Elliot Rudwick, *Race Riot at East St. Louis, July 2, 1917* (Urbana: University of Illinois Press, 1982), 4.

23. Ibid., 5.

24. Ibid., 16–30.

25. Ibid., 134–36, 138–41; Ernest Kirschten, *Catfish and Crystal* (New York: Doubleday, 1960), 368–75; Wright, *Discovering African American St. Louis*, 125.

26. *Fourteenth Census of the United States, 1920* (Washington, D.C.: U.S. Government Printing Office, 1922), 2:47.

and churches were segregated. Glennon claimed he did not want to offend wealthy patrons of the church.[27]

Business and Institutional Landmarks

In spite of racial tension and because of discrimination, St. Louis African Americans, one small group at a time, seldom together, but never relenting, continued to strive for advancement, integration, and for the equal protection guaranteed to all by the U.S. Constitution. For instance, in 1910 blacks and whites organized the Committee for Social Services among Colored People to help black migrants from the South. In 1918 the committee became the Urban League of St. Louis. St. Louisans established a branch of the National Association for the Advancement of Colored People (NAACP) in 1914.[28] Joseph Mitchell began a weekly newspaper, the *St. Louis Argus*, in 1912. In 1916, after St. Louisans passed the segregation ordinance, Mitchell and theater owner Charles Turpin and law partners Homer G. Phillips and George L. Vaughn formed the Citizens Liberty League to focus on specific political goals. By 1920 the league had accomplished many of its goals, including electing the first African American to the Missouri General Assembly: tall, thin Walthall Moore, who walked everywhere he went.[29] Because the St. Louis Bar Association excluded African Americans from membership, black lawyers organized the Mound City Bar Association in 1918. George L. Vaughn was the first president.[30]

African American businesses and institutions flourished. In 1917 Annie Turnbo Pope Malone, probably the richest self-made woman in Missouri, built Poro College at the corner of St. Ferdinand and Pendleton Avenues in the Ville. Annie Malone manufactured Poro System beauty products, and her college, housed in a three-story classical revival brick building, included an instructional department, a beauty parlor, offices, an auditorium, a cafeteria, a dormitory, an apartment, and a roof garden for summer parties. The auditorium was used for performances of the Poro Symphony Orchestra and as a movie theater. Storefronts on the Pendleton Avenue side contained a barbershop, the Poro Ice Cream Parlor, and a millinery shop.[31]

In 1919 the Pine Street YMCA opened at the corner of Ewing and Pine in Mill Creek Valley. Several branches of the YMCA had served St. Louis African Americans before the Pine Street Y was built. In 1887 the first YMCA for blacks met in St. Paul AME Church at Eleventh and Green Street. It moved to 1408 Morgan Street, then to 1739 Lucas, then to 2633 Lucas, and finally it met at a previous location on Pine Street. The new Pine Street Y, under the leadership of the Reverend James E. Cook, surpassed them all, becoming a dynamic social center for African Americans. It offered a swimming pool, a gymnasium, meeting rooms, a cafeteria, dormitories, Camp Rivercliff, and the Y Circus. Reverend Cook also brought distinguished lecturers to speak at the Public Affairs Forum. Pullman porters from out of town stayed at the Pine Street Y, which was less expensive than the Booker T. Washington Hotel at Jefferson and Pine, where black musicians stayed.[32]

In 1920 attorney and politician Homer G. Phillips asked Mayor Henry Kiel to assign black physicians to the staff of the City Hospital to treat black patients. Mayor Kiel responded by opening City Hospital No. 2 in the old Barnes Hospital at Garrison and Lawton in Mill Creek Valley. Phillips continued to press for a better city hospital for blacks, especially when his political machine was asked to support the city's $87 million bond issue in 1923. Black doctors treated private patients at Peoples Hospital at Theresa and Pine, established in 1894 as the Provident Hospital, and at the Catholic St. Mary's Infirmary on Papin, opened in 1922.[33]

In 1922 the St. Louis Colored Orphans Home, founded

27. Dreer, "Negro Leadership in St. Louis," 88; Donald J. Kemper, "Catholic Integration in St. Louis, 1935–1947," *Missouri Historical Review* 73 (October 1978): 1–22.

28. Wright, *Discovering African American St. Louis,* 51, 92.

29. Dreer, "Negro Leadership in St. Louis," 96, 98–103.

30. "Black Professionals in the Mound City," *Proud* 12, no. 1 (1981): 21; Herman Dreer Papers, Collection 167, folder 13, Western Historical Manuscript Collection, University of Missouri–St. Louis.

31. When Mrs. Malone moved her business to Chicago in 1930, the Poro College building became a hotel; Toft, *The Ville,* 12.

32. Wright, *Discovering African American St. Louis,* 35; YMCA Records, Collection 473, folders 43, 60, 64, Western Historical Manuscript Collection, University of Missouri–St. Louis. Conversation with Bennie Rodgers, 1997.

33. Dreer, "Negro Leadership in St. Louis," 146–49; Wright, *Discovering African American St. Louis,* 32; oral history interview with Dr. Frank Richards, 1994, Western Historical Manuscript Collection, University of Missouri–St. Louis.

in 1888, moved to the Ville. The community celebrated the dedication of the large colonial-style building on May 1 with a May Day Parade down Aldine Avenue and up Cote Brilliante. Annie Malone donated the land and money for the new building, and she served on the board of directors from 1917 to 1943, even though she moved her business to Chicago in 1930. In 1946 the board renamed the institution the Annie Malone Children's Home. The Annie Malone Parade and the accompanying festivities, still held on the first weekend in May, have become a popular tradition and continue to raise funds to support the children's home.[34]

The Peoples Finance Building, at 11 North Jefferson, in the heart of Mill Creek Valley, opened in 1926. Doctors, lawyers, photographers, the J. Roy Terry School of Music, the Moving Picture Operators' Union, the Brotherhood of Sleeping Car Porters, and the NAACP had offices in that important professional building. The first floor housed the Peoples Finance Bank, Ernest Harris's Pharmacy, the *St. Louis American,* the Inge Real Estate Company, and the National Baptist Association and Bookstore. Mrs. Kittrell's Restaurant was in the basement, and there was a ballroom on the top floor. Black leaders gathered in the NAACP office to plan strategies for civil rights battles, especially when NAACP attorney Thurgood Marshall came to town.[35]

Jazz, Swing, Policy, and Baseball

Across the street from the Peoples Finance Building, Jesse Johnson owned the DeLuxe Restaurant at 10 North Jefferson. The ever-popular DeLuxe Restaurant attracted a mixed clientele of blacks and whites. Next door Johnson owned a shoeshine parlor and the Deluxe Cab Company, and upstairs he operated Club 49, a private club where Duke Ellington, Billy Strayhorn, Juan Tizol, and Herb Jeffries held jam sessions and wrote music. Johnson owned a record store at Twenty-second and Market, one of the first in town, and he scouted talent for several record labels, including Victor and Decca. He promoted dances on the *St. Paul* steamboat on Monday nights and dances at the Coliseum at Jefferson and Washington, at the Castle Ballroom at Ewing and Olive, and at Sauter's Park on South Broadway; and he brought Ella Fitzgerald to Rodenberg's Grove across from O'Fallon Park. When Johnson brought big bands to town, he drove them through the city in the back of an open truck, while the band played music to attract a crowd.[36]

During the 1930s and 1940s people flocked to the Elk's Rest at Cardinal and Olive, to eat in the open-air garden or swing to Eddie Randle's dance music in the ballroom on the second floor. Billy Swanson opened the West End Waiters Club on Vandeventer, where musicians such as Ben Webster, Harry Carney, and Johnny Hodges held jam sessions and a bottle of beer sold for fifteen cents. Swanson, a leading Democratic politician, had been a bootlegger during Prohibition.[37]

During Prohibition many people held "Saturday night rent parties" on Chouteau and Lucas Avenues and in every neighborhood where blacks lived. The host charged admission to collect money to pay his rent, and he served bootleg whiskey and invited someone to play the piano or the guitar and sing the blues.

After Prohibition ended, nightclub owners got liquor licenses, and many of them ran "after-hours clubs," bringing entertainers from out of town and staying open long after the hour when liquor establishments were required to close. Lenny Johnson had an after-hours place at Twenty-first and Gratiot, where he served both alcohol and water by the pitcher, and the clientele mixed their own drinks.[38]

African Americans also established private clubs, including the Broadway Sports Club, the Twentieth Century Club, the Foxes, the Lambs Club, and the Vagabonds. Many of these exclusive private clubs disappeared in the sixties when white establishments such as the Tenderloin Room at the Chase Hotel began admitting blacks.[39]

During the Depression, the Policy Game brought a spark of excitement and hope to many people. Twice a day men came through the black neighborhoods with strips of paper, about a foot long, with numbers printed on them. People paid fifteen or twenty-five cents, or maybe even fifty cents, to bet on the

34. Toft, *The Ville,* 13; *Washington University Alumni News,* winter 1989, 4–5.
35. Conversation with Bennie Rodgers, 1997.
36. Herman Dreer Papers, Collection 167, folder 13; conversation with Bennie Rodgers, 1997; conversation with Bill Greensmith, 1997.
37. Conversation with Bennie Rodgers, 1997.
38. Oral history interview with Bennie Rodgers, 1997, Western Historical Manuscript Collection, University of Missouri–St. Louis.
39. Ibid.

numbers. The policy men turned in their numbers receipts at a hotel in the Mill Creek area where a machine chose the winning numbers. The policy men collected the money for the winning numbers and returned to pay their clients. The Policy Game was much like bingo or the lottery, except that it was run exclusively by blacks. People were excited to win three numbers, because they received forty or fifty dollars, which in those days was enough to buy rice and bread for a week. The Policy Game began before World War I, and although it began to wane in the fifties, it did not disappear until the numbers runners died and the Missouri Lottery took its place.[40]

Baseball drew crowds during the summer afternoons and evenings. The professional St. Louis Giants began playing at Finley Park, at Grand and Laclede, in 1909. In 1920, the Giants and seven other midwestern teams formed the Negro National League. In 1921, a new group of owners—Richard Kent, owner of Calumet Cab Co., Dr. Sam Shepard, and Dr. G. B. Key—purchased the Giants and renamed the team the St. Louis Stars. In 1922 the St. Louis Stars moved to Stars Park near Compton and Market. Fans still remember first baseman Willie Bobo, third baseman Branch Russell, shortstop Devil Wells, and outfielder James "Cool Papa" Bell, one of the fastest men ever to play baseball. They played the Kansas City Monarchs, the Birmingham Black Barons, the Chicago American Giants, the Detroit Stars, and the Memphis Red Sox at Stars Park, and the crowds in the stands went wild when a right-handed player hit a home run over the trolley barn that cut into left field. In 1929 Stars Park installed the first permanent lights for night baseball in the country. The St. Louis Stars won the Negro National League Championship in 1928, 1930, and 1931. But after 1931 the team broke up because of the Depression. The St. Louis Stars reorganized to play in the Negro American League, but they were never as good as before, and ball fans preferred amateur baseball on Saturday and Sunday afternoons, watching the Scullin Mules at Tandy Park and the Compton Hill Cubs at Compton and Chouteau. About a year after Jackie Robinson broke the color barrier in baseball in 1947, Quincy Troupe, catcher for the Compton Hill Cubs, became a scout for the St. Louis Browns.[41]

Early Civil Rights Activities

The first issue of the *St. Louis American* hit the streets on March 17, 1928. St. Louis now had two black weekly newspapers, the *St. Louis American* and the *St. Louis Argus.* The *St. Louis Palladium,* an earlier black weekly, lasted from 1897 to 1911. Attorney Nathan Young ran the *St. Louis American* and wrote the editorials. Young hired Nathaniel A. Sweets, a graduate of Lincoln University, as the business manager, and Sweets eventually became publisher. The *St. Louis American* preached reform, while the *Argus* became more conservative. When A. Philip Randolph tried to organize the Brotherhood of Sleeping Car Porters in 1928, the Pullman Company offered large sums of money to the *Argus* and the *American* if they would avoid support of Randolph and his union. The *American* declined and covered Randolph's story. The *Argus* published articles against the Brotherhood of Sleeping Car Porters, paid for as advertisements by the Pullman Company.[42]

By 1930 African Americans made up 11 percent of the 821,960 people in St. Louis.[43] In 1931, the *St. Louis American* began its "Don't Buy Where You Can't Work" campaign, encouraging blacks to support businesses that hired African Americans. The campaign led to the boycotting and picketing of a new Woolworth's Five and Ten Cent Store on Franklin Avenue (now Easton) in 1931. The store manager had refused to hire black salesclerks, even though most of his customers were black. By early summer the first black economic picket in St. Louis had achieved its goal: the store manager hired two black salesclerks. With help from David Grant, an attorney, and Theodore McNeal, a field organizer for the Brotherhood of Sleeping Car Porters, the picketers organized the Colored Clerks Circle in 1933, under the leadership of Frank Jones. The Colored Clerks Circle picketed other stores on Franklin Avenue to open employment to blacks in that neighborhood.[44]

40. Ibid.
41. Robert W. Peterson, *Only the Ball Was White* (Englewood Cliffs, N.J.: Prentice Hall, 1970), 257, 267, 269; Wright, *Discovering African American St. Louis,* 54; conversation with Bennie Rodgers, 1997.

42. Oral history interviews with Judge Nathan Young, 1970, N. A. Sweets, 1970, and Theodore McNeal, 1970, Western Historical Manuscript Collection, University of Missouri–St. Louis; Wright, *Discovering African American St. Louis,* 59.
43. *Fifteenth Census of the United States, 1930* (Washington, D.C.: U.S. Government Printing Office, 1933), 2:71.
44. Oral history interviews with Nathan Young, 1970, and David Grant, 1970, Western Historical Manuscript Collection, University of Missouri–St. Louis; conversation with Bennie Rodgers, 1997.

On June 18, 1931, civil rights suffered a blow when two assailants shot and killed Homer G. Phillips as he waited for a streetcar on the corner of Aubert and Delmar, near his home. Law partners Phillips and Vaughn had organized the campaign against the Segregation Ordinance of 1916 and had helped organize the Citizens Liberty League the same year. Phillips managed George Vaughn's unsuccessful campaign for Congress in 1920. He persuaded city officials to establish City Hospital No. 2 in 1920, and he continued to press for a better city hospital for blacks. And Phillips proposed that African Americans divide their votes between Republicans and Democrats, so the parties would compete for their votes, rather than taking their votes for granted. Recent historians suggest that Phillips was killed because of a disagreement over his professional fees, but the police never solved his murder.[45]

Politics and Patronage

In 1932 St. Louis African Americans decided to flex their political muscle. Initially, black St. Louisans had supported the Republican Party out of loyalty to Abraham Lincoln and hatred for the anti-Lincoln landowning Democrats in the South. At the turn of the century Republican President Theodore Roosevelt insisted on patronage jobs for blacks and supported an antilynching law, further strengthening black support.[46] But attorney David Grant made African Americans in St. Louis realize that for all their loyalty, blacks had received nothing from Republican city officials, not even the new hospital that had been part of a successful 1923 bond issue. In 1932 Grant convinced many blacks to vote for Bernard Dickmann, the Democratic candidate for mayor, who promised to build that hospital for African Americans. Dickmann became the first Democratic mayor of St. Louis in twenty-four years and immediately began work on the new city hospital in the Ville. Dickmann appointed David Grant assistant city counselor. Because of his friendship with Democratic President Franklin Delano Roosevelt, Dickmann obtained many public works programs for St. Louis. The

PWA (Public Works Administration), the WPA (Works Progress Administration), the CCC (Civilian Conservation Corps), and the NYA (National Youth Administration) got thousands of blacks off the dole and gave them jobs they were proud of: building roads, building parks, and tutoring students to keep them in school. By the next election, in 1934, because of Mayor Dickmann and President Roosevelt, almost every African American in St. Louis had become a Democrat.[47]

Dickmann, like every large-city mayor, had many patronage jobs to award, and he passed that powerful responsibility on to those who had helped him get elected. Jordan Chambers, owner of the Peoples Undertaking Company on Franklin Avenue, used the patronage system and the many jobs available through Roosevelt's New Deal to become a very successful political boss. Chambers had an uncanny ability to organize and mobilize voters. Through his block captains, he knew the needs and interests of every voter in the Nineteenth Ward. He provided jobs, coal, and food to his constituents, and in return they registered and voted as he instructed. New York Congressman Adam Clayton Powell called Chambers one of the greatest politicians of all time. In the 1940s Chambers opened the Club Riviera on Delmar. He brought great black entertainers to perform there—Cab Calloway, Duke Ellington, Louis Armstrong, Count Basie, Sarah Vaughan, Jimmie Lunceford, Lionel Hampton, Nat King Cole, Dinah Washington, Jackie Wilson—and for almost twenty years made the Riviera one of the hottest nightspots in the country.[48]

Separate but Equal Education

Plessy v. Ferguson, the 1896 Supreme Court decision upholding the right of the state of Louisiana to segregate public transportation, established the legal basis for states to provide separate but equal facilities for the education of black students and white students. From that time on, St. Louis African Americans fought constantly to improve educational opportunities for their children. In 1918, three men from St.

45. Wright, *Discovering African American St. Louis,* 79; Dreer, "Negro Leadership in St. Louis," 102, 150, 272, 304–7; Greene, Kremer, and Holland, *Missouri's Black Heritage,* 152.
46. Christensen, "Black St. Louis," 217.

47. Oral history interview with David Grant, 1970.
48. Oral history interview with Oscar Farmer, 1994, Western Historical Manuscript Collection, University of Missouri–St. Louis.

Louis County, Frank Stone and Augustus Ewing from Webster Groves and William Jenkins from Kirkwood, filed a suit that went all the way to the Missouri Supreme Court demanding high school educations for their children and for all black children in the state of Missouri. The Missouri Supreme Court ruled that any public school district that provided a high school education for white children must provide a high school education for black children. School districts in the St. Louis area complied with the ruling by paying the tuition for their black students to attend Sumner High School.[49]

As Sumner became overcrowded, the Webster Groves school board in 1925 began creating a high school department at Douglass School, which was completed in the fall of 1928. Parents in the city lobbied for a second high school, and in 1927 the Board of Education opened Vashon High School on Laclede Avenue in Mill Creek Valley. The first class graduated from Vashon in 1928. Black parents also lobbied for a vocational high school, and in 1931 the Booker T. Washington Vocational High School opened on North Nineteenth Street. In 1937 George Vaughn stopped the Board of Education from building an elementary school on the grounds of Vashon High School, thereby saving the athletic field and keeping young children separate from teenagers.[50]

The St. Louis Board of Education operated two institutions of higher education to train teachers, mainly for the St. Louis public schools. Harris Teachers College trained white teachers, and Stowe Teachers College trained black teachers. Stowe Teachers College began in 1890 as a two-year program called the Sumner Normal Department. For years, Stowe held classes at Sumner High School. Starting in 1928, it moved to Simmons Elementary School in the Ville. After much community pressure, the Board of Education built a new Stowe Teachers College on Pendleton Avenue, across from Sumner High School and Tandy Park, in 1940. Stowe produced outstanding teachers and, because it was inexpensive, provided upward mobility for African Americans.[51]

In spite of these advances in public education and the long tradition of excellent higher educational opportunities for white students in St. Louis, there was no liberal arts college for African Americans in St. Louis. Northern churches had founded some of the great Negro colleges in the South, including Howard University, Fisk University, Talladega College, Tougaloo College, LeMoyne-Owen College, and Huston-Tillotson College, all founded by the American Missionary Association of the Congregational Church after the Civil War.[52] Many African American St. Louisans attended Lincoln University in Jefferson City, the school funded by the state of Missouri to provide a separate education for blacks, equal to the education for whites available at the University of Missouri. Whenever an African American student wanted an education in a field not taught at Lincoln, such as medicine or law, the state of Missouri paid that student's tuition to a school outside the state.

Realizing the need for a liberal arts college in St. Louis, Herman Dreer, author, historian, and educator at Sumner High School and Stowe Teachers College, opened Douglass University at 4300 West Belle, south of the Ville, in 1934. Douglass University used Sumner faculty, part time, and occasionally invited outstanding speakers, such as historian Carter G. Woodson, to lecture, until it closed in 1942.[53] Dr. Dreer's interest in African American history led him to write a Ph.D. dissertation for the University of Chicago entitled "Negro Leadership in St. Louis: A Study in Race Relations."

A major battle over education began in 1936, when Lloyd Gaines, a graduate of Vashon High School and Lincoln University, applied to the University of Missouri Law School. The University of Missouri rejected his application and offered to pay his tuition to attend law school in another state. Gaines went to the NAACP, and attorney Sidney Redmond took his case all the way to the U.S. Supreme Court. In 1939 the Supreme Court ruled that either the University of Missouri had to admit Gaines or the state had to provide a law school for blacks. The state responded by creating Lincoln University Law School in the old Poro College building in St. Louis, in the summer of 1940. Lloyd Gaines disappeared mysteriously before the law school

49. Morris and Ambrose, *North Webster,* 13.

50. Ibid., 20–21; Wright, *Discovering African American St. Louis,* 30, 49; Dreer, "Negro Leadership in St. Louis," 131, 142; conversation with Bennie Rodgers, 1997.

51. The building on Pendleton is now the Turner Middle School. Wright, *Discovering African American St. Louis,* 38, 83; oral history interview with Doris Moore Glenn, 1997, Western Historical Manuscript Collection, University of Missouri–St. Louis.

52. *United Church of Christ History and Program* (New York: United Church Press, 1978), 13.

53. Herman Dreer Papers, Collection 167, folder 4.

opened and was never heard from again.[54] Many St. Louisans attended Lincoln Law School in the Ville, until it closed in 1955.

Homer G. Phillips Hospital, another important institution of learning, opened in the Ville on February 22, 1937. Mayor Dickmann, state and federal officials, and a jubilant African American community attended the dedication. City architect Albert A. Osburg had designed the beautiful Art Deco building, and city and federal New Deal funds had built it. Interns came to Homer Phillips from medical schools all over the country, especially from the two black medical schools: Howard University Medical School in Washington, D.C., and Meharry Medical College in Nashville, Tennessee. Interns learned and practiced under the Homer Phillips medical staff and under doctors from Washington University and St. Louis University. Homer G. Phillips Hospital also provided an outstanding school of nursing.[55]

Organizations Seeking Equality

As the Great Depression continued, the Urban League and the NAACP toiled constantly to obtain jobs and equality for African Americans. From its office in the Peoples Finance Building, the NAACP reflected the militant intellectual philosophy of its first leader, W. E. B. Du Bois, and provided legal assistance to those who sought to test the constitutionality of segregation laws and practices. The Urban League emphasized vocational training and hard work, reflecting the philosophy of educator Booker T. Washington. It provided job training, employment placement, and other social services from its headquarters on Delmar. John T. Clark, director of the Urban League from 1926 to 1950, continually appealed to local industries to open jobs to blacks. He created block units to improve neighborhoods, and he encouraged black workers to organize. He also supported African American artists by sponsoring an annual art exhibit, by putting pressure on the City

Art Museum (now the Saint Louis Art Museum) to welcome black patrons and artists, and by helping to establish the People's Art Center on Delmar (now Grandel Square) in 1942.[56]

In spite of the constant pressure for more jobs, by the end of the Depression, African Americans still found jobs only in certain professions and with certain companies, and they were not allowed to join white trade unions.[57] In 1941, as the country moved closer to war with Germany, Chicago civil rights leader A. Philip Randolph, president of the Brotherhood of Sleeping Car Porters, called for a march on Washington by one hundred thousand Negroes from all over the country, seeking an end to discrimination in government, military, and defense industry jobs. Theodore McNeal and David Grant organized a St. Louis chapter of the March on Washington Movement. Fearing unfavorable publicity, or even violence, in June 1941 President Roosevelt signed Executive Order 8802, which prohibited discrimination in hiring in defense industries and in the federal government and created the Fair Employment Practices Commission to monitor hiring practices. Randolph called off the march.[58]

But the St. Louis chapter of the March on Washington Movement continued its activities, holding a huge rally at the Municipal Auditorium on August 14, 1942, attended by nine thousand people. A. Philip Randolph and David Grant inspired the crowd with eloquent speeches. During that summer, the St. Louis chapter of the March on Washington Movement picketed the United States Cartridge Company on Goodfellow and the Carter Carburetor Company on Grand, demanding more jobs and better promotions for blacks. The next year, members of the March on Washington Movement picketed Southwestern Bell Telephone Company and paid their telephone bills in pennies to protest the company's policy against hiring black telephone operators. As a result, Southwestern Bell opened an office with black employees in a black neighborhood.[59]

World War II created more gains in black employment. Well-paying jobs for African American men and women

54. Wright, *Discovering African American St. Louis,* 60; oral history interview with Sidney Redmond, 1970, Western Historical Manuscript Collection, University of Missouri–St. Louis.

55. Wright, *Discovering African American St. Louis,* 79; Greene, Kremer, and Holland, *Missouri's Black Heritage,* 152; oral history interview with Dr. Frank Richards, 1994.

56. Urban League of St. Louis Annual Reports, 1938 and 1942, Urban League of St. Louis Records, Collection 93, Western Historical Manuscript Collection, University of Missouri–St. Louis.

57. Conversation with Bennie Rodgers, 1997.

58. Louise Elizabeth Grant, "The St. Louis Unit of the March on Washington Movement: A Study in the Sociology of Conflict" (Master's thesis, Fisk University, 1944), 42–48.

59. Ibid., 49, 61; Wright, *Discovering African American St. Louis,* 14.

opened in defense industries, such as airplane manufacturer Curtiss-Wright, and many positions became available when soldiers went to war. As during World War I, African Americans from the South migrated to St. Louis to fill those positions.

Although all branches of the military were segregated during World War II, St. Louis African Americans served their country with distinction. Some served as Tuskegee Airmen, the valiant pilots who flew thousands of missions over North Africa, Sicily, Italy, the Balkans, Romania, Czechoslovakia, Austria, France, and Germany and never lost a plane of their own. And some St. Louisans drove in the famous, fearless black motor transport brigade, nicknamed the Red Ball Express, which sped across France, defying the blackout, carrying fuel and supplies to General Patton's army as it advanced into Germany before the deadly winter snow.[60]

Integration

St. Louis struggled with segregation during the 1940s. In 1943, after a violent race riot in Detroit, Michigan, Mayor Aloys Kaufmann created the Race Relations Commission, to which he appointed seventy-two St. Louis citizens. The integrated commission, headed by Edwin Meissner, owner of the St. Louis Car Company, had great potential because of the quality of its members, including community leaders such as David Grant and Theodore McNeal. However, the commission did little except promote goodwill. In January 1944, the Reverend Jasper Caston, the first African American elected to the St. Louis Board of Aldermen, introduced a bill to end discrimination in the lunchrooms at City Hall and the Municipal Court Building. The Board of Aldermen voted 22-4 to integrate the municipal lunchrooms.[61]

A larger breakthrough took place that same year. Father William Markoe, the priest of St. Elizabeth's Parish; Father Claude Heithaus, S.J., a professor of classical archaeology at St. Louis University; and black Catholics put pressure on St. Louis University to open its doors to African Americans. In the fall of 1944 St. Louis University became the first school, at any level, to integrate in Missouri, and the first university to integrate in any

of the former slave states. Father Patrick Holloran, S.J., president of St. Louis University, integrated the classrooms but did not allow blacks to attend social events. St. Louis University High School integrated in 1946, and in 1947 Archbishop Joseph Ritter ordered the other Catholic high schools to admit blacks. Catholic elementary schools integrated in the early 1950s.[62]

In 1948 attorneys David Grant, George Vaughn, and Robert Witherspoon brought a lawsuit against Washington University to force the university to admit African Americans. The lawsuit claimed that Washington University should lose its tax-exempt status on real estate owned in the city, a form of tax support, unless it was open to all. The lawsuit stalled until 1952, when students pressured the Board of Trustees to desegregate the university, and the lawyers dropped their suit.[63]

In 1944, Pearl Maddox, a widow, and Henry Wheeler, a postal worker, organized the Citizens Civil Rights Committee, a group of black and white women who sat in at lunch counters at the city's leading department stores—Stix, Baer, and Fuller; Famous-Barr; and Scruggs-Vandervoort-Barney—in an attempt to end discrimination at their lunch counters. Fred Harvey's Restaurant at Union Station had always served blacks, but otherwise it was still necessary for an African American to pack a lunch when going downtown. In 1947 another group of black and white men and women organized the St. Louis chapter of the Congress of Racial Equality (CORE), the nonviolent protest group that James Farmer had started in Chicago in 1942. The St. Louis members of CORE sat in at lunch counters in department stores, drugstores, and dime stores. The St. Louis daily newspapers did not cover those early civil rights activities, because editors did not want to inflame the public or antagonize advertisers.[64]

Soldiers returning to St. Louis after the war, with the benefits of the GI Bill of Rights and the optimism created when President Truman integrated the armed services in 1948, still met with segregation in restaurants, hotels, theaters, department

60. Morris and Ambrose, *North Webster,* 36–37.
61. Pat Adams, "Fighting for Democracy: Civil Rights during World War II," *Missouri Historical Review* 80 (October 1985): 69.

62. John M. McGuire, "Jesuits Have Left Mark on St. Louis History," *St. Louis Post-Dispatch, Everyday Magazine,* September 15, 1991.
63. Amy Pfeienberger, "The Struggle to Desegregate Washington University in the Postwar Era," *Gateway Heritage* 10 (winter 1989–1990): 23–24; oral history interview with David Grant, 1970.
64. Adams, "Fighting for Democracy"; oral history interviews with Theodore McNeal, 1970, and David Grant, 1970; Richard Dudman, "St. Louis' Silent Racial Revolution," *St. Louis Post-Dispatch* editorial, June 11, 1990; conversation with Irv and Maggie Dagen, 1995.

stores, public education, employment, and housing. In 1945 African Americans made up 13 percent of the population of St. Louis, yet they occupied only 7 percent of the housing stock. The Real Estate Exchange effectively confined blacks to certain neighborhoods by counseling whites living near those neighborhoods to put restrictive covenants in their deeds, thus prohibiting the future sale of their property to blacks.[65]

In 1945, J. D. Shelley bought the duplex at 4600 Labadie Avenue, in an attractive, integrated neighborhood. Louis Kraemer sued Shelley for violating the restrictive covenant in the deed to 4600 Labadie. Realtor James Bush hired attorney George Vaughn to defend Shelley all the way to the U.S. Supreme Court, hoping to end the use of restrictive covenants. The national office of the NAACP wanted to take over the case, but James Bush and David Grant, now president of the local NAACP, had faith in the ability and persuasive eloquence of Vaughn. In 1948 Vaughn argued Shelley's case before the U.S. Supreme Court, and the justices decided unanimously that when a court upholds a racial restrictive covenant it denies the equal protection guaranteed by the Fourteenth Amendment to the Constitution. The landmark decision in *Shelley v. Kraemer* ended the legal enforcement of racial restrictive covenants in the United States.[66]

With the end of restrictive covenants and with the postwar housing boom, African American neighborhoods expanded west and north, as whites moved to the suburbs. The area around Fairgrounds Park at Grand Avenue and Natural Bridge Road experienced dramatic change, and so the use of the park began to change. The St. Louis Parks Department observed an unofficial policy of segregating playgrounds, community centers, and swimming pools, while no longer segregating picnic areas, golf courses, or tennis courts. As a neighborhood changed, officials changed the policy for the area's recreation facilities.

During the summer of 1949 a new municipal swimming pool opened in the suburb of Webster Groves, and black residents of Webster Groves decided to sue the city for permission to use the pool. A court injunction against operating the pool for whites only and the intransigence of Webster Groves city

officials kept the pool closed for three years. But in 1949, as that battle was just beginning, reporters asked how such a situation would be handled at the Fairgrounds Park swimming pool. St. Louis city officials said they would open the pool to African Americans. Newspapers and radio gave extensive coverage to this policy change, and on June 21, 1949, when black youths arrived to swim, a crowd of white teenagers and adults gathered outside the pool fence and yelled threats at the swimmers. Park officials had to summon police to escort the black youths out of the park. By evening, when other blacks came to swim, a huge crowd had gathered. Many boys carried clubs or baseball bats, and grown men encouraged them to fight. A riot ensued, and the crowd grew from five hundred to five thousand, as people getting off streetcars to attend the Cardinals baseball game at nearby Sportsman's Park joined the crowd. Police arrested seven people and hospitalized twelve for knife wounds or injuries caused by beatings. When the pool reopened later that summer, the policy of integration remained, and police maintained the peace.[67]

Although change was painful, lack of change was worse. By 1952, something had to be done about the overcrowding in the black public schools. David Grant carried a child's coffin as he led a group of parents picketing the school board, and Josephine Baker returned to St. Louis for a sold-out performance at Kiel Auditorium to benefit the schools. She insisted that the management of Kiel Auditorium allow an integrated audience, and she did not miss the opportunity to chastise the city for its segregated hotels.[68]

The schools finally changed. In 1954, Thurgood Marshall, head of the NAACP's legal staff, argued the case of *Brown v. Board of Education of Topeka* before the U.S. Supreme Court, which ruled that "separate educational facilities are inherently unequal." In the fall of 1954, the St. Louis Board of Education began to integrate its schools by merging Harris and Stowe, the white and black teacher-training colleges, and opening all high schools without regard to race. The board integrated the

65. Dreer, "Negro Leadership in St. Louis," 8–12; Jamie Graham, *Shelley vs. Kraemer: A 40th Anniversary Celebration, May 1988* (St. Louis: Girl Friends, 1988), 8.

66. Graham, *Shelley vs. Kraemer,* 31–37.

67. George Shermer, "The Fairgrounds Park Incident: A Study Conducted for the St. Louis Council on Human Relations" (Mayor's Interracial Committee, Detroit, Mich., 1949), 10–31; Health and Welfare Council of Metropolitan St. Louis Records, Collection 434, folder 282, Western Historical Manuscript Collection, University of Missouri–St. Louis; Morris and Ambrose, *North Webster,* 38–40.

68. David Grant Papers, Collection 552, folder 5, Western Historical Manuscript Collection, University of Missouri–St. Louis.

grammar schools in September 1955. However, because the St. Louis Board of Education assigned children to the nearest neighborhood schools, residential housing patterns still separated most black students from white students.[69]

Urban Renewal and Public Housing

In the 1950s, the city of St. Louis took advantage of federal housing programs to clean up its most embarrassing slums. As early as 1941, Mayor Bernard Dickmann had dedicated Carr Square Village at Eighteenth and Cole, the oldest and finest public housing project in St. Louis. Mayor Joseph Darst built public housing projects with funds from the Federal Housing Act of 1949, and Mayor Raymond Tucker continued building low-income housing with funds from the Federal Housing Act of 1954. Cochran Gardens, at 1112 North Ninth Street, opened for white senior citizens in 1953. Pruitt-Igoe, at Jefferson and Cass, opened in 1954. The Pruitt Apartments, named for World War II Tuskegee flying ace Wendell Pruitt, included twenty eleven-story buildings for black tenants, and the Igoe Apartments, named for Democratic Congressman William Igoe, included thirteen eleven-story buildings for white tenants. When Pruitt-Igoe opened in 1954, urban planners hailed it as one of the largest and best-designed public housing projects of the postwar period. In 1957, the George L. Vaughn Public Housing Project opened between Cass Avenue and Carr at Eighteenth Street, and the Darst-Webbe Complex opened at Twelfth and Park.[70]

In 1958 and 1959 the city, under Mayor Tucker, undertook the ambitious Mill Creek Valley Urban Renewal Project. The St. Louis Land Clearance for Redevelopment Authority condemned and cleared five hundred acres of old tenements, from Eighteenth Street to Grand Avenue and from the railroad tracks to Olive Street, to make room for new industries, businesses, town houses, and the expansion of St. Louis University. The former residents of Mill Creek Valley dispersed, some to the housing projects, some to North St. Louis. With them went the votes of the Sixth Ward, part of the political power base of Jordan Chambers. And with them went the history and the memory of Mill Creek Valley, as haunting as the melodies of ragtime and the blues.[71]

Most of the housing projects were segregated, but other aspects of St. Louis life began to integrate. Nathaniel Sweets, publisher of the *St. Louis American,* integrated the outdoor Municipal Opera in 1954, simply by reminding ticket sellers that there was to be no discrimination in a public facility belonging to the city of St. Louis. Henry Wheeler, then president of the St. Louis NAACP, picketed in front of the American Theater, off and on, for seven years, until the American opened all seats to everyone in 1955. In 1957 the Metropolitan Church Federation and the Urban League pressured some hotels to admit minorities, to accommodate ministers from all over the country who were attending the General Assembly of the National Council of Churches in St. Louis. Members of CORE picketed restaurants and movie theaters that would not admit blacks. Finally, in 1961, the St. Louis Board of Aldermen passed a public accommodations ordinance prohibiting the exclusion of anyone in places open to the public: restaurants, hotels, theaters, department stores, swimming pools. The state of Missouri passed a public accommodations bill in 1965.[72]

Martin Luther King Jr.

In 1957, Martin Luther King Jr. organized the Southern Christian Leadership Conference in Montgomery, Alabama, and began a new civil rights effort throughout the South, based on nonviolence. King spoke in St. Louis on several occasions. In April 1957, he electrified eight thousand listeners at a rally at Kiel Auditorium. In 1958, he addressed two thousand people at the United Hebrew Temple. In June 1961, he spoke to the National Baptist Sunday School and Baptist Training Union Congress at Kiel Auditorium. On May 28, 1963, three thousand people heard him speak at a Freedom Rally at the Washington Tabernacle Baptist Church, several months before the historic March on Washington. And during two visits to

69. Dreer, "Negro Leadership in St. Louis," 224; Kirschten, *Catfish and Crystal,* 452.

70. Kirschten, *Catfish and Crystal,* 440; Wright, *Discovering African American St. Louis,* 19, 30, 103; James Neal Primm, *Lion of the Valley: St. Louis, Missouri* (Boulder: Pruett, 1981), 488.

71. Kirschten, *Catfish and Crystal,* 440.

72. Dreer, "Negro Leadership in St. Louis," 135–36; Wright, *Discovering African American St. Louis,* 19; Metropolitan Church Federation Records, Unprocessed Collection, Western Historical Manuscript Collection, University of Missouri–St. Louis; Adams, "Fighting for Democracy"; Greene, Kremer, and Holland, *Missouri's Black Heritage,* 178.

St. Louis in 1964, King spoke to crowds at Christ Church Cathedral, Washington Tabernacle Baptist Church, the Protestant Episcopal Convention at the Sheraton Jefferson Hotel, and St. Louis University. Dr. King praised St. Louis for its gains in integration. "This city," he said, "has shown what can be done to help bring about the American dream when people act in good faith. I often use St. Louis as an example of what other cities could do." But in 1964, he warned that St. Louis must eliminate job discrimination and the housing segregation that perpetuated segregated schools.[73]

St. Louisan Ivory Perry led several local demonstrations in sympathy for civil rights workers in the South. In March 1965, Perry and nineteen busloads of St. Louis demonstrators traveled to Alabama to join the Freedom March from Selma to Montgomery.[74]

In 1955, Ernest Calloway, the research director for the St. Louis Teamsters Union and later a professor of Urban Studies at St. Louis University, became president of the St. Louis NAACP. He began holding informal brainstorming meetings with leaders of the black community at his home on Sunday afternoons. Calloway and his constantly changing group of ten or twelve disciples discussed the problems of the black community. Sometimes Calloway assigned writing topics addressing those problems to his students at St. Louis University, and he often shared the students' papers with his Sunday afternoon disciples. Calloway identified the powerful, but unofficial, leadership of the city of St. Louis, and he encouraged individual members of the group to seek membership on boards of directors where they could exert a positive influence for change.[75]

It may have been at one such meeting that the idea of picketing the Jefferson Bank came up. In 1963, when the Jefferson Bank and Trust Company opened a branch at 2600 Washington Avenue, in a black neighborhood, members of CORE and others picketed the bank, demanding that it hire black tellers. The bank got an injunction against the picketers. When the picketing continued, police arrested nine ringleaders of CORE and sent them to jail. Those nine civil rights heroes were Robert Curtis, Lucian Richards, the Reverend Charles Perkins,

Alderman William Clay, attorneys Raymond Howard and Charles Oldham, and teachers Marian Oldham, Herbert Thompson, and Norman Seay. After seven months of demonstrations the bank hired five black clerical workers.[76]

In the mid-1960s Percy Green and other former members of CORE organized ACTION, a group whose purpose was to demonstrate, with a militant flair, the need for jobs for blacks and the need for further integration. Green climbed a leg of the Jefferson National Expansion Memorial Arch while it was under construction, to protest the lack of black construction workers on that federal project. Green also startled many mainstream citizens out of their complacency by interrupting Sunday services at white churches.[77]

In 1968 William Clay won election to the U.S. Congress and became the first African American to represent Missouri in Washington, D.C. But that same year Dr. Martin Luther King Jr. was assassinated in Memphis, Tennessee. All over St. Louis, black and white churches held memorial services and schools had special programs. A coalition of civil rights groups sponsored a funeral march from the Arch to Forest Park; the St. Louis Symphony Orchestra performed a memorial concert at Powell Symphony Hall that was free to the public; and Norman Seay founded the Dr. Martin Luther King Jr. Holiday Committee. In 1971, Mayor A. J. Cervantes signed a bill making St. Louis one of the first cities in the country to observe Martin Luther King's birthday as a legal holiday. Easton Avenue and part of Franklin Avenue were renamed Dr. Martin Luther King Drive in 1972, and the Veterans Bridge across the Mississippi River was renamed the Martin Luther King Memorial Bridge.[78]

Trouble in the Projects

In 1967 and again in 1968, the bankrupt St. Louis Housing Authority raised rents. Instead of basing the rent on a tenant's income, the Housing Authority began to charge according to the size of the apartment. Missouri's low welfare payments made

73. *St. Louis Argus*, April 12, 1957; *St. Louis Globe-Democrat*, April 6–7, 1968.

74. Wright, *Discovering African American St. Louis*, 70.

75. Oral history interviews with Norman Seay, 1995, and Anita Bond, 1996, Western Historical Manuscript Collection, University of Missouri–St. Louis.

76. Wright, *Discovering African American St. Louis*, 39; *St. Louis Globe-Democrat*, September 4, 1963.

77. Oral history interview with Percy Green, 1996, Western Historical Manuscript Collection, University of Missouri–St. Louis.

78. *St. Louis Globe-Democrat*, April 6–7, 1968; Wright, *Discovering African American St. Louis*, 4.

the change a grave hardship for residents of public housing. On top of that, St. Louis public housing had fallen into extreme disrepair. In desperation, in 1969 tenants from all of the housing projects went on strike. With leadership from the Reverend Buck Jones, Ivory Perry, and Jean King, the tenants paid their rents into an escrow account, withholding the money from the Housing Authority until conditions were improved. After nine months, Teamsters Union President Harold Gibbons resolved the tense situation by bringing together civic leaders—including August Busch, owner of Anheuser-Busch Brewing Company; Paul Reinert, president of St. Louis University; Maurice Chambers, president of Interco; David Calhoun, chairman of St. Louis Union Trust; David Worley, director of the United Auto Workers Union; Oscar Ehrhardt, president of the St. Louis Labor Council; Dr. Donald Suggs, owner of the *St. Louis American;* and Jean King and other leaders of the tenants—to form the Civic Alliance for Housing. They negotiated a settlement to the rent strike by locating money to renovate the housing projects and establishing a tenant management corporation to run each of the housing projects. The St. Louis tenant management corporations became models for similar projects in public housing throughout the country.[79]

But tenant management could not solve the problems at Pruitt-Igoe. As Congressman William Clay said: "Pruitt-Igoe was doomed the day it left the drawing board. You can't concentrate almost three thousand low-income families into thirty-three high-rise buildings and expect them to survive in an area that provides no shopping facilities, no health service, inadequate transportation, a minimum of job opportunities, and almost nonexistent schooling, playground, and recreational facilities." In 1976 the St. Louis Housing Authority relocated the residents of Pruitt-Igoe and demolished the "largest and best-designed public housing project of the post–World War II period."[80]

The Desegregation Program

Eighteen years after *Brown v. Board of Education of Topeka,* most school districts in St. Louis County had made an effort to integrate; however, the St. Louis public schools were still segregated. The Board of Education claimed that the demographic trend of whites moving to the suburbs caused de facto segregation in the schools. But the board itself, when closing schools or dealing with overcrowding, bused entire classes of black children, intact, to white schools, where it maintained separate classes and separate lunch periods for the black students, so that black and white students never interacted.

In 1972, the parents of Craton Liddell filed a lawsuit charging that the Board of Education denied African American students an equal education. During the lengthy trial and appeals, the list of participants in the lawsuit grew to include the NAACP, the state of Missouri, the U.S. government, the city of St. Louis, and a group of citizens supporting neighborhood schools. Finally, in 1983, the Eighth Circuit Court of Appeals approved the decision of the U.S. District Court, which stated that the only way to overcome years of segregation and discrimination was for the St. Louis school system to work together with suburban school districts to establish magnet schools, and for the state of Missouri to pay to bus students to the schools of their choice. The court established the Voluntary Interdistrict Coordinating Council to oversee the process.[81]

The End of the Twentieth Century

With schools and neighborhoods no longer segregated by law, African Americans have moved to neighborhoods throughout St. Louis and to the suburbs. The Ville, once a bastion of the black aristocracy, has taken on an aura of seedy decadence, with many houses in disrepair and vacant lots where buildings have been torn down. Successful blacks have moved to the Fairgrounds Park neighborhood of tidy postwar brick bungalows, to the Kingsway neighborhood of older brick town houses with stained-glass windows and spotless lawns along North Kingshighway, to mansions in the Central West End, and to West St. Louis County.

For more than a century, St. Louisans have worked to change laws and practices that denied an equal opportunity to all. Some successes affected one business at a time; others affected

79. Metropolitan Church Federation Records, Unprocessed Collection, Western Historical Manuscript Collection, University of Missouri–St. Louis.

80. Wright, *Discovering African American St. Louis,* 103.

81. David Colton and Miriam Raskin, "Democracy and Public Education," *Focus Midwest* 14 (September 1980): 11–13; conversation with Susan Uchitelle, director, Voluntary Interdistrict Coordinating Council, 1997.

laws throughout the nation. Today, black leaders hold positions of power in major St. Louis corporations. Black businessmen can obtain financing for black business ventures. African American educators serve as administrators and faculty in colleges, universities, and public schools throughout St. Louis and St. Louis County. In 1978 the St. Louis Public School Board transferred Harris-Stowe Teachers College to the state, and it was renamed Harris-Stowe State College. African American doctors serve on the staffs of all the great hospitals in the St. Louis metropolitan area, and, to the sorrow of many, in 1979 the city closed Homer G. Phillips Hospital.[82] African American lawyers have become judges of the U.S. District Court, the Eighth Circuit Court of Appeals, and the Missouri Supreme Court. And in 1993 St. Louisans elected Freeman Bosley Jr. as their first black mayor.

The stories of individual African Americans serve as metaphors for the struggle and the progress of the human spirit. Each event in St. Louis history is part of a continuing saga, building on what has gone before. That history can inspire us to undertake impossible dreams. St. Louis African Americans have fought discrimination with perseverance and an unconquerable spirit. On the following pages, one hundred St. Louis African Americans lift their voices and sing, passing on to future generations stories of heroes, great and small, who contributed to St. Louis in the twentieth century.

82. Wright, *Discovering African American St. Louis,* 79.

Portraits **and Narratives**

Bennie G. Rodgers

Editor, *St. Louis American*

I was born in Tutwiler, Mississippi, April 1, 1914, and thank God, when I was two years old my father moved us to St. Louis. My father was Joseph D. Rodgers, and the reason he brought us from Mississippi was he was an engineer on the railroad and his white boss called him a nigger, and my father gave him a heavy blow, and then he had to catch the next train to St. Louis. He couldn't live down there after whipping a white man. My father was a butcher at the Krey Packing Company for forty-two years. My mother's name was Frances Stanford Rodgers. There were twelve of us.

I attended L'Ouverture School and Vashon High School during the Depression. My brother graduated from Illinois Wesleyan University, and I went to stay with him and enrolled in Illinois State Normal University, which is now Illinois State University. I majored in commercial industrial art, but because of the Depression I came back to St. Louis and worked with Jesse Johnson of Deluxe Enterprises. I went on the road promoting bands like Duke Ellington and Count Basie and all those bands.

And then when the war started I got a job at Curtiss-Wright. The federal government forced Curtiss-Wright to employ blacks. Curtiss-Wright set up a school for blacks in a building that is now McDonnell Douglas. We learned about aircraft, and I graduated as an assembler. I worked on the wings, and because of my work at the Normal School, studying blueprints, I could have been a foreman, but they would only give that position to white boys. That's the reason I am working at the *St. Louis American* today. While I was working at Curtiss-Wright I wrote stories about discrimination in the plant and in the union. We were forced to be off from work when the union was on strike, but we could not belong to the union because we were African Americans. It did not matter how smart a black individual was, or how great the work he was doing, he could never advance. I could never be a foreman. I was writing stories like that, and Mr. Sweets promised me that when the war was over I could have a job. He knew we would be the first fired when the war ended.

So I came to work at the *St. Louis American*. Judge Young, the founder of the *American*, graduated from Yale University and knew a lot about journalism. Mr. Sweets was the manager and editor. The newspaper was very small. There was only one other reporter there, and that was Everett Nelson David. He went to California, and then I was the only reporter. I wrote the stories, I made up the pages with hot type, those lead slugs, and I had the screens made for the photographs. Years ago we had cases of type, and I had to take the type out by hand to make the headlines. Sometimes it took two hours to make up the headline. And sometimes I would start a headline and I would discover that a letter was missing from our alphabet. Then I would have to change the headline and make it something where I had the correct letters. For the pictures, I would take the pictures on Monday and send them to an engraving company in Indianapolis by Greyhound bus, and they sent the engraving cuts back to me on Thursday. Then I would mount the cuts and get the newspaper printed. It was really difficult. I don't know of any other person who did everything for a newspaper. I was the reporter, the circulation manager, I got the ads out, and I made up the newspaper. I had to do it all from the beginning for it to hit the street. The St. Louis Association of Black Journalists honored me in 1977 for my lifetime achievements.

The highlight of my journalism career was meeting Martin Luther King Jr. and having a personal interview with him at the Jefferson Hotel. I had been to Mississippi, and I had seen the church that burned down, and I knew how dangerous it was. I asked Dr. King if he felt he was on a dangerous mission. He said, "It is a dangerous mission, and I know I am not going to live long, but I think what I am doing is worth it." That is what he told me.

I like to tell people that the reason I turned out to be a reporter was that when I was about ten years old my brother and I went to the Coliseum for the *Globe-Democrat*'s Christmas party for children. They gave us an apple, a pair of socks, and a ticket to the St. Louis Theater in January. I walked all the way from my house on Hickory Street to the St. Louis Theater on Grand and Lucas Avenue when the temperature was below zero. When I got there and gave the man my ticket, the guy said, "We don't admit colored children." And he gave me a pencil box with pencils and an eraser. So I took that box of pencils and I went home and started learning how to write. I am still bitter about the discrimination of that day. Both my feet were frozen. I had walked all the way across town. Young people don't have a personal reason to fight discrimination like I do.

I didn't learn journalism at a journalism school—I got it the hard way. I hate it when people say you can pick yourself up by your bootstraps, because I remember a lot of days when I was a kid that I did not even have any shoes. When I'm barefooted, there is no way in hell you can tell me about some bootstraps.

Lorraine O. Gasaway

Seamstress, St. Louis Police Department

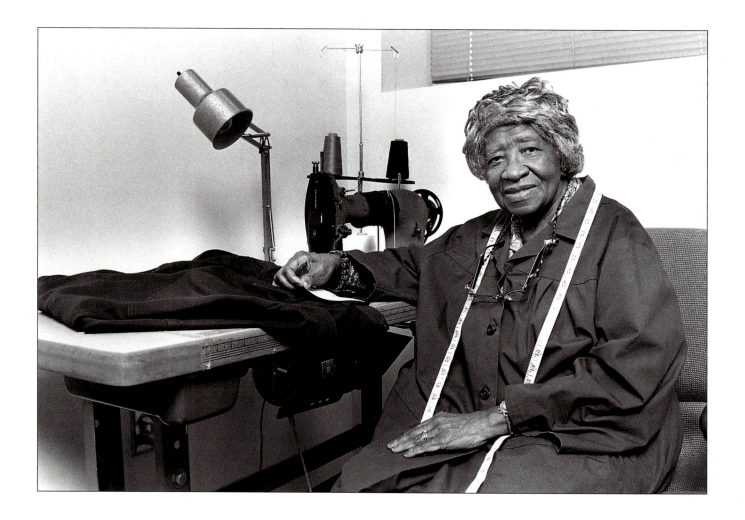

Grandfather had a brother and one or two relatives who came from St. Louis to Arkansas and told him there was plenty of work in St. Louis, because they were getting ready for the World's Fair. It took Grandfather two or three years to make up his mind to move to St. Louis, because he had a wife and seven children. When they moved here, in 1902, my mother was age eleven. My grandfather was a man among men. He didn't leave my grandmother and seven children and say, "When I get enough money I will send for you." He said, "We will go together to St. Louis. We will make it together, or we will starve together."

He brought his wife and seven children to the Italian Hill. There was work for blacks in walking distance of the Hill: the Liggett and Myers Tobacco Company and Seagram Industry, a whiskey factory. Grandfather worked in some of those industries. Black men did the hard labor. That's all there was.

Back then colored people were not invited to worship at St. Ambrose or other Catholic churches. Mother said they worshiped in a tent from 1902 to 1904. Then the men put their money together and they paid down on a three-room frame house, 5128 Pattison Avenue. Grandfather and some of the other men converted that three-room frame house into the Pattison Avenue Baptist Church, so colored people would have a place to worship God. That church remained there until Highway 44 took the church and a lot of the Italians' homes. The Pattison Baptist Church moved to De Baliviere, not too far south of Delmar.

My brother and I went to Simmons School through the sixth grade. And then we went to John Marshall Junior High School, 4300 Lucky Street. It was changed to Aldine, but when I was a child it was Lucky Street. The girls wore white middies and navy-blue pleated skirts for graduation. And we were all very proud. And then I entered Sumner High School, January 1927. Sumner High School was still the only public high school for blacks west of the Mississippi.

With a high school education, I should have been able to get more than just maid work, but that's the way it was for colored people. Department stores hired young colored women to operate the elevators, but they had such a long list of applicants they might never get around to hiring me. Life was so different in those days. After I finished high school I was a part-time maid, doing laundry, scrubbing, and some cleaning for a family which was transferred by Nugent's Department Store to Hayes Department Store in Newark, New Jersey. Mr. McGrath was appointed manager of that large department store, and he and his wife said if I wanted to come I could still be their maid.

I moved back to St. Louis, before the war, and I did domestic work. After Pearl Harbor, work opened up at the small-arms plant, the aircraft companies, and the military bases in Illinois, as well as St. Louis. The defense plants were hiring any people who wanted work. And that is when Barney's Army Store opened. So many soldiers from the base in Illinois and Jefferson Barracks came looking for chevrons and whatnot, that Barney's needed a seamstress, and I saw the ad. And that's how I got my first sewing job. And I was thirty years of age. By the end of the war I could look at a serviceman from his collar down and tell you right away what his rating was.

But after the war, there wasn't much work in Barney's Army Store, because people were not buying chevrons and military clothing. So I started working for a Jewish tailor in the Holland Building. I was the only black person, but, after all, I was experienced in sewing. I worked in the garment industry as a power machine operator, and I took courses with the Singer Sewing Machine Company. I became an expert slipcover maker and drapery maker.

Finally I was working part-time at a cleaning shop when my daughter Jeanie saw in the newspaper where the police department was trying to hire a seamstress. I was hired to do the sewing for fifteen hundred police officers. It was that military sewing of World War II! I never attended college, not even one semester. But God gave everybody some talent. So find your talent, and try to develop your God-given talent.

Robert Carter

Musician, Singleton Palmer's Dixieland Six;
President, Local 197, American Federation of Musicians

My first regular job was with Fate Marable. I played on the riverboats for the Streckfus Company. At that time they had two boats down on the riverfront, the *St. Paul* and another boat. And blacks could only go on the *St. Paul* one night a week, on Monday nights. All the other nights, it was reserved for whites. Blacks didn't go on the other boat. Later, that company built the *President* and the *Admiral*.

I worked three seasons with Fate, '37, '38, and '39. We took a train down to Cairo, Illinois, where they docked the boat during the winter. We got on the boat and went down the Mississippi to where the Ohio emptied into the Mississippi. Then we went up the Ohio, all the way to Pittsburgh. We were gone all summer. They booked towns along the way: Paducah, Cincinnati, towns on the riverfront. They booked school picnics in the spring. We went out on excursions and played for the schoolkids, and then we'd come back. That night, we would have a moonlight excursion for adults. The boat had a bandstand, a dance floor, and all that. When we came back we would have to fill up with coal, because they used coal at that time for steam. The stevedores hauled the coal onto the boat with wheelbarrows and lit the stokers. Then we'd go up the river to the next town, where we had another booking, and we would do all the little towns like that until we got to Pittsburgh. We stayed there all summer, playing the excursions from Pittsburgh down the river and then back.

Fate Marable was one of the pioneers in big-band music. He played for the Streckfus people for years, and he was responsible for bringing Louis Armstrong from New Orleans. Louis was a kid, about nineteen, when he started with Fate.

I joined the musicians' union around 1935. You had to join the union to play at the better places, to play with Fate Marable and with other bands. I didn't really have much training myself. Most of my training was from other musicians. I was lucky to have been in contact with good musicians most of my career. We learned from each other. There's more to music than just reading the notes. It's a "feeling." It's an art.

When the war came I went into the navy. This was in 1942. At that time, the only thing that blacks did in the navy was handle the food. They were stewards. This was during Roosevelt's administration, and his wife, Eleanor, was a good liberal. She recommended that blacks in the navy have duties other than being stewards. So they recruited twenty or more bands. A chief petty officer came to St. Louis to recruit musicians, and he recruited most of us from the union. There were thirty or forty musicians who left from St. Louis.

I was stationed at Lambert Field. The navy was conducting flight training for cadets from England for the RAF at Lambert Field. Of course, segregation was still bad. All our band did was play music. We played for bond rallies, we played for the cadets when they paraded, and we played concerts. There was a white band stationed here, and, since they were regular seamen, they had to do other duties, like scrubbing floors and handling the food. The white seamen figured that the blacks, who were rehearsing and playing for bond rallies and concerts, could do some of the other work, like cleaning up the rec hall and the johns. Then in the summer of '44 they built a swimming pool, but the only day the blacks could use the pool was the day they were going to drain the pool and put fresh water in it. There were a lot of little things that piled up and became a conflict. When they ordered us to clean the johns, we refused to do it. They put us all under house arrest, and they broke the band up. All of us were sent out as replacements to other bands scattered all over the world.

I was sent to Hawaii. My son was only four months old when I shipped out, and I was bitter and lonesome and homesick. I played in a big band over there, until they dropped the bomb on Japan. I wonder if they would have dropped the bomb on the Germans, since they are white. But I think Truman was one of our better presidents. He integrated the armed services, and things started improving for blacks from then on.

When I came home I got my job back at the St. Louis Medical Depot in the Mart Building. We warehoused all the medical supplies for the army. But I knew they were not treating us right. They were promoting the whites, and I was still the same little GS-2, earning ninety-nine dollars a month.

But I didn't do too bad. I retired in 1973 after working for the government for thirty-two years. I have three children, and I put them all through college. I was able to do that because I still played music, part-time. I played with George Hudson's Orchestra, and I played with Singleton Palmer in Gaslight Square.

Olivia Calloway

Democratic Committeewoman, Eighteenth Ward

I have lived in St. Louis, Missouri, all of my life. I grew up at 1300 Gay Street. Gay Street was located between Franklin Avenue and Morgan Street and ran from Twelfth Street to Fourteenth Street. It was only two blocks long. And of course, it was all inhabited by colored people. There were several teachers living there, particularly the Wallace family. Cozy Wallace was a teacher in the public schools, and she had a brother who lived with her, also a sister, Angie, who did not marry. Up the street on Gay Street were the Logan sisters, who were related to my uncle, Zeno Hamilton, who married my aunt Mary, who I stayed with during my early childhood. Everybody knew everybody. Everybody looked out for each other. It is a very pleasant memory. Facing Gay Street, looking west, was St. Elizabeth's Catholic Church. I was baptized there on June 6, 1906.

My mother's name was Thomina Young, and my father's name was George Ellis. My mother was born in Sparta, Illinois. My father was born in Jefferson City, Missouri. They met in St. Louis, and to that union were born four boys and one girl. My brother George was the oldest. I was next. And I had a brother Zeno. Then there was Allen, and then there was Stevie. Unfortunately Stevie and Allen passed when they were very young, and George passed when he was twenty-two. My brother Zeno Ellis lived till he was eighty-one. He died about twelve years ago. Now I'm the only living Ellis.

In 1921 St. Elizabeth's Church moved to 2721 Pine Street. And I lived at 1411 Morgan Street, with my uncle and my aunt, because we were taking care of the convent there, which housed the Oblate Sisters of Normandy, which was a colored order of nuns. I stayed with my mother during school days and attended Banneker School. I remember Mr. Williams, the principal at Banneker. He was the nicest, kindest man. He was like a father. He talked very softly, but with command. You knew he meant business. We were taught to respect our elders and to mind when we were spoken to. We had wonderful teachers. I went to John Marshall School for seventh and eighth grades and then Sumner High School. In 1925 I went to Sumner Teachers College, which was a two-year course in the same building as Sumner High School.

I first got involved in politics when my children were in school. I met Harry Small, a member of the Democratic Party who had a nightclub in the 3400 block of Franklin Avenue. It was on the bottom level of a three-story building, and he and his wife lived upstairs. The club had a bar, which was the Nineteenth Ward Democratic Headquarters. Jordan Chambers had not been elected yet. And Harry Small invited me to the nightclub. So I went to the meetings, and I served the drinks. Harry got me a job at City Hospital No. 2. Jobs were important, because in those days if you weren't a teacher, you could not get a job anyplace, unless you worked downtown at a department store, running the elevators, making eight dollars a week.

City Hospital No. 1 was for whites; City Hospital No. 2 was for colored. I worked in the kitchen at City Hospital No. 2. Later I moved to the X-ray department. I stayed there for quite a while. Finally, Homer G. Phillips was built, and oh, it was a beautiful hospital. They had an X-ray tube which cost fifteen hundred dollars. WPA workers were building that hospital, and they wanted me to watch the tube to make sure that nothing happened to it. For three months all I did was sit and watch that tube while the WPA workers worked.

After I moved to Homer G. Phillips, I really got into politics. Jordan Chambers had become the committeeman in the Nineteenth Ward. He was the first black committeeman in the city. Jordan Chambers owned the Peoples Undertaking Company, at 3100 Franklin Avenue, and he owned the building where he started his organization. Later, he had the Club Riviera in the Eighteenth Ward. It was a beautiful nightclub. He had outstanding entertainment, all the big bands and everything. I went there many nights after meetings. I'd sit with Sable, Jordan Chambers's girlfriend, and have a drink and listen to the show. I knew everybody.

I worked in the Probate Court for seven years. Mayor Darst appointed me to the school board in 1948, but I had to refuse it because it was a conflict working in the Probate Court. Then in 1954, Jordan wanted to increase the black leadership in the Nineteenth Ward, the Eighteenth Ward, the Fourth Ward, and the Sixth Ward. When I moved up onto Page, that put me in the Eighteenth Ward. I ran for committeewoman in the Eighteenth Ward, and Fred Weathers ran for committeeman. Fred and I both won in the Eighteenth Ward, and, of course, Jordan won in the Nineteenth Ward.

Politics has changed since then. Today much of the political leadership in St. Louis is black. We should be training our young people to be leaders. But first young people must get a good education. If our minds have not been trained for something better, or to know there's something beyond tomorrow, how are we going to be prepared for what comes?

Weldon Young

First Engineer, Vashon High School

I was born in Spartanburg, South Carolina, January 3, 1902. My father was a tailor, and he made clothes for most working people in Spartanburg. I had two brothers. Harold came to St. Louis in 1935 and opened a photographic studio. My youngest brother, Moses, went to Howard University Medical School and then received a Ph.D. in neural anatomy from the University of Michigan. He went back to Howard in 1933, and he stayed there until 1973.

I came to St. Louis in June of 1920 to take a job as a moving-picture projectionist. I started showing pictures when I was about fifteen. I left Spartanburg to go to Claflin College in 1918 with thirty dollars in my pocket. I told the president of Claflin my predicament, and he said, "Well, what can you do?" I told him I was a moving-picture operator. He gave me a job showing movies in the chapel, every other week. Back in 1918 many of the students had never seen a moving picture. I stayed there two years, and then I heard that a Mr. Austin in St. Louis needed a moving-picture operator. I wrote to him, and he sent me a telegram saying he would pay me thirty-five dollars a week and send me a railroad pass. That was a lot of money in 1920, so that is the reason I came to St. Louis.

Then I went to the New York Electrical School in 1922, and I came back to St. Louis and worked in the Pullman car shops. There had been a strike in the car shops in 1921, and the Pullman Company was so bullheaded that they went all over the country recruiting Negroes to work in the Pullman shop, instead of bargaining with the union. They started us at forty-seven cents an hour, and the maximum was seventy cents an hour.

When they started up Vashon High School, there was a colored fellow out there, Bill Alexander, who had studied electrical engineering at the University of Pittsburgh. He told me he was going to try to see if he could get Negroes in the power plant at Vashon, and he asked me if I'd like to go to work there. He took me by and introduced me to one of the Vashons. Mr. Vashon told me to go down to the Board of Education building and ask for Mr. Hallet, the chief engineer. He said he'd tell him who I was. He told me to put in an application. So I did. When I saw Mr. Hallet, a year later, I knew that Mr. Hallet hadn't seen the application, nor had Mr. Vashon said anything to him about me. And so I told him what my qualifications were. He said, "New York, that's a good school. Sorry I didn't know about you. But I already hired the personnel: two white engineers, one white oiler, and one colored

oiler. We want to put colored in there." I dismissed it as a brush-off, and I went back to the Pullman shops.

The next year, 1928, I got laid off and I went down to see about the job. Mr. Hallet told me that Alexander had done well, they liked his work, and he was glad I'd come back. He said, "You are the most qualified, and I've got seven men that recommended you." Some politicians were pushing for more of us to get in. I didn't care for politicians because you had to pay politicians, and I couldn't see doing the work and paying somebody.

I got the job as an oiler, and after I started, the board passed a rule that all stationary engineers must have a license by September 1, 1930, in two years. Everybody said that no Negro would get a license in the city of St. Louis because in order to get a license you had to have a licensed stationary engineer sign your application. And no white man would sign the application of a Negro.

I found out that the fellows they had at Vashon were inadequate. The old man who was chief engineer at Vashon was so scared they were going to promote me to second engineer that he told the chief engineer downtown that either he or I would have to go. That old fossil wouldn't even pay attention to what the manufacturers of the machinery recommended for its operation. I had written for one of the manuals, and I showed it to the chief engineer downtown. I said, "You better be prepared to get another plant out here, because the chief engineer is going to tear it up in another month." And they fired him.

In August of 1930, the chief engineer offered me a job at Sumner High School, but he said I had to have my license. I had made friends with one of the assistant chief engineers, and I said to him, "I am going to get a license, and I don't know anybody who will sign my application but you. If this will cause you any embarrassment, or you don't think I'll make a good engineer, don't sign it. We'll still be friends." He looked straight in my eyes for a minute, and then he said, "Get your application. I'll sign it." I got my license. And right now, I'm the oldest licensed engineer.

Early in the fifties I got our union, the International Union of Operating Engineers, Local No. 2, to start an integrated training program to train men to pass the examination to obtain a license. When I retired in 1972, more men had obtained their stationary engineer's license who had worked in the Vashon power plant with me than from all the other ten plants of the Board of Education put together.

Oscar C. Farmer

Lieutenant, St. Louis Police Department;
Chief, Wellston Police Department

I was born and raised right here in St. Louis, and I attended school here. I checked in at Lincoln Law School, but I'm what you might call a dropout, because I didn't go but a quick little while. My dad had a business hauling coal during the Depression, when almost everybody heated with coal. I worked before and after school, and then it got important for me to practically run the business. I had three brothers and four sisters. My mother, you know where her time had to be with eight kids. My father worked at the Armour Packing Company. He had a pretty stable job there, so I ran the business, hauling coal all night. Sometimes I thought my dad was getting cheated, because people were unable to pay their bills, and he would still supply them with coal. I recall one lady came to my dad on a day that was about ten below zero, and my dad told me to give her what she wanted. She had her son there with his coaster wagon. I called my dad aside and told him she hadn't paid her bill. He looked me straight in the eye and he said, "Well what should we do, son? Should we let her and her kids freeze to death?" That shows you how compassionate he was about people. I worked with my dad to send all of my brothers and sisters to college. I was the only one that had to work, but I helped him get them all through.

I participated in sports all through high school. Even though I didn't go to Sumner, Mr. Garrett and Mr. Beckett came and talked to my dad about sending me to an Ivy League school on a scholarship because of my athletic ability. But I didn't take it up, because during the Depression we were doing pretty good. I was running the truck, making money. I wasn't interested in nothing else. When I did quit and moved on, my dad sold the business.

I went to work for a bowling company, Tom Carbone Bowling. We operated bowling alleys in St. Louis, and then they transferred me to Chicago. It was a pretty good thing because I was pioneering bowling among blacks. I opened it up in Chicago and then New York. Tom Carbone started with a duckpin alley here in St. Louis. Then Uncle Sam got after me to go into the service. So I went into the navy. I trained recruits at Great Lakes and at an air base in New York. When I was discharged I went back into bowling.

When I was home on vacation I would go over and talk to Mr. Chambers. He wanted me to help him with the Club Riviera, which was just blooming. I never had been a nightclub worker before. I knew nothing about it. But I went to help him, and you catch on quick to those kinds of things. I took care of the reservations. I worked with him until it looked like things were getting a little dull, and then I told him I wanted to go into the police department. He hit the ceiling. He said, "I thought you had more ambition than that." About a month or so later I told him I still wanted to go into the police department. He said, "Well, if that's what you want, I'll see if I can get you in." That night when I got home, I had my orders to report. That's the type of guy he was.

When I went on, I went on full of vinegar. I had a new uniform and a shiny badge. I was going out and I was going to put somebody in jail. I got out there and people had never seen a black policeman before, and they treated me with courtesy. They wouldn't charge me for my coffee, and the people would greet me on the street and it got to be family. When I got down to the Bureau, it was a challenge for me, I mean, like a game. If you try to get away with something in the city, I'm going to catch you. I worked with the major-case squad, worked the other districts and everything. It was just my life. Police work is not for a guy who just wants to make a living. If you go into police work it takes dedication. You've got to want to do it. It's for a person who really wants to see things better.

My civil rights connection was Mr. Chambers. I told him when things weren't right. He changed a lot of things in the police department. We didn't have any policemen in the department in uniform. They were all plainclothed if they were sergeant or more. He made them put a uniformed sergeant and a crew in the black area. He made them open beats north of Clark Avenue. And he made them appoint a black captain. Mr. Chambers was fair. I remember they offered him money under the table about the charter. But he wouldn't support the charter unless they put something in it that would help his people, the poor people. He defeated it twice. He was a politician. Adam Clayton Powell said Mr. Chambers was one of the greatest politicians in the country.

Famelia Kennedy

Registered Nurse, Homer G. Phillips Hospital

I graduated from grade school in the rurals of Arkansas. I've always enjoyed school, but the schools were very poor. The first school I attended had only one teacher, and it was in a church. It had four benches arranged around the heating stove. For first grade the teacher had maybe four kids, two on each side. She taught fourth-grade reading and then maybe eighth-grade math to just one student. We had no electricity at all in the school. We had no windowpanes, just shutters like a door. When it was a dull day, we used an oil lamp. But it worked.

At that time, there weren't any high schools available for blacks. I had a chance to go to Arkansas State to a summer conference when I finished the seventh grade. That was my first visit into a formal school setting. While I was there, I won a contest and was able to stay and finish the eighth grade at Arkansas State. Then, back to the country, with nothing else to do. At that time my parents lived in a very small house in the country. The only thing that you could see was the sky, because all the way around was the woods and a running stream that was close to the road to the store. I took a look at the situation.

I had an uncle who lived in a small town of about nine hundred, and he wrote to my parents and told them that I could come and live with him, if I wanted to go to high school. My older cousin told me that I could make some money by chopping weeds out of the cornfield with him. Which I did. I made ten dollars a week. And that was the hardest money I ever earned in my life. It was hot; it must have been July. And when corn is growing, the leaves are fuzzy, and it gets all on you and irritates your skin. But I stayed for the five days, and I repeated the poem:

Beautiful, beautiful world,
With the beautiful grass upon your breast,
Oh world, you are so beautifully dressed.

And I stood and looked at the world, and I said: "God, I know this is your world, and it is pretty, but this part of it, I just don't like."

I spent six dollars for a train ticket to go to Vienna, Illinois, to my uncle's small town, and I had four dollars left. Oh, that high school was fantastic. There weren't any black students there. But they were really nice to me. The summer after I finished high school, I worked for a Caucasian lady who took in boarders. She helped me get into SIU Carbondale. I went there one year, and I also went to summer school.

The next fall, I came to St. Louis to see if I could get into the nursing program. I just walked into my aunt's house in the 4200 block of Easton Avenue, and she just pushed back until she found someplace for me to stay. I got a job with a private family where I worked until February, when I was admitted into the next class at City Hospital No. 2. City Hospital No. 2 became Homer G. Phillips Hospital.

City Hospital No. 1, down on Lafayette Street, was for Caucasian people, and they didn't have facilities for black people. During the thirties a tremendous number of black people from the South migrated to St. Louis, because the cotton crops in the South had failed and cut all the farming to the nitty-gritty. People traveled from the South, coming north as far as they could get, and a lot of them stopped in St. Louis. Well, a black politician, named Homer G. Phillips, started fighting for a hospital for blacks, and we got City Hospital No. 2, which was segregated. And as the years went on, that hospital became crowded to capacity. When I came we had beds down the aisle and all that. Homer Phillips fought for a larger hospital for blacks, but he didn't get a chance to see it. He was killed on the Hodiamont tracks. The new hospital and nursing school were named for him. My nursing pin says City Hospital No. 2. But in 1937, Homer Phillips was opened, and all the new nursing pins say Homer G. Phillips.

When I first went to Homer Phillips, I was a psychiatric nurse. Then I supervised in the delivery room. In 1950 the Board of Education opened a new program for young adults at Simmons Grade School, and I taught nursing there. When the schools integrated in 1954, nursing came under vocational education, so we moved to Hadley Tech. We stayed at Hadley until O'Fallon opened for vocational education. Then I taught health education at the State Community College in East St. Louis.

I didn't know anything in the world about nursing as a little girl. There were no hospitals where I grew up. I never saw a hospital until I was in college. And then I met this nurse. She lived near the lady I worked for when I was in college. She showed me a picture of her aunt who was a nurse. And I decided that I would like to be a nurse. Then, when I visited my aunt in St. Louis, my aunt told me about the nursing school that became Homer Phillips. And that's how I became a nurse.

Madeline S. Turner

Registered Nurse, Homer G. Phillips Hospital
and St. Louis County Hospital

I worked in a drugstore in Cincinnati. It was owned by a black pharmacist named Sky Johnson. A lady came into the drugstore, and she was a nurse from St. Louis. She was on vacation visiting her sister, and I inquired of her what type of school she attended. They were building Homer G. Phillips at that time. She worked at City Hospital No. 2. So, after she told me that, I started making my plans. I knew that I wanted to be a nurse, but I hadn't decided on that until I talked to her. It was the early thirties, I believe.

When I moved to St. Louis I lived down on Lawton in the nurses' home. There were three houses that nurses lived in on Pine and on Lawton. It has all been torn down now. We weren't far from the hospital at that time, because City Hospital No. 2 was down on Lawton. That's all closed up. Then we moved into Homer G. Phillips Hospital while they were building the four wings on each side. They built the center section first, and we took classes there.

Miss Helen Kamp was the superintendent of nurses. She was Caucasian. The lady under her was also Caucasian. They taught us nursing services, and then we'd go on the ward and do our academic work. We took care of patients under supervision. Our teachers were doctors and nurses. Most of the doctors were from Meharry and Howard University in Washington. When we graduated they were short of nurses, at that time, so we were employed right there.

When the war came a lot of the doctors went in the army. Then there was a shortage of anesthetists, so I studied anesthesia under Mrs. Caldwell. I did anesthesia during the time that the doctors were gone. By the time the war was over I was on twenty-four-hour call with Mrs. Caldwell, my superior, and it was kind of hectic during that time.

I worked in Isolation when it was on Arsenal. I worked there after I graduated. Our staff was mostly white, and people would walk all over you because you were black. I remember one instance when some people came to visit somebody, and I had my cap and white uniform and pin on, and they still asked me, "Is there a nurse on the floor?" They had not been accustomed to seeing black nurses. And I said, "Well, I'm a nurse. What would you like?" They wanted to see where such and such a patient was, but they'd walk all over you, because they didn't know anything about black nurses.

I worked in the emergency room at St. Louis County Hospital, and I remember we even got airplane crash victims at that emergency room. I worked nights, because by this time I had a couple of children and I didn't want to be away from them all day. My mother came to live with me when I divorced Mr. Franklin. I didn't have a car, so I took the bus and the streetcar to County Hospital to work at night. There hadn't been many blacks that worked there. I worked in the emergency room, and I set up the operating room with my supervisor. Of course, being black, I had to do the work. I set up the operating room and then came back down to the emergency room. I worked there for at least three years. I also worked at DePaul, which was on Kingshighway. I worked nights there too, because it was convenient for me to be home with the children in the day.

And then I went into public health, and I worked for the city of St. Louis. Our purpose in public health nursing was to get patients to come into the clinic, pregnant mothers and newborn babies and tuberculosis cases. We had to follow through on tuberculosis cases and see that they got institutionalized or had good care.

Nursing was a hard job in my days. At that time we had to do everything, take care of the patients, make up the beds, and do the procedures. Now they have other people that do those procedures. When I did anesthesia during the war, I was on twenty-four-hour call. That was rugged. But I enjoyed it. It was challenging for me. I think it's important to have a goal and follow that route. I wanted to be a nurse, and I followed it through. Nursing today isn't near as hard as it was when I came along. But I wouldn't exchange my experience for anything in the world. I loved nursing.

Clyde S. Cahill

Judge, U.S. District Court for the Eastern District of Missouri

The horrible days of the Depression left an indelible mark upon me. My dedication to the poor, particularly the poor who are black, was born during the Depression. During those years when we were all little children, we were evicted from our home, we slept in the park, we had no food. Instead of making me bitter and angry, it made me determined that this should not happen to other people.

When I was in high school in 1942, the last lynching in Missouri took place in Sikeston. Cleo Wright, a black man, was accused of molesting a white woman, and he was lynched by a mob. The U.S. attorney, here in St. Louis, could not get any witnesses to testify against the crowd that lynched him. Mr. Guy Ruffin, who taught me history at Vashon, drove me and a couple other high school students down to Sikeston, to try to find witnesses. And I will never forget the difficulty we had. We drove into the Negro part of town, and a police car followed behind us. They didn't interfere with us, but they followed behind us. Every time we knocked on a door, the shades would be pulled down, and nobody would talk to us. The people were so frightened when they saw the police car behind us that they wouldn't come out and talk to us. And Mr. Ruffin said, "If you students will become lawyers, maybe you can fight this and make changes in the law." And that was one of the things that motivated me to go to law school.

I was also involved in the Fairgrounds Park swimming pool case. I hadn't graduated from law school, but I was a plaintiff. Dave Grant was the lawyer. At that time, you could go into certain parks in St. Louis, even though you were black, but you couldn't swim in the swimming pools, you couldn't go into the community centers. They were kept for whites. So Dave Grant filed a lawsuit to end segregation in public facilities paid for by tax money. The police department was having trouble up at Fairgrounds Park. There were riots and beatings, and several people were killed. That neighborhood was changing. The blacks were moving up to Natural Bridge, but not beyond it. The whites had all of the area north of Fairgrounds Park. So this park was right on the cutting edge of integration.

Dave Grant called me one day and said, "The judge has called a meeting of all the lawyers to discuss this thing, and I want you to come with me." I had never been in a judge's chambers. So we went to see Judge Rubey Hulen, and Dave presented his argument about why there should be no segregation in a public facility paid for by city money. Hulen was a tall guy with big glasses. He looked like Ichabod Crane. He sat at his bench and towered over everybody. And the chief of police said, "Judge, we can't let these blacks come in and swim. There's crowds out there, spitting, cussing, and throwing rocks. We've had several people killed. They're mad at the police and they may hurt some of our officers. We can't control them. Why don't you let it cool down for several months?" The judge pulled down his glasses and said, "Chief, how long have you been chief of police? Do you want to remain chief of police? By God, if you can't control that crowd, I'll get a chief of police who can!" And there was dead silence. Dave Grant was smirking. The chief didn't say a word, he just stood there like he was paralyzed. And I thought, that's what I want to be, I want to be a federal judge.

It was my job, as president of the NAACP Youth Council, to swim in the park. So I went to Jim Cook, president of the Pine Street Y, and asked him for some boys to go with me. And he said to some boys, "Listen, this young man needs help. Who will go to Fairgrounds Park and swim with him?" The next day about ten of us met at the corner of Grand and Natural Bridge, and here came the paddy wagons. The police were nasty. "Get in the paddy wagons! Hurry up! We don't have much time!" And they drove us to the park. When we got to the park, crowds of people were lined up on each side of the pathway, and the police drove us through the crowd, real slow, with the crowd hitting the police cars. We went into the dressing room and changed and came out and jumped into the pool. All the whites got out. The crowd on the outside was yelling and calling us all kinds of names. And we did that for several days. Each day, we swam in the swimming pool to prove that we could do it.

I think the law is on the cutting edge of change. And I think the law can provide the opportunity for change in America. America with all its faults is still a great country. It has great potential. The law can make America live up to the principles that it espouses. And then it will be the greatest country in the world.

John F. Bass

Principal, Beaumont High School; Comptroller, City of St. Louis;
Missouri State Senator

I grew up in the Ville. My grandparents had property on Easton Avenue and Aldine Avenue, which was originally called Lucky Street. Easton Avenue had a lot of tenement houses, probably four-room flats. We lived up over a grocery store and a used furniture store. When we lived on Fairfax we had three rooms with an outdoor toilet. That was the last year before the city outlawed outdoor plumbing.

I attended Cole School and Sumner High School. Those years were years of development for me. Sumner High School had some of the finest black minds in the country. That was my first contact with black professionals, and I was inspired by their knowledge, by the disciplined people who were our role models. They gave me a sense of what I wanted to be.

At that time, community life was different. There were people on your block who were respected, whether because of occupation, or because of their practical wisdom, or because they were successful parents, or they had some kind of success through what they were doing. Those were the people who were your counselors. They took time, and they took part in your growing up.

In high school I was on the track team, and I was in the city neighborhood athletic program. I was boxing at the Slaughter Athletic Club. I got into it because I was small and because I lived in a tough neighborhood. We had gangs back then, too. We had the Unmerciful Hulks, the Termites, and the Swanks. I was part of a couple of those groups. Gangs served a sort of social purpose. They showed your neighborhood prowess. I also was a drum major for the Spirit of St. Louis Drum and Bugle Corps, sponsored by American Legion Post No. 77. We marched in the Annie Malone Parade every year.

I started teaching in the public schools in 1950. In 1968, after a crisis about a flag burning at Beaumont High School, I was appointed principal of Beaumont High School. I was able to settle the student unrest because I was young and had a lot of energy. I could keep up with the students.

Then in 1970 some black politicians came to me and said they were ready to run a black for mayor, a black who could get white votes. They got me a job at City Hall as the director of human resources. After two years in that job I was ready to run. But Mayor Cervantes decided to run again, and Poelker, the comptroller, ran against him. I was not interested in running if it would be divisive, because I already had a good job at City Hall, so I ran for comptroller. I went to Mayor Cervantes and told him I was going to run for comptroller, and he tried to discourage me. He said that since he and Poelker were both Democrats I would still have my job no matter who won. I told him that the black community was ready to test its political might. It was time for an African American to be part of the decision-making process.

Getting into politics took a lot of image building, especially in South St. Louis. We had help from Sorkis Webbe and from the Pipe Fitters Union. I was the comptroller from 1973 to 1977, and then I worked at CEMREL, the think tank, and I was a city alderman. In 1980 I was elected to the state senate. My district ran from the Ville on the north to Highway 44 on the south, and from Goodfellow on the west to the Mississippi on the east. I represented the business district, the hospital district, the Central West End, the Grand Center arts district, and part of North St. Louis. I represented blues, booze, and Bach; the Big River City where the Good Times Flow.

Then Bill Clay asked me to come to Washington as the chief of staff of the Subcommittee on Libraries and Memorials. That included the Library of Congress, the Smithsonian Institution, and the Kennedy Center. The Library of Congress employs a large number of researchers, many of whom have Ph.D.s, to do research for congressmen and senators. Sometimes those researchers have to find out all about some issue in twenty-four hours.

We need to ask ourselves, who are we going to turn the gauntlet over to? Who will stand on the shoulders of those who have gone before? Young people who get involved in politics need to understand about coalition politics, about working together with other groups. They need to develop a council of elders to advise them. You must stay informed about politics. Know who is representing you, who is affecting your life.

J. B. "Jet" Banks

Missouri State Senator; Senate Majority Leader

I grew up in southeast Missouri, in the little town of Hermondale, on the Arkansas and Missouri state line. My dad owned a small farm where he raised cattle, hogs, cotton, soybeans, alfalfa, all the things you do on a farm. My mother was a housewife. She did a lot of gardening and sewing, and she loved fishing. She belonged to a fishing club, and she and the other ladies would clean and cook the fish right there on the riverbank. As a youngster, my job was to build the fire for them.

I had one brother and one sister. I was the youngest of the family. We all went to the Hermondale School in southeast Missouri. James Brody, the principal, had a big influence on me. He started sports at the school and took us places we had never been before. He taught us etiquette. He was a good educator, and he was a good role model. He turned my life around.

My family moved to St. Louis so that my father could make more money. My father got a job working for the city. In those days you had to have political connections to get those jobs. He worked for the city for fifteen or twenty years.

In my childhood we lived in a segregated society. There were places in southeast Missouri where we could not go to eat. There were Jim Crow train cars. As a youngster I simply accepted it, not that I wanted to, but it was just a way of life. Then we moved from southeast Missouri looking for equality, looking for better treatment. The heroes who impressed me over the years were Martin Luther King, Jesse Jackson, and A. Philip Randolph, who organized the March on Washington. I admired them for what they were trying to do. I wanted to do something like they were doing, because I thought it was needed.

When I left school and went into politics, my mentor was Jordan W. Chambers. He was the first black justice of the peace and the first black constable in the city of St. Louis. He was a Republican at one time, and then in 1932 he joined the Democratic Party. He was recognized from coast to coast as a great leader. I wanted to be a politician like him. I admired the things he did and the things that he stood for. He opened doors for African Americans. He got jobs for African Americans on the police force and in the fire department, and he integrated the hospitals in St. Louis. A large number of African Americans went to work in City Hall because of Mr. Chambers. He got us jobs we never had before.

The opportunities are a lot better than they were in the past, particularly if you have education and skills. But if you want to get ahead you have to be better than average. My dad was not an educator, but he instilled that in me. You may be able to get out of school or college with a C, but when you're trying to get into the job market you've got to be better. Kids have got to work hard, and they have got to have a sense of pride. And when you get to the fork in the road, there's a dead-end street over here and there's a light at the end of the tunnel over here. Which one are you going to take? If you go over here, you've got fast money that will not last. On the other side, if you get your education, there is a job, there are things that are waiting for you. The road is much slower, but that's the route to choose. The dead-end street looks rosy, you know, fancy cars, fancy jewelry, fancy ladies, and everything else. But it's a dead-end street. When you get to the end, where do you go?

I served in the house for four years, and I served in the state senate twenty-two years. I have been majority leader of the senate for eight years. I was the first African American elected to that position, and I will possibly be the last, because now we have term limits, and you can only serve eight years in the senate. I passed over two hundred bills that have been signed into law. The one that I am most proud of is Senate Bill 307, which changed Harris-Stowe from a city college that was ready to close into a state institution that is one of the best in the area. The reason it is so important is because of the cost. Harris-Stowe provides a quality education for a lot less than Washington University, St. Louis University, or even the University of Missouri–St. Louis.

I came out of southeast Missouri, from the capital of the cotton fields, where I couldn't ride in the front of the bus. In the city of St. Louis I was able to own thirty-five buses. They were my buses. I put together a business that provided employment for thirty-five or forty people. I graduated from Lincoln University, where I majored in mathematics and minored in physics. I had intended to become a doctor, but I ended up in politics.

You can do a lot of things as a legislator, even if you are in the minority. I'd like to sit down and tell young people how important politics is. It affects our lives from the moment we come into this world until the moment we go out. Young people should learn as much about the political system as possible. They should start at the grass-roots level and work up through the organization. They should get involved to try to help somebody. See, you don't go into politics for yourself. You go into politics to make yourself available and to make changes in the system.

Joyce M. Thomas

President, Cardinal Ritter College Prep High School;
President, St. Louis Board of Education

I grew up at 4255 West Kennerly in the Ville. My mother died when I was four years old, and I was raised by my aunt and uncle, Bessie and William Morton. They were my inspiration. They made me understand that going to school would help me become independent, that it was important to be a good student, and that learning was fun. They also taught me the importance of community service. My uncle was a Mason and my aunt was an Eastern Star.

Growing up in the Ville meant that you were among people who cared. Those were the days when any adult in the neighborhood could call your attention to something you were doing wrong and discipline you if necessary. The neighborhood was like an extended family. It was a very secure feeling. I feel sad about the children who don't have concerned adults who support them and help them and nurture them.

Let me describe the Ville. The first thing I would mention is Poro College. The building was constructed in such a way that you could go in the door of Poro College that was sort of angled on the corner of St. Ferdinand and Pendleton. And on the Pendleton side there were storefront businesses. And they were all black owned. There was a barbershop and Billie Burke's, a sandwich shop that was really popular with the college students and the high school students. There was a movie there, the Amethyst Theater. And then coming onto St. Ferdinand the rest of that part was Poro College. Annie Malone built Poro College. It was a school of beauty culture. My mother learned beauty culture there. And my mother knew Annie Malone.

I attended Simmons Elementary School, Sumner High School, Stowe Teachers College, which was right across the street from me, and Lincoln University. And I had some memorable teachers. Thelma Meaux was my third-grade teacher, and she was always kind and warm and smiling and encouraging. She gave us big hugs to comfort us if we were sad. I knew I wanted to be a teacher since the third grade, and that was because of Miss Meaux. My other favorite teacher was Dr. Julia Davis. Dr. Davis was my eighth-grade teacher, and she didn't just teach regular subjects, she taught black history. She built it into the curriculum on her own. That's when I began to get a sense of my own cultural heritage.

I attended all-black schools all the way through Lincoln University, and I just came through at the right time. Dr. Herman Dreer was at Stowe when I was there. And when I went to Lincoln, Dr. Lorenzo Greene was the professor of black history there. He subsequently wrote a book about the black contributions to the state of Missouri. In high school it was more informal. Wirt Walton helped us to understand the beauty of our black gospel music; Nan Walton helped us understand the beauty of our black literature.

There was a fraternal organization in the Ville called A. U. K. & D. of A., the Ancient United Knights and Daughters of Africa. I thought of Africa as the mother country very early, when I was young. It was fascinating! What I remember about that group was that they worked together to help one another. They recognized their lineage to the mother continent of Africa, and they worked to spread that message. But also fraternal organizations worked to help one another in times of distress. What is hard for some people to understand was that there was a time when our people had little or no life insurance, so they had fund-raisers to help their brothers and sisters in distress, and they supported children in the Annie Malone Children's Home. My cousin and I marched in the Annie Malone Parade each year with the Ancient United Knights and Daughters of Africa. We wore white dresses, and the boys wore white shirts and pants, and we wore white shoes and socks, and we wore blue capes trimmed in yellow over one shoulder. We thought we were great stuff!

Sumner High School was fun. There were only two high schools for blacks, Sumner and Vashon. And therefore there was a great competition between those two schools. The Thanksgiving Classic was the Sumner-Vashon football game. It was held in the St. Louis Public School Stadium. Sumner sat on the west side of the stadium, and Vashon sat on the east side of the stadium. And most of the time that I was there Vashon won the football game, and Sumner won the fight. There always was a little jostling after the game. I didn't live far from the stadium, so walking back and forth was fun because I ran into my buddies and we walked together. And during those times there was a lot of snow on the ground. In those days we had a lot of winter in St. Louis. The snow started in early November, and it might be on the ground until February or March.

I married Joe Thomas from that little house on Pendleton. Growing up in the Ville was comfortable. School was fun, and adults looked out for you. I came along at a fantastic time, the thirties and the forties.

Theoplis "Ted" Hudson Sr.

Owner, Hudson's Embassy Records, Tapes, and Videos

When I was growing up, the Ville was one of the most respected neighborhoods in the city of St. Louis. Everybody in the area was a home owner. The area was anchored by the educational facilities and Homer G. Phillips, which was a top medical teaching facility. Blacks out of Africa, Asians, and Orientals were trained to be doctors and nurses at that institution. In fact, it has a heck of a history. Homer G. Phillips was a black attorney who lived in North St. Louis. He fought in the political arena to get a good hospital for blacks, and that is what caused his death. He was killed by white racists. And he is the one the hospital was named after.

We only had two high schools, Sumner and Vashon, so everybody was friends with everybody. In fact, it was a neighborhood that really preached education and social behavior. There were plenty of social activities where we had fun as youngsters. At that time, we weren't allowed to go to white places of enjoyment, so we created our own fun. We had house parties and dances at the school. It was a cohesive neighborhood. There was a unity there that I yearn for now.

The Ville began to change in the middle 1950s, when blacks began to move out. We had broken the barrier in terms of restrictive housing. Blacks began to move west and north, and the exodus from the Ville began. But up until that time, everybody lived in the Ville. Teachers lived next door to steelworkers. Steelworkers lived down the street from postal workers. Your doctor lived around the corner. In fact, everything was in that community. And it stayed in that community until the mid-fifties.

Because our community was such a tight unit, we really didn't encounter racism until we became adults. When I came home from the navy, in 1945, I bought a truck, and I had my first business. It was an express company called American Delivery. When I tried to solicit business I realized that I could not get white companies to do business with me. So I reverted to black businesses. At that time, we had quite a few black businesses. We had a black furniture store and appliance dealer. I had him for my customer. We had florist companies, and I had them for my customers. They were all black owners from the black north side, along Delmar and Taylor, from Kingshighway east. You ran into racism in the white business community, and you also ran into the racist structure of the unions. The unions were even more rigid than the white businessmen. There was no way you could haul for white companies and not be a union driver or a unionized company. So I reverted to black-owned and black-operated businesses. And I did very well. I was able to buy two more trucks.

Then I diversified. I had the trucking company, and I hauled freight and furniture. So then I diversified into furniture and appliances. I ran into racism with furniture and appliances in terms of volume buying. At that time companies would sell to black dealers at the same price that they sold retail. It was almost impossible to compete with white people who were getting a wholesale discount. I was being charged the same price that the white retailer was charging. So when the whites wouldn't give me a wholesale price, I opened a wholesale company and called it Ted's One Stop.

At that time black schools didn't teach business classes. I just had to get it the best I could. So I went through white businessmen's trash cans. I'd take the correspondence and I'd study it. Then I'd know where they bought products. That's when I started buying furniture from South Carolina. I had seen correspondence from there in the trash cans behind Jewish businesses. So I started buying bedroom sets and living room sets from South Carolina. And from furniture and appliances I moved into the record business. I turned the appliance store into a record store in 1959.

I would like to see more young people interested in entrepreneurship. I don't see anybody involved in commercial development in the Ville. I would like to see that. I would like to see businessmen who own land in the Ville develop the land commercially. I would like to see the Ville get stronger, like it used to be.

Alfred J. Ford

Owner, Turf Grill; Broker, Ford Brothers Insurance Brokers
and Marsh and McLennan Inc.

I'd say that my whole life, my interest has always been business. That goes for my brother too. We used to get put out of school for bootlegging candy. We sold Baby Ruths and Snickers out of our lockers. We bought candy, bagged it, and sold it to teachers, so when they had their parties, they would have bags of candy.

After college I worked in the post office for about six months, but that really wasn't for me. And then I had a friend who got me on as a waiter on the National Limited, the fastest train on the Baltimore and Ohio Railroad. It went from here to New York, carrying politicians and big shots, and to Washington, D.C. I worked on there for about a year and a half. That was an experience that I would never trade.

Then my brother Lafayette and I decided to open a restaurant, a sandwich shop. We opened a restaurant at 1010 N. Vandeventer, and we named it the Turf Grill. I'd seen that name on a place in Times Square, in New York. Our restaurant was a twenty-four-hour deal, where you were served short orders, chili, pork chops, eggs, fried chicken, and hamburgers. That was around 1936 or 1937. Then in 1939, we opened up Turf Grill number two, on the northeast corner of Jefferson and Chestnut. And this was a very fine place. It was built like White Castle, with nothing but white porcelain and chrome trim. It went well. You have to understand that during that period, if blacks went downtown, the only place they could eat was Woolworth's, where they stood up at the counter and ate a hamburger, and if they had something to drink, it was out of a paper cup. Otherwise they had to come all the way out to Jefferson and Chestnut and stop at the Turf Grill. And then there was the Deluxe Restaurant, which was owned by Jesse Johnson, which was on the southeast corner of Jefferson and Market.

Then, when World War II started, Lafayette was inducted into the army. He didn't stay long. He was in and out because of his flat feet. I was inducted in '43. Near the end of the war, it must have been '44 or '45, I had a cousin who lived in Chicago who operated a french-fried-shrimp shop where he sold nothing but french-fried shrimps, no potatoes or anything, just french-fried shrimp by the pound. And I sent my sister Emma up there to learn that business. I was still in the army, and my brother was handling the restaurants. Emma went to Chicago and learned the secrets of how to make the batter, and we opened up Ford Brothers French Fried Shrimp, on Jefferson Avenue between Pine and Olive Streets. That was before the Mill Creek area was torn down.

I was discharged in '45. We opened up Ford Brothers Appliance and Record Company. We sold phonograph records, and we sold appliances. Then one day, Lafayette and I were talking about all the people who came in and asked for advice, and we decided to open up a consulting service and charge for it.

So we went out to Frank Blumeyer, who carried all our insurance. He and Chris Muckerman were running the largest insurance brokerage firm in the Midwest. We told Frank about this consulting service we were going to start. He swiveled around in his chair and said, "How would you and Lafayette like to be in the insurance business?" I said, "I don't know, we run these restaurants and everything now." He said, "I think it would be a good thing. You know everybody, everybody knows you. And you know a lot about insurance because you're carrying all kinds of insurance yourself: burglary insurance, plate-glass insurance, automobile insurance." And we found ourselves in the insurance brokerage business. That was around 1950.

We were associated with General Insurers, and we operated as Ford Brothers Insurance Brokers. We had to liquidate our other businesses, because in order to have an insurance broker's license you have to be a full-time broker. By coincidence that was the year the Vagabonds bought a house for a clubhouse, and we donated a lot of things to the Vags. The counters from the record shop became the bars at the Vagabond Club.

In 1968 Lafayette and I switched from General Insurers Incorporated to St. Louis Insurers Incorporated. In 1970 we joined Lawton-Burn-Bruner Insurance Agency, and that same year Lafayette had a heart attack and died. I moved into the Equitable Building in 1971, and Marsh McLennan bought out Lawton-Burn-Bruner in 1987. Marsh McLennan handles all of the insurance for McDonnell Douglas. It's the largest insurance brokerage in the world.

When I think about the youth today, I think many of them get started off on the wrong road by following someone else. I think more young people need to think for themselves and let themselves become leaders. Integrity is very important. If you are going to do something, don't just talk about it. Do it.

Antoinette C. "Toni" Robinson

Democratic Committeewoman, Seventeenth Ward

I was born in New Orleans, Louisiana, and I came to St. Louis when I was eleven. I was one of fourteen children. We had a big family, a wonderful family, eight girls and six boys. Of the fourteen children, there are only six of us living now. My father was a singer. He sang with the internationally famous LaBoule Sisters. The four LaBoule Sisters were from Europe. They performed all over the world, and we lived back and forth from New Orleans to Florida to St. Louis, and then my parents decided to settle in St. Louis. My mother was from New Orleans.

I was baptized Catholic. The whole family was baptized Catholic. When my family moved to St. Louis around 1925, the colored people were being invited to join St. Elizabeth's Church. Father William Markoe and Father John Markoe and Father Austin A. Bark were the first ones to come to my home. We lived at 1126 North Whittier, that's at Whittier and Cook, that big, beautiful, white stone house. We had the basement, first, second, and third floors. They asked us if they could start a school there, a Catholic school for black children, because at that time St. Louis had not reached the stage yet that whites would consider letting black children go to school with white children. That was the first black Catholic school in the city of St. Louis. The Helpers of the Holy Souls, the little French sisters, taught the children at the school. The Helpers of the Holy Soul did a lot of parochial work throughout the city, getting Negroes to become Catholics and join St. Elizabeth's Church. They lived at 4012 Washington, but the Mother House called them back to Philadelphia a few years ago because they were getting old. The Sisters of the Most Blessed Sacrament worked with us, too. The Catholic Church has played an important part in improving race relations amongst all, because they started integration in the city of St. Louis. They were the first to integrate their schools, starting with St. Louis University in the forties.

I went to the school at our home first. Then I went to the West Bell School, and then to John Marshall School, and then to Sumner High School. And then I received a scholarship from the Jesuit fathers to go to Xavier University in New Orleans. The Jesuit fathers at St. Louis University saw to it that my sister Rosabelle and I both got scholarships to Xavier. That was great. Imagine what our poor mother had to go through, rearing fourteen children.

I married Pellon Robinson in 1942. He was following in his dad's footsteps. His dad graduated from Loyola University in Chicago. Pellon Robinson handled all types of businesses. He filled out people's income taxes for them and helped less fortunate families to get on their feet. He owned ten drugstores, but he didn't name all of them Robinson's Drugstore, because some of the neighborhoods asked us to leave the old names when we bought them. Then the Mill Creek Area Redevelopment Corporation came through, and they tore everything down. We lost several of the stores that way. But God has been more than good to us, and because of that, we reached out to help others. We helped many, many children through school. We had two children of our own, a boy and a girl, and I have three grandchildren. But we also helped other children go to college.

When we moved to 4953 Maffit Place, we were the second black family over there. Clarence and Dorothy Hunter moved in a week before we did. This is where we lived when my children went to school at Blessed Sacrament. When we moved to 4953 Maffit Place, it so happens that the politicians in that area were all white. When the neighborhood began to change, I held a meeting at my home. I called Clarence Hunter, and I said, "Our area has become predominantly black, so why don't we get together and become organized and we can have our own political leaders." This is when we got in there and got some black politicians.

Jordan Chambers was really among the very first black politicians. Jordan Chambers and Fred Weathers—they were really the beginners of the black politicians in the city of St. Louis. It was after that that Leroy Tyus and Bill Clay and all of us began to come in. Jordan Chambers was the first person who really and truly got the black man interested in politics and working on it. He was a great guy. He was our really top man. We owe a lot to him.

Black politicians did not really and truly have a voice until Jordan Chambers organized us in the thirties. Before that St. Louis was a very prejudiced city. Now a lot of our politicians are growing older, and our younger generation is going to have to carry on from where we are. We have to pass on our political ideas to the younger generation, so that we'll be able to stay in the picture. I hope the younger generation will remember the accomplishments of those fathers who have gone before.

God made us all, regardless of race or color. He made the human race like a beautiful flower garden. What a strange world it would be if everyone was the same color.

Clifton W. Gates

Owner, C. W. Realty Company and Lismark Distributing Company;
Chairman of the Board, Gateway National Bank

I was born in Pine Bluff, Arkansas. I lost my mother when I was three, and my father's sister and brother brought me to St. Louis to rear me. We lived in the Ville. In those days Taylor was the western boundary of the Ville. There was no better neighborhood available for blacks anywhere in St. Louis. Many professionals lived in that neighborhood: schoolteachers, doctors, lawyers, postal workers, porters for the railroads. It was a very stable neighborhood.

I went to Cole Elementary School on Enright close to Vandeventer. Cole School was built right after the tornado of 1927, and my class was the first class to go all the way through Cole. I remember the teachers and Mr. Langston, the principal. We knew them all well and respected them.

I went to Sumner High School. Class of '42. I had four wonderful years there. Pop Beckett and Lucian Garrett taught physical ed., and Wirt Walton was the music director. I sang in the a cappella choir, and Robert McFerrin, the opera star, sang baritone in the choir with me. Upon graduation, I crossed the street and attended Stowe Teachers College. But I didn't graduate. What happened was, during my second year at Stowe, Uncle Sam decided he couldn't end the war without me.

I was drafted in December 1943. I went into the army, and after completing my training at Fort McClellan, Alabama, I was put into an ordnance and trucking outfit and shipped overseas. We went to England and were part of the invasion of Normandy, landing on Omaha Beach on D day plus eleven. We hit the beach just after the invasion and followed through with supplies and ammunition. Our trucking outfit was known as the Red Ball Express. We supplied General Patton's army all the way through to Germany.

After the war I worked at the post office for a number of years, until I decided that I was not earning sufficient income. Then I began to sell real estate for P. C. Robinson Realty. I left P. C. to manage another company, and then I formed my own company in 1959, C. W. Realty Company. I built it into the largest black-owned real estate company in the city.

Then I began to think about the need for a mortgage company, a place where blacks could borrow funds to buy a home. I bought stock in a Kansas City group, Mid-Central Mortgage Company, and I opened a branch office here, in Clayton. After five or six years, I sold out to a larger mortgage company. Now

I was thinking about a bank, a commercial bank. I helped to form Gateway National Bank in 1964. Our first board of directors included Howard B. Woods, publisher of the *Sentinel*; Leo Bohanon, director of the Urban League; Joyce Montgomery; Dr. Jerome Williams; and Judge Clyde Cahill. We opened Gateway National Bank in 1965.

In the 1970s I was still involved in real estate when the interest rates went crazy. No one in his right mind wanted to buy property when he had to pay 18 or 20 percent interest. So as the real estate business began to taper I began to look for something else to do. I thought of the liquor business, and I went to New York to talk to Seagram's, but they decided that they were adequately represented in St. Louis. Then came the idea of a beer distributing business, Miller in particular. I approached them, and it seemed that it was the right time. They asked for a formal application giving five-year projections for their product in this community. I contacted a number of people and put together a proposal. I became the first and only black beer distributor in the St. Louis area. Fifteen years later I was still the only black beer distributor. Miller has over eight hundred distributors, but I think there are only four black distributors. Budweiser has a thousand beer distributors, and they've got about four blacks. That shows you how difficult it is.

I would say the Urban League and the NAACP were the two organizations that brought about the most change for blacks. I was president of the Urban League in the sixties, and I was always a board member of the NAACP. I was chairman of the Job Negotiation Committee of the NAACP, and I successfully negotiated jobs for blacks at Southwestern Bell Telephone as installers and linemen. I give a lot of credit to some of the earlier leaders of the Urban League and of the NAACP, Ernest Calloway and people of that sort, who had the foresight and wisdom and desire to see change and took the leadership role that made it possible for many of us, in turn, to follow.

There is really no difference in people, basically. We're all alike. It's how we interact with one another and how we relate to one another that really counts. We shouldn't treat each other differently based upon status or color or what have you. Basically, inwardly, we are all very much alike. I treat all people alike, from the president of an institution to the one who cleans the floors.

Bettie Mae Taylor

Owner, Taylor's Sausage Company

I was born in Coffeeville, Mississippi, Yalobusha County. My parents were sharecroppers, and I grew up on the Newberger Plantation. My mother had seven girls and three boys.

We moved from Coffeeville down to Elliott, Mississippi, where I married my husband. His grandparents owned a little farm, fifty-two acres of land, and we stayed there and farmed about five or six years. We moved to St. Louis in 1938. His father was here. He had been here for a while. But his grandfather died, and he came back to Mississippi to take care of his grandmother, and we got married. He always said he would never be a farmer, but he would stay in Mississippi as long as his grandmother lived. When she passed that August, we gathered the crop and sold out and moved, because we didn't like his bosses. He was independent, and I was independent. I had four children, and I said to him, "John Wesley, if we move to the city, how are we going to feed these kids?" He said, "We'll open up a grocery store, and we can feed them wholesale." His father had one of the biggest grocery businesses in the city at one time, but he got into trouble and got out of the business.

When we moved to St. Louis, we moved to 2816 Adams, and then they changed the name to Spruce. We had the store right at 2816 Adams Street. We ran that store for a long time, and we made sausage in the back of it. We kept growing until the city decided that we would have to move. We bought the building next door, 2818 Adams, and all my children were there. He and his daddy opened a store on Market Street, and they stayed there for a while. But they didn't get along too well, and they broke up. I said, "St. Louis is big enough for both of you to make a living," but his father moved to East St. Louis and opened up a sausage company.

We moved here, to Grand Avenue, in 1960. My husband passed in 1963, and I've been a widow ever since. I was lucky I had my sons. They had learned the business, and we carried on. My husband learned how to make sausage in the country. People who lived in the country always made sausage, sauce, and headcheese. We make sauce and headcheese now. My husband bought the different spices and mixed his own seasoning. He made a barbecue sauce for rich white people. And when that man died, you ought to have seen us trying to hoard and save barbecue sauce that was left, because I didn't know how to make it. He knew just how to season it, just how many spices.

When he would put the sausage in the mixer downstairs, you couldn't stay down there. You had to come outside to catch your breath, because those peppers and all those spices were too strong. He got a company to mix it for him, and they've been doing it ever since. But he knew how to mix the spices to make his sausage taste like he wanted it. We started out mixing it in tin tubs with our hands, putting paper on the scale and weighing up pounds, and foil wrapping it. We did that for a long time, and then he decided that we would get a machine to package it.

I went to school in Mississippi, down from where we were living on the plantation. Then I went to school at Tie Plant, Mississippi. I finished the eighth grade there. I was always a person that was after whatever was there. I thought, if it was in a book, I could learn it.

I went into cosmetology. I won a free course here, and then I passed the state board. That was really good because I had some of my children, and I wanted to be here when my children came home from school. I had my little shop right here where we took out a closet. Then I had a little store two doors down the street. I cooked in the back and washed in the back. Then I ran home at night, and I didn't have to cook. But we had the sausage company downstairs, so I gave up the store. The children said, "Oh, Mama, what are we going to do?" And I said, "It's just like kicking an old man out when he's worthless." My husband said, "We make enough with the sausage to live."

When I took the Cosmetology State Board, my husband said, "You probably won't get it." I said, "Why don't you wish me luck and hope I do?" When the mailman dropped the license in the door, I tell you, I picked it up and I slapped my husband all over the place. I said, "You said I couldn't do it, but I got it!"

I've been busy all my life. I just love to be doing something. I'm not used to sitting around. I say, if you have it in your mind that you want to be somebody or do something, you work to that effect. That's what I did. I had in mind what I wanted to do, and I believed that if you can read you can learn. If you don't try, you will never make it. But if you want to be somebody, then just get with it. That's what I say.

Virgil Akins

Welterweight Champion of the World

I grew up downtown, around Broadway and Mullanphy and Eighth and Clark. My mother didn't want me to be a fighter. When I won the amateur title my picture was in the paper, and she almost fell over. She said, "That's my boy." She didn't know what to make of it. But it was nice. It was good. She said I was always too wild. That's what made me a good fighter, being wild. Nobody could whip me, no way.

St. Louis was rough, like it is now. There were gang wars, and youngsters ganging together and fighting each other from different parts of town. My mother was always telling me not to run with those boys. That's how I started liking boxing, going to the community centers. I wanted to wrestle and punch the bag. I liked it, and I stayed with it. I started at Vashon over there on Laclede, then I went to Carr Square because it was close to my home. I worked out at Slaughter's Athletic Club at Sarah and the Hodiamont tracks. I knew all the fellows that were up there.

But I had a hard time, as I said before, and I'm not bragging. They said I didn't know how to work out, because I used to work hard all the time, you know, and they didn't like that. They liked to mess around. I didn't like to mess around. If I wanted to box I wanted to be good at it. My ring name was Virgil "Honey Bear" Akins. A sportswriter named Ray Smith gave me that name. He said when I went to work on my opponents I was vicious as a bear and smooth as honey.

I started boxing professionally in 1948, when I was eighteen. They had a show in Kansas City. A kid who had ducked me in the amateurs had had three fights up in Kansas City and won, and they said, "Why don't you send down to St. Louis and get a fighter?" They sent down, and my friend Johnnie Tocol was running the gym over on Blair and K. He said, "Hey, Virgil, we've got a good fight for you. Why don't you turn pro up in Kansas City? We're getting good money for it." He said he was getting a hundred and a quarter for a full round of fighting. He said he'd give me that much cause they liked me and I brought boys up there all the time. I said,

"Okay, it's all right with me, as long as it's fair." And so I went up there. And when I signed in at the doctor's office, and he was taking my pulse and my blood sample, he said, "Sign right here. Put your ring name down there." I said, "Virgil Akins." And everybody looked around. "Akins," they said, "we know about him. He's tough."

I was the first homegrown champion that ever came out of St. Louis. I was born here, went to school here, and won the title here. I fought as a lightweight and a welterweight. And I fought some middleweights. Middleweight was 160, and at the time I was 147. Before that I was lightweight. And then they put me on welterweight, which was 147, and I wasn't but 135, 136, at the time. They called me the uncrowned lightweight champ, because I couldn't get a title fight. So I just moved up into the next weight and won that.

Boxing needs more regulation. When you're training, you take a severe beating, because you're not in shape when you're getting punched all around. Even though you have head gear on and big gloves, you get hurt even when you're training. If they would supervise it properly, boxers wouldn't sustain such terrible blows, you know. I would also like to see a deputy commissioner, to be there at the weigh-in, not just a doctor. Because, it's just like anything else, they slip a little money under the table if he can't make the weight. You should have a deputy commissioner there to see that the weights are right.

When I had a restaurant down there at 2000 Martin Luther King, Archie Moore used to come by. I had his picture up on the wall. Every time he was in town he'd come by. He loved the spaghetti, and he loved the fish. He was a champ.

I was thinking about this the other day. When you want something, you have to go after it, hook, line, and sinker, with all you've got. You might not get it right then and there, but you've got to stay on it, and you've got to put your whole soul and body into it. Anything, I don't care what it is, if it's good, it's not going to come easy. It's going to be hard if it's worthwhile. You've got to stay with it.

Thelma Jackson Bates

Beautician

I grew up in downtown St. Louis, right at Jefferson. I was born at 2652 Morgan, in the rear. It was Morgan then, but now it's Delmar. I lived next door to the Scott Joplin House. I had one brother and one sister. My sister died when I was eighteen, and my brother died about seven years ago. My mother died in 1965, but she raised me and my children. She was a beautician before me.

I attended Banneker School and Sumner. I graduated from Sumner High School in 1926. Mr. Herman Dreer is a teacher I'll always remember. He taught history at Sumner. He taught black history along with the history of the states. He encouraged me to be in one of the religious plays he put on with his theater group. He was a good Christian. My other favorite teacher was Julia Davis. She was a strong leader and very strict. She encouraged me to be a good person.

My mother started as a beautician when I was five years old, and I helped her. I stood on boxes to wash people's hair for my mother. I've been doing hair that long. I've been doing hair for eighty years.

There weren't any schools for training at that time. But there was a lady named Mrs. Gregory who taught me everything. All this is before Poro College. I knew that Poro College, the beauty school, was there, and different people that I knew went there, but that was after I had learned beauty culture. Mrs. Gregory taught me everything.

I was one of the first black women to receive a cosmetology license. My mother and I received the first licenses that were out. They had just started giving them, and we were the first. I am the oldest beautician still working. I have one customer left.

I was the first person to receive a relaxer in St. Louis, a perm as we know it now. I've forgotten what year that was. Ardell gave me my first permanent. I knew him real well. He had several little beauty shops down on Newstead. I remember all the little beauty shops down on Newstead.

I've always had my shop in my home. I bought my products from Miller Supply. I was always very close with Miller Supply. When I came along, you know, it was much cheaper. At that time it was fifty cents for a shampoo, press, and curl. Now, it's much higher.

I was president of the beauticians' organization. I was one of the first presidents of the Hairdressers and Cosmetologists. We had meetings, and then we would do practicing work. We'd do hair as charity work. We set up a beauty shop at the Truman Center on Arsenal Street, and we'd go once a month to do the patients' hair. We did it for free. Also I was a model for charitable organizations, beauticians' organizations, and churches. I drove from church to church.

My daughter Perita was a model also. I have three children, three girls. Jacqueline is my oldest daughter. She retired as a principal at Mark Twain. Racine Maddox is my youngest daughter, and she retired from schoolteaching. And Perita has the beauty shop, and she was a model. *Ebony Magazine* featured her one time.

The organization that has been most important to me is the NAACP. In fact, I was one of the first members, when it started in St. Louis. I have a lifetime membership in the NAACP.

In 1956 I joined Lane Tabernacle. I go to Sunday school every Sunday and stay on through. I was vice president of the Usher Board, and I taught Sunday school. I was president of my Sunday school class.

I've always had my own business at the house, and I used to participate in the beauty shows. Beauticians would always have shows, and I used to compete in those shows. I did quite a bit of that.

I have been a beautician for eighty years. Eighty years, how about that? Yes, when I was a little girl I'd stand up on the boxes and shampoo. Doing hair is a talent. That is definitely what it is. It's a good profession to be in. I mean, you are on your own. If you think you would like to be a beautician, continue to go to school, because it is a beautiful career.

I am the longest still-active beautician in St. Louis… eighty years.

Paul L. Miller Jr.

President, P. L. Miller and Associates, Inc.

I was born in Starkville, Mississippi, and we moved here in 1947, when I was about five. When we first moved here from Mississippi, we lived on the south side of Rutger Avenue, down near Compton. But I grew up, principally, in the Ville. My parents were both born in Mississippi. My father worked for a black insurance company, Universal Life Insurance Company. He was the assistant manager of the local office here. And later he became a traveling salesman for a company called E. F. Young Manufacturing Company, which was based in Mississippi. E. F. Young Manufacturing Company was one of the first companies that produced a hair-straightening product for African American consumers. Beginning around 1949 or 1950, my father traveled in a twelve- or fifteen-state area, selling these goods out of the back of his car.

My father started his own business in addition to what he was doing as a traveling salesman for E. F. Young Manufacturing Company. He traveled mostly in the South and the upper Midwest, selling products to beauticians and barbers and other beauty-supply companies. Along the way he began selling items like pressing combs, electric heaters, bobby pins, hairpins, shampoo capes, and all those kinds of things. He carried those items in the back of his car, during his travels for E. F. Young Manufacturing Company, and he worked out an agreement with Young so that he could carry items that didn't compete with their products. As an outgrowth of that business, he developed a mail-order business. We sold products to beauticians and barbers outside the St. Louis area, principally in states like Missouri, Arkansas, Alabama, Kentucky, Tennessee, Louisiana, Mississippi, North and South Carolina, and all over the Deep South. He would take orders for any items that he didn't have in his car, and each evening my mother and I packed up the orders. Then in the morning, before I went to school, I took the orders to the post office and shipped them C.O.D.

We lived right on the corner of Sarah and Garfield, in the heart of the Ville, and we carried the inventory for most of these items in the basement of our home. When my father was in town, we would call on beauty shops and barbershops. I went with my father on the days that I wasn't in school. On Fridays and Saturdays, he would solicit orders from beauticians in East St. Louis, Alton, Madison, Venus, and all of the little towns over on the east side. Then he opened up a shop in the basement of the house where we not only packed orders, but where beauticians could pick up the products that he carried. And that's how we got started.

From 1955 until 1961, we operated from the basement of our home. Then in 1961 the city inspector indicated that we could no longer operate our business in the home. So we moved the business from Sarah Street to 4125 Easton Avenue, which later became Martin Luther King Boulevard, between Sarah and Belle Glade. From that location we developed a pretty good local following.

In 1962 my father had a serious automobile accident on the way to a trade show in Philadelphia. My mother and my sisters and I kept the business going for a couple of years while he was incapacitated. That was during my junior and senior years at St. Louis University. My father changed the name of the company from Miller Beauty Supply to Miller and Son Beauty Supply, because I had kept the business together while he was ill.

During the sixties we helped to organize the Gateway National Bank, and both my father and I served on the board of directors of the bank. We were also early customers of the bank. We supported a lot of community and civic activities throughout that period.

I think St. Louis offers an interesting number of opportunities for almost anybody, if they are willing to take the initiative to pursue those opportunities. As youngsters, we learned from my father and mother that you can do almost anything that you set your mind to. We learned that education was important, and both my sisters and I went to college.

I started school at Marshall Elementary, and I transferred to Riddick when I was in the sixth grade. I graduated from the eighth grade at Riddick in 1956, and then I attended Sumner High School. After graduating from Sumner, I attended Harris Teachers College for two years in the junior college program. I graduated from St. Louis University with a degree in accounting in 1965. Later, I participated in a graduate program in New York, underwritten by the American Management Association, and then I got an MBA from Washington University, here in St. Louis.

Any success that I have enjoyed has been due to the start that my father provided. He started off serving beauticians and barbers, and we expanded to where we shipped to chain stores in a thirteen-state area, from warehouses here in St. Louis and in Louisville and in Birmingham, Alabama. We sold the business in 1986, but a lot of what I'm doing now is an outgrowth of the business he started in 1954 and his early admonitions to do something that would not only benefit myself, but that would benefit the community at large.

Ivan C. James Jr.

Engineer, St. Louis Housing Authority

My father was from Russellville, Arkansas. He went to Meharry Medical College and became a dentist. A park and the public housing in Russellville are named James Park and the James Apartments after his father, who was the professor of the African American school. My mother grew up in Nashville, and she graduated from Fisk University. They came to St. Louis before I was born.

We lived on West Bell, and I went to West Bell School. So I only had to walk a block to school. Looking back now, segregation and integration weren't emphasized too much in our family. As children, we were never put in a situation where we had to run up against segregation. All of our activities were limited within the family, within the neighborhood. We had a neighborhood show that was in walking distance. I never thought about going downtown. Everything revolved around the family.

My Mom and Dad were good readers, and they had a lot of books by African American writers. Mama liked to recite poetry, and when we went to bed, if we had been good that day, she would leave the door open, and she would recite poetry for us. She could recite most of Paul Laurence Dunbar's poems. One of my favorites was "They had a party down at Tom's house." Another of my favorites was "Hiawatha." She could recite that, but the ones she couldn't remember, she would read.

I attended *the* high school of St. Louis. Sumner…ah, Sumner High School. During the early period of segregation, Sumner was the only African American high school in St. Louis. The teachers had master's degrees or above. At one time there were more Ph.D.s on the faculty at Sumner than at all of the other high schools in St. Louis put together. I went to Sumner in '28.

I was really inspired by the faculty. I was interested in science and math. One of my favorite teachers was a Mr. Anderson who taught math. Another teacher who made a great impression on me was Mr. Davenport. He had us write a paper weekly. I noticed that the subjects were such that we had to go to the public library to get the material. I think on Friday he went to the school library and looked to see what books they didn't have, and those were the books that he picked our subjects from, so that we had to go down to the public library. And that was my introduction to the public library and to researching.

And then I had an English teacher, Mrs. Alford. In her reading list she would have readings from African American writers. Also our history teachers would emphasize the contributions that African Americans made. Our teachers were dedicated. Our teachers saw that we not only got the history, but that we saw the part that we played in developing the history of our country. I feel that I was very fortunate to be able to go to Sumner.

After Sumner I went to the "Big One" college of Missouri: Lincoln University. Then after Lincoln I went to the Milwaukee School of Engineering. That was an all-white school, and three of us from Lincoln went there. One day we asked the president of the school why there were only three African American students, and he said, "You three are the first who applied." So we recruited more African American students.

I was the first African American hired by Emerson Electric for any job other than porter. I ran a punch press when they were doing a lot of government work for the Lend-Lease Program and then for the war. But I wanted to be a stationary engineer. A stationary engineer does the same thing as an engineer who runs a train, except he sits still and runs a power plant. You have to become licensed, and you have to take an examination. The only place in St. Louis that an African American could get a job as an engineer was with the public schools, and only the high schools had engine rooms. I took some engineering courses at Washington University and some correspondence courses, and I worked with Weldon Young at Vashon High School to study for my exam. Then I got a job as a fireman at Homer G. Phillips Hospital. After I got my license I left the hospital and took a job as stationary engineer for the St. Louis Housing Authority down at Carr Square Village. Then I was transferred to Pruitt-Igoe, and I became supervising engineer for Pruitt-Igoe. I stayed there for a number of years, and then I was transferred to supervising engineer for the south side, which included the Darst-Webbe-Peabody complex. I retired from the Housing Authority around 1982 or 1983.

I was the sixth African American to become a licensed engineer, and I had to wait about three or four years before I could get a job. At that time the only places African Americans could work as engineers were the two high schools or for the Housing Authority at housing projects that were for African Americans. At that time the housing was segregated. Today African American engineers can work anywhere that they can qualify. Even in the private sector, the jobs are not limited by color, but by ability. So don't give up. Education is the key, and just keep plugging, plugging, plugging.

Vivian E. Dreer

English Teacher, Vashon High School

I'm a native St. Louisan. I grew up in the Ville, and I went to the Cottage Avenue Elementary School, in the portable classrooms next to Sumner High School. My father came to St. Louis from Virginia in 1914, to teach at Sumner High School. He taught English and some of the social sciences and languages. After working as assistant principal at Sumner for thirteen years, he began teaching at Stowe Teachers College. He kept his students attuned to the achievements of blacks and the history of blacks. He made all of us proud of our heritage. My father knew Carter G. Woodson, the historian, and was instrumental in bringing him to St. Louis to speak. He started the Pushkin Publishing Company to disseminate Woodson's books. My father and Lorenzo Greene helped Carter G. Woodson with his first history of blacks in America.

My father also wrote two novels, *The Immediate Jewel of His Soul* and *The Tie That Binds*. My father was an ordained minister, the pastor of the King's Way Baptist Church, as well as being an educator. He wrote religious plays, which he presented through his dramatic clubs at the high school and at the college. I loved to write plays, too. I started writing plays when I was in first grade. I would produce my plays in my backyard with other neighborhood kids, especially Shirley Riddle and Hattie Sawyer, my best friends, who lived across the street. My interest in dramatic productions led me to start a children's theater so my niece and nephews and their friends would have a summer program that developed their talents and their self-esteem.

After starting college at Stowe, I went to Fisk University, and I graduated with a bachelor of arts in 1937. I got my master's in English from Fisk in 1939.

I went to Fisk because I had heard of W. E. B. Du Bois and James Weldon Johnson, who lectured there. Reverend Faulkner, our college chaplain, had people like James Weldon Johnson and Aaron Douglas, the artist, come to lecture in the chapel. Sometimes we were invited to a fireside chat, where we sat around and talked with these prominent black leaders. I was editor of the *Fisk Herald* and vice president of the dramatic club. One gets a sense of involvement and the inspiration to be a leader from attending a historically black college.

When I came along, few positions were open to me. I could have been a librarian, a nurse, a social worker, or a teacher. I thought I would teach for five years, but instead I found I got great pleasure from teaching. So I continued teaching English literature and dramatic arts at Vashon, and had a dramatic club for nearly twenty years.

I took a leave of absence from the St. Louis schools in 1948, because I was disenchanted with segregation in St. Louis. I didn't want to teach students that life would be equal, or that they would get social justice, when it wasn't true. So I went to Cleveland. I thought it was the place to go, because the Underground Railroad had operated there. I worked as a public relations secretary for the Urban League. I wrote scripts for a radio program called *The Urban League Hour*. Langston Hughes was one of the people on our program.

In 1948 CORE was just beginning in St. Louis. Marian Oldham was volunteering her time to type my father's dissertation on Negro leaders in St. Louis, and she encouraged me to work with CORE. When I came back from Cleveland, about 1950, CORE was in full swing. That's when I became active. We tried to open up public facilities, like restaurants. I would picket or do whatever they assigned me to do.

We had an experience at Howard Johnson's that I will never forget. We got up very early one morning and went there, the white members of CORE and the black. The black members held newspapers up to their faces so no one would notice us until we sat down on the stools. When we sat down they wouldn't serve us. The whites would order something and pass it down to us. The manager had the police come and make us leave. We left peacefully. That was one of the things that I liked about CORE—it was nonviolent.

I served on the board of the Urban League, here in St. Louis, when Leo Bohanon was the director. And I served on the board of the NAACP when Ernest Calloway was the president. I taught at Vashon High School from 1939 to 1958, except for the two years when I took a leave and went to Cleveland. After I got an M.A. in counseling, I moved to New York and worked with young people as a College Discovery Counselor at New York City Community College in Brooklyn for sixteen years.

But the thing that has impressed me the most, in my various careers, is the impact that the faculty must have had on the young people who came through Vashon High School. Many of those former students are community minded, service minded. They are determined to give something back to the community. Many of them hold important positions in the community. I am always happy to go to their reunions and to find out what they have been doing. I am very proud of them. And I am very proud to be one of the teachers who touched their lives.

Joseph M. Robinson

Owner and Pharmacist, Robinson Drugs

I was born at Union and Page. Dr. Johnson, from Ferguson, was taking my mother to the hospital in his Model T Ford, and he couldn't make it all the way down to the black hospital in the city of St. Louis, so they stopped at St. Ann's Hospital at Union and Page, and I was born. My mother was a very light-complected lady. She could have passed. See, there were no black doctors in the area then. So I was born. When my dad showed up, he was a dark man, and they moved us straight down to Provident Hospital in St. Louis.

I grew up in Carsonville, in St. Louis County, next to Normandy. My mother was from Ste. Genevieve, Missouri. Her name was Luella Elizabeth Robinson, and her maiden name was Brooks. My father was from Paducah, Kentucky. One of my brothers married Toni Robinson. And I have plenty of other brothers. All my brothers and sisters are retired now. I'm the only one who is still working.

We moved from Carsonville down to Wellston, Missouri, where I attended the W. E. B. Du Bois School from the first grade through the eighth grade. We had only two teachers then, but there weren't many students to a class, maybe six or seven in each class. It was a good school. Then I went to Sumner High School. We walked to Sumner High School from Wellston. That was quite a walk, wasn't it? Sometimes we would walk, but usually we caught a streetcar.

I finished high school in 1936, and I went to Lincoln University. After going to Lincoln University, the army grabbed me. We had the war, you know. I went into the army, through basic training, and then they selected me to go to the Army Specialized Training Program at the University of Pittsburgh. They took three of us out of the whole camp and shipped us up to ASTP at the University of Pittsburgh. It was kind of rough. We had a lot of classes in physics, chemistry, and math. We were working on the atomic bomb. It was top secret. We had a good time up there, too. There were only three black students among all those soldiers. The University of Pittsburgh was like several big downtown department stores with elevators, and we stayed on the twenty-first floor. The people in Pittsburgh were very nice to soldiers. We went to the clubs, and they gave us free drinks, just like that. And then they dropped that bomb, and the war was over.

I stuck around St. Louis maybe two or three years, and then I went to pharmacy school at Xavier University in New Orleans. I came back to St. Louis and I worked with my brother, who was in the pharmacy business. He owned several pharmacy stores in St. Louis. His store at Compton and Laclede was called All Drugs. That store was well known throughout the community. Then he acquired a store called the Druggist's Store, on Channing and Laclede. He had a store in Kinloch, called Kinloch Pharmacy. And he had a store in the Peoples Finance Building. I worked at the store in the Peoples Finance Building. And he had stores on Sheridan and Garrison, and Vandeventer and West Bell.

After I worked with him, I bought the store across the street from here, at Page and Taylor, in 1956. Then I moved across the street to here. This is the forty-first year of being on this corner.

We had a fountain in the drugstore, a nice long fountain where you could get malted milks and banana splits and sandwiches. Every drugstore had a fountain. You don't see them now. I remember I had the drugstore across the street the first time Martin Luther King Jr. came to town. He was here for a Baptist Association meeting. They didn't allow blacks to stay in the hotels, so they stayed in different people's houses. We had the fountain in our store, and the girls working for me cooked up a lot of chicken dinners for the people from out of town. See, they couldn't go to the restaurants. The Baptists had a parade through here, and Martin Luther King rode in the parade. But it was before he was well known.

We filled quite a few prescriptions back in those days. All the black pharmacists used to belong to the Mound City Pharmaceutical Association. Now we can join the St. Louis Pharmaceutical Association, which was for whites, and we've kind of let the Mound City Pharmaceutical Association go. I am a member of the National Pharmaceutical Association, made up of black pharmaceutical associations from all over the country.

A lot of blacks have gone out of business since integration. We didn't used to have superstores around here, no Walgreens, no National. We had the whole area sewed up. And we did a lot of business then, because we didn't have any competition. You don't see much of a black image in St. Louis now. The Peoples Finance Building was a black building. Homer G. Phillips was a black hospital. Those were great images for black people. But there's not much left. I think young blacks should get an education so they can enhance our image. I have worked with a lot of young people, and I try to encourage them to stay in school. Some of them come back and they have their master's degrees. Some are nurses. Some are school principals. Some of them are teachers or social workers. And that's what we've got to do—encourage our youth to go to school, encourage them to finish college.

Eddie Randle Sr.

Bandleader, Eddie Randle and the Blue Devils;
Owner, Eddie Randle and Sons Funeral Home

I was born in Pulaski County, Illinois, seven miles north of Cairo, Illinois. I came to St. Louis when I was sixteen, in 1923, and went to Sumner High. I'm still in the process of growing up. My parents were fine people. They had to be; look what they produced! My grandparents did the most toward raising me. My grandmother called me her little man, and I tried to do everything I could to please her. My grandfather, Elzie Buren, was a musician, a minister, and a schoolteacher. When he was young he was so far back near slavery, that I don't know where he learned as much as he knew. He was a very smart old man. He had seventeen children, and he taught them all music. His youngest son, my uncle, taught me. I was seventeen when I got my own trumpet.

Back in 1964, after I quit playing music, my son was taking music lessons over at Community Music School on Washington Avenue. One day he couldn't go, so I took my horn and went in his place. The teacher had never heard of such a thing, especially at my age, but he sat down with me, and we started playing duets. I took lessons for a month, and when I told him I wasn't coming back anymore, the old man almost cried. He told me I had a good sound and asked how I got that sound. So I told him about my parents and my experience, and I told him that music was just in the family. I used to practice six to eight hours a day, every day. I used to tell young people that no matter how much you pay for your instrument, no matter how much you pay for your lessons, or what school you go to, if you don't practice, you're not going to get anywhere.

For a while I stayed with my aunt in Kinloch. She was my mother's twin sister, and she was married to Reverend Harrold. She had a group called Baby Sis and the Harrold Singers, and when they sang with the choir, I played the trumpet, my cousin George played the saxophone, and my uncle played the clarinet. I guess that's how I got started. Then I started Eddie Randle and the Blue Devils. We worked schools and special affairs, dances. We worked at the West End Waiters Club on Vandeventer and the Chauffeurs and Butlers Club on Lawton. I didn't play at the Plantation Club much, because that was a white club, owned by racketeers. I liked to be my own boss, so we did a lot of one-nighters. We traveled extensively in Missouri, Illinois, Indiana, and Kentucky. We played on the radio a lot, on WEW and KMOX. We were very popular. When Count Basie was appearing in Columbia, Missouri, and we were appearing in Moberly, an hour away, we outdrew Basie.

My father started the funeral home in 1932, the same year I started the orchestra. We had a barbershop, tailor shop, shoeshine parlor combination. Business was slow, and my father decided to close down all of our businesses and start the funeral home. So naturally, being a country boy, I did whatever my parents were doing. An opportunity to do anything worthwhile was welcome. So we did what was worthwhile, profitable, interesting—we did it.

I thought that I was pretty lucky to be able to start playing music, but I still kept up with my father. The reason I appreciated him so very much was that, when I got older and the style of music changed, when it was switching to rock 'n' roll, I needed something else to do. I learned the business, and I am very happy that I did, because now, at the age of eighty-seven, I still have a part in the business. I'm fortunate that my children are carrying on the same business.

I think a parent should teach a child anything and everything he knows. If you give a child the knowledge that you have, and then he acquires other knowledge, you give him a good start in life.

Miles Davis says that I taught him, that I inspired him. But when I heard him, I knew he was a natural. I showed him a few points, how to do a few things differently. And later on, he showed me. He had this talent, a talent bestowed on him by God. Nobody can teach anybody that talent. I'm happy, though, that he appreciated what he got from me. It makes me feel good that I contributed something to him. I gave him a chance. I worked with him. I gave Ernie Wilkins his first chance. I bought him his first ream of paper, and he turned out to be one of the greatest arrangers in the jazz field. Clark Terry always calls me Pop. Once upon a time we had horns, and we just played together. The good Lord gave him talent, and we took ideas from each other. Another talent was Jimmy Forrest. He memorized most of my arrangements when he was a kid. He played the fourth-part harmony to my three saxophones, and he emphasized every phrase as though he were reading a sheet of music. He was that gifted. And Clyde Higgins was really gifted.

Everybody can't be a musician, and everybody can't be a funeral director. Whatever you do, you owe it to yourselves to do your best—you owe it to yourself. I don't think too much about integration, because integration won't help anybody. You have to help yourself. Integration does give you the opportunity to go where you couldn't go, but who wants to go there anyway? A lot of times, we have to try a little harder. What's wrong with being twice as good?

Frank Harrold

Director, Memorial Lancers Drum and Bugle Corps

I have fifteen brothers and sisters. I was born in 1922. I was the twelfth child. We traveled all over the United States as a family, singing gospel songs. We were brought up in the church. I attended Dunbar School in Kinloch, and then we moved, and I attended Vernon School in the Ferguson School District. I graduated from Vernon Grade School in 1932. When it's the onliest graduation you had, you remember that. I attended Kinloch High School for three and a half years. Then I got a job working in a lumberyard, and later I worked at the Krey Packing Company. That was when we were coming out of the Depression, and with that big family we just needed the money.

Then I got married. I had five children by that marriage, but we divorced. Then I married a girl who I met when we were singing in New York. We were married for thirty years. No children were born to this marriage, but we adopted all these children. Oh, boy, how many kids was it? Fifty-some. Some of them graduated from high school, and some of them didn't. Some of them made a success in life, and some didn't. We offered them the opportunity to go to school and to be children. That is kind of hard in these days, because kids want to be grown so fast. I was the same way. The raw truth of life was just so enticing, so inviting, that I couldn't get going fast enough. I understand the kids' frustrations, because I've been there.

When Kinloch incorporated, I served eight years as sergeant of the Kinloch Police Department, and I taught Sunday school at the Memorial Baptist Church in Kinloch. Officer Eddie Lee Dalton and I started a boxing club, because the kids in Kinloch had no recreation facilities, no place to play, and they were getting in trouble.

Then I went to New York, and I saw that every church had a drum and bugle corps. I thought that was pretty fascinating, and I talked to our pastor concerning a drum and bugle corps. That year I got an income tax refund. I bought three snare drums, two bass drums, two pair of cymbals, and ten bugles, from St. Ann Music, right over on Page. They cost all of eight hundred dollars. And we organized this drum and bugle corps. And then whenever I approached a child, whether he was in trouble or not, I invited him to come to my house, after school, and learn how to play drums, learn how to blow a horn. The kids would come to my house, right after school— they couldn't wait.

When I was a kid there was a group called the Tom Powell Post Drum and Bugle Corps, and I wanted to be in the Tom Powell drum corps so bad. My cousin is Eddie Randle who

owns the funeral home, and his daddy, James Randle, sponsored me in the Tom Powell Post. But there came a matter of fifteen cents a week dues, plus seven cents carfare to go to the practice and seven cents carfare to come back home. People seem to forget that it was hard to get fifteen cents during those times. Mr. Holloway put us out of the drum corps because we couldn't pay our dues.

So I make sure that for our group money is not the predominant thing. I try to make the drum and bugle corps accessible to all children, and I try to bring out the best talent and put the best face forward with what we have. And somehow, some way, through all of these thirty-five years, the Lord has seen fit to see that we sure had a good time with the little funding that we had. I tell the kids, you've got the best drum corps that people with no money can have.

We marched in the Annie Malone Parade for thirty-five straight years. I always think that's wonderful. There are some kids who fall through the cracks, but not a lot. Some of the first members of the corps are in their forties now. One of our corpsmen, Jerry Joe Thomas, he's a school professor in Memphis, Tennessee. Darryl Hudson is working at ECHO. Bertie Smith is an executive at Monsanto. David Ivy was the first Negro manager of a department store in Denver, Colorado. Ruth Ann Ivy is in California. She's a computer technician there.

But the most exciting of all is when one of my guys walks across the stage, the high school stage. When they get through high school I call that tenacity. I do not want them to pattern their lives after me—I did not get an education. I point to the road and say, "Go on by me. Keep your eyes high." We have a creed for the corps: "If every corpsman was just like me, what kind of drum corps would this be?"

If a child gets good parenting at home, right away you can tell it. A lot of parents, today, don't have time to be parents. They say, "Here's some money, now I'm on my way, and you be good." Now if a child comes to the drum corps, walks up to me with his hat on, all slouched over, pants down around his back, I know he ain't getting good parenting at home. So now my love for him has to be much more than for the child who's been groomed at home and everything's good.

The important thing is finding the person that's inside each child. Goodness is inside of most people. But they have to have a holding place where they can stay until the goodness pours forth. They have to have something that interests their minds until they catch ahold of themselves. Everybody's got a handle, and my job is finding that handle.

Clarice D. Davis

Artist; Art Educator, Sumner High School

I grew up in St. Louis, in the Ville. My father, Herman Dreer, taught at Sumner High School and at Stowe Teachers College. My mother and father were beautiful people. They loved people and were concerned about helping others. They were Baptists, and we spent every Sunday in church. They were strict with the two of us, my sister and me. My father was almost Victorian in his thinking. When other children my age were going to movies, I was restricted to going only when the theater had Sunshine Sammy or Rin-Tin-Tin on the screen. Sunshine Sammy was a little black boy. I could only go to those productions if my parents took me. It wasn't until college that I had a chance to really break loose. I mean to tell you, when I had a lull, when I didn't have to study, I was in and out of those theaters, because, you see, theaters in Philadelphia weren't segregated like they were in St. Louis.

As a youngster, I went to Cottage Avenue and Simmons Elementary Schools, and then to John Marshall School when we moved to our new home. I went to Sumner High School and graduated from there. That was the only high school for blacks when I was young. We did not have Vashon High School until 1928.

I went to the University of Pennsylvania in Philadelphia from 1930 to 1934, where I majored in fine arts. My parents sent me there because I was only sixteen, and they wanted me to live with my mother's sister and her husband. They had been missionaries to Africa. I guess another reason for me staying with relatives was that blacks could not stay in the dormitories, although we could go to theaters and eating places in the City of Brotherly Love. I had no qualms about going to a university that was practically all white, even though it was right in the heart of the city, because my father had drilled into me that I could do anything and that I was as good as anybody. He made me feel important and proud of my heritage.

When I graduated from the University of Pennsylvania in 1934, it was in the midst of the Depression and jobs were scarce, so instead of going into the field that I had trained for, I became a social worker here in St. Louis. My life had been sheltered up to that point, and casework gave me a chance to see how other people lived. My clients were people who lived east of Grand Avenue, between Sheridan and Cass Avenues, and many of the homes were equipped with outdoor toilets. I only did casework for a year.

In 1935 and 1936 I got my master's degree in art education from the University of Iowa. From 1936 to 1938 I taught English, French, home economics, and music in Brooklyn, Illinois. I got married in 1938 and went back to casework. In those days women could not teach and be married. That changed during World War II. In 1950 I went back to teaching full-time. I taught at Sumner High where George Brantley was the principal, and I finally got my chance to teach art. Then in 1966 I helped to integrate the teaching staff at Southwest High School. From there, I went to Harris-Stowe, where I taught art until I retired.

I had three children, born between 1941 and 1948. When they were growing up, I was teaching school, coming home, cooking dinner, taking them to music lessons, grading papers, and attending sports events. As if I needed more, in the sixties, when my daughter was in college, she became involved in the civil rights movement. She telephoned one evening and said, "Mommy, if I have to go to jail, will you and Dad bail me out?" I said, "Listen! Indeed I will. You are doing what I would be doing if I didn't have family responsibilities. Yes, I will help you, and of course, we will get you out of jail. As you march, you march for me, too."

It has been a struggle. I remember when my father would take us to see plays at the American Theater. We had to sit up in the buzzard roost. We climbed up steps that seemed never ending. From our seats we had to lean over to see the stage. I hated that. Even though we paid for first-class tickets, we were treated like second-class citizens. You see, that was when St. Louis was segregated. We couldn't do a lot of things that we are enjoying now.

I hope young people will think in terms of helping others. They should get as much education as possible, and then reach out and help others. They should ask themselves, "What is my potential? How can I make a difference?" They should never forget where they came from. They are where they are because somebody else made it possible.

Earl E. Nance Sr.

Pastor, Greater Mount Carmel Baptist Church

I grew up in Alma, Arkansas, fifteen miles out in the country from Fort Smith. My father, Willis Nance, and my mother, Betty Perry, were the parents of eighteen children. Eleven boys and seven girls. My daddy was a country schoolteacher, and I went to school under him. In the country, there weren't too many families. My daddy had eighteen children, Hayes Emory had seventeen children, Will Clark had fourteen children. And that's what made up your community.

I left home when I was fourteen and went to Fort Smith, Arkansas. I went to high school at Lincoln High School in Fort Smith. I was fourteen years old, but I was still in school. You see, at that age you were supposed to be out of school, at fourteen. But I was just beginning. I was eighteen or nineteen when I finished high school. When you go to school only three or four months out of the year, my God, I was lucky to get out then.

See, we had to plow and farm. There were enough of us so that we could pick seven bales of cotton a day. And if that white man wanted his cotton picked before my Daddy's, that's what would happen. If his crop needed to be chopped while we were in school, we had to go. Youngsters don't know what people went through then. I had to work when I was young. My daddy didn't have nothing to give us eighteen kids, eleven boys and seven girls. There wasn't no money to give nobody. He could barely make it and feed us all. I worked at night at a restaurant and went to school in the day, at fourteen.

I was working at night and going to school, and one time Nixon Patilla, one of the well-to-do boys who had a car and everything, was going to tell about his travels. I wanted to go home and get some rest, but the teacher told me, "You're not going anywhere. You ain't going to be nothing." Now she said that to me, and I was saddened—everybody laughed. Here I was from the country with a pair of patched overalls on. All the other kids were dressed up, and I said that I wanted to go, that I had a job. And the teacher wanted me to stay and listen to Nixon's travels, because I was never going to go nowhere. But God let me finish school and go back and speak at that assembly.

I started college at Lincoln University in Jefferson City, Missouri, but then I went into the army. After I got out of the army, I went to Morehouse College, and I was in Martin Luther King's class. I was a junior when he came, but we were in some classes together. He was only sixteen, and he was smart. He lived at home with his parents, and I was in charge of the dormitory, and he would come and stay there sometimes.

When he came here and spoke in 1963, I introduced him, at the Washington Tabernacle—Martin Luther King, himself. When he said "We shall overcome," I got on him about that. I thought he should explain that. I think we should overcome our backwardness. We should overcome fighting one another. We should overcome killing one another. That's what we need to overcome.

I started preaching in the country when I was sixteen. After I got out of school at Morehouse, I preached at Big Bethel in Atlanta. Then I was the associate minister at Galilee Baptist Church with Reverend Orange in 1947. A church on Newstead asked me to be their educational director, but I didn't want to work for someone else. I wanted my own church. Then this church became vacant. It only had eleven members when they called me. I am the forty-first preacher here, and the church was only thirty-nine years old when I came. That was in 1951.

Robinson owned all those drugstores all over, and he had one of them right over here on the corner. I used to borrow money from him to do things at the church. He was very helpful to me. He had a flourishing business, all black. A lot of blacks had their own stores, and blacks traded with them. They were open on Saturday and Sunday mornings. They had boys working, delivering groceries and working. As soon as integration came, blacks started leaving the black businesses and trading with the white businesses. We shouldn't have given that up and let the white man take over everything. But wherever there is a black man and a white man competing, the white person is going to get the better end of it.

Our black social organizations don't help. They get together and have parties and give themselves awards, but they should be giving scholarships, sending young people to college. We are not responsible for the way other folks treat us, but we are responsible for how we treat others. Put yourself in the other person's shoes and ask yourself, "How would I like them to treat me?" The principal thing is to treat people as you would have them treat you.

Lloyd A. Smith

Musician; Music Educator; Owner, the Musicians Club; Director of
Public Relations and Community Affairs, Colonial Baking Company

I was born in Lexington, Mississippi, in 1914. My father was a cotton buyer in Mound Bayou, Mississippi, an all-black town. That was something, to work in an all-black town. My mother was a housewife, and I have two sisters. I was five years old when we came to St. Louis, in 1919. I went to school in St. Louis, all the way through Sumner High School.

During my childhood I always loved music. When I was about four or five I would step out into the night to hear a band play or to listen to the blues. They sang some nasty songs, but I listened to them anyway. I first started playing music on a violin. I took private lessons from a man who played in the St. Louis Symphony. But as time passed, I noticed that my buddy, who played the saxophone, was getting to be real popular with the girls. So my dad bought me a saxophone. I started playing the saxophone when I was thirteen, and then I played the clarinet, the oboe, and the French horn, all woodwinds.

I studied music at Juilliard and at the Boston Conservatory of Music. I went to Roosevelt College in Chicago for a music course. And I'll tell you something, two of the greatest sax players in the world were in Chicago: Charlie Parker and Johnny Hodges. When I was young, I idolized musicians. I thought everybody could play. I learned to copy them, and I got so I could play. But music didn't rush into me.

I played with most of the major bands. I was in and out. Whoever paid the most money, that's where I went. I started with Eddie Randle. We played all the small towns in Missouri, Illinois, Iowa, and Wisconsin. We broadcast every Tuesday and Thursday on the radio. That was 1932, '33, '34.

I played all the major clubs. I played the Club Plantation. It was a segregated club. We played white clubs, the Castle Ballroom, the Dance Box, the Pigeon Hole, East St. Louis, Brooklyn, Illinois. I played the Cotton Club in Harlem.

There were all kinds of fine musicians during that time. The bands I stayed with the longest were Earl Hines, Eddie Randle, and Dewey Jackson, a local band. But I played with Fate Marable, Louis Armstrong, Fats Waller, Cab Calloway, Billie Holiday, Paul Whiteman, Duke Ellington, Count Basie, Jeter Pillars, Josephine Baker....Let me see...Cecil Scott, Mose Wiler, Nat King Cole. Nat Cole was my friend. I played with everybody.

I had so many buddies, all the way down the line. Redd Foxx went to Sumner High School when I did. He left the school in a cloud and went to Chicago. Robert Carter was a friend of mine. George Smith went to Sumner High School. And so many, many more. Some of them got to be famous. Some of them ended up in the coop. I knew Josephine Baker well. But she'd be about ninety-something years old now. I was a young man, a boy, when I knew her. She was fantastic.

I had an "after-hours club" from 1947 to 1955, the Musicians Club, on Delmar. It was half a block east of the Club Riviera on the south side of Delmar, 4414 Delmar. After-hours clubs were kind of outlawed, because they were open after the curfew, when they were supposed to be closed. All the celebrities who came to town came to my club. Movie stars like Frank Sinatra and Ava Gardner came there. Everybody who was somebody came there...Dinah Shore, Dinah Washington, Spider Burks. I had a big sign by the door that told who would appear that night: Duke Ellington, Louis Jordan, Andy Kirk, Count Basie, Earl Hines. Benny Goodman passed through on a double nighter.

At first I wasn't too interested in civil rights. But as time moved on, Percy Green and his group talked to me. He was an average type of guy who looked like hell, but I could see the good he was doing. White people hated him. The *Post-Dispatch* hated him. The *Globe-Democrat* hated him. And if it weren't for him, I wouldn't be where I am today. Percy Green did a lot to make it better for people like you and me. I didn't do any marching, but I got Percy out of jail. People sort of forget about it, but Percy's been a hero. That goes for Norman Seay, too. Norman Seay opened a lot of doors. We've had a lot of heroes. Percy Green, Norman Seay, and Ivory Perry, too.

Most blacks get in a good position and they forget about the fellow behind them. That isn't true with me. I have played with some of the greatest bluesmen all over the world. I played with them when I was a young man. Most of them are dead, so many of them are gone. I knew all of them. I played with them and lived with them. There are many good musicians in St. Louis today. But the important thing is to be in the right spot at the right time. And if success comes, remember to help those who are coming along behind you.

Zella Jackson Price

Gospel Singer

My mother was Alberta Waterford Robinson, and my dad was Zelman Robinson. I'm one of four children, the only girl. So I got a lot of love. Dad was uneducated, but he was amazing. Back in the forties he worked at Chevrolet Shell. He went to work dressed up in a suit and tie to make people think that he had an office job. And he was a porter! He put on a blue collar. He would mop, sweep, clean, and then he'd wash up and get back into his suit and tie and come home. Man, he had pride. My mother was twenty-five years younger than he, and she was his queen, you know? I remember a lot of laughter.

My mother was a singer. She traveled with Willie Mae Ford Smith for about ten years. I admired her, I looked up to her, and I wanted to be like her and Willie Mae. They seemed to enjoy what they were doing. My parents separated and divorced when I was about ten years old, and Mama remarried. They may have divorced each other, but they didn't divorce me. I remember a very happy childhood.

I went to four elementary schools—Carver School, Cole School, Washington School, and Cupples School—and I graduated from Sumner High School in 1957. My grade school teachers were dedicated and involved. They played an important role in our lives. I looked up to my teachers.

We lived on Vernon Avenue, and before that at 3657 Cook. The women stayed home; they washed on Mondays and ironed on Tuesdays. On Monday everybody's clothes hung on the line, down through the backyards and alleys. On Tuesday women would iron on the back porch and talk to each other. They didn't need the phone, they'd holler. You'd hear them talking to each other down the street. I remember everybody's house smelled like beans on Wednesday, and fish on Fridays. I don't remember women cooking on Saturdays. I know what we did—Chinese food! We went to a Chinese store on Taylor and Page or one on Page and Walton. Best Chinese food in the world, fifteen cents a box with plain rice. And we had big chicken dinners on Sundays. Those were the days. Our neighborhood had pride.

We lived in a four-family flat. My grandmother had nine children, and four of them lived at home. My mother returned home after her marriage with my father broke up. My aunt Nezzie taught the neighborhood girls how to crochet and how to embroider. We had a close neighborhood. There was no such thing as kids staying out after dark. The neighbors would say, "What are you doing out after dark?" and they would take

us home. We sat on the front porch awhile, and everybody came in at a certain time to get a bath. It was a happy routine.

I grew up surrounded by great women, Willie Mae Ford Smith, Clara Ward, Martha Bass, Mahalia Jackson, and my mother. In the winter I stayed home with Grandma, but in the summertime I'd go with my mother when she traveled with Willie Mae. I'd fall asleep on the pew, and I'd wake up, and they were still singing. And I admired them. I loved the joy they brought to the audience when they sang.

I love to sing. It's more than forty years since I began singing as a career. I've appeared at concerts with the O'Neil Twins, James Cleveland, Edward Hawkins, Walter and Tramaine and Al Green. I sang at Carnegie Hall and I sang at the Whitney in New York, at the Superdome, at the Delta 88, which was a sellout, and for the Bicentennial in 1976 in Washington, D.C. I was in an exhibit at the Smithsonian and one here at the History Museum. I was on the air at KIRL for fourteen years. And I was in the film *Say Amen Somebody*. I was one of the stars. Willie Mae Ford Smith, Sally Martin, the Barrett Sisters, the O'Neil Twins, and yours truly, Zella Jackson Price. It was filmed here in St. Louis and in Houston and in Chicago. That film went all over the world.

I love that old-time religion, and I love the bridge that brought us across. Some people would describe the songs that our ancestors sang as depressing, songs like "Nobody Knows the Trouble I've Seen," "Meeting on the Old Campground," and "Steal Away." But those were not songs of depression, those were codes for the Underground Railroad. When you look into the history of the old-time religion, you find it was also a language, and it makes you appreciate that bridge.

I like to learn about other religions. I like to broaden my horizons. I like to understand why each person attends church. Everyone has a reason. I have sung for many people, many races, many religions. It is strange that segregation has been so important in America, since there are so many Christians here. But music is a language that for a moment makes everybody equal. Everybody listens and receives it at the same time, in the same way. For that moment you are all together. Sometimes I've sung in places where I couldn't shake hands with the audience because the audience was white. But I didn't change my song. Singing became a ministry. I think gospel singing has played a role in breaking down the barriers of segregation. Music has a way of bringing people together. I'm thankful that at certain times I was an instrument that mended people and brought them together.

Melba A. Sweets

Columnist, *St. Louis American*

I was an only child, and I grew up in the Ville. My father finished high school in Tennessee, and then came to St. Louis and started as a porter for Union Electric. At the turn of the century he couldn't get any better job than being a porter. He took chemistry by correspondence, and I grew up smelling queer odors in the kitchen where he did chemistry experiments. He had a boss who encouraged him, and he became the first black chemist at Union Electric. He retired as the chemist at the Union Electric Ashley Street Plant. My mother went to Sumner High School and Sumner Teachers College, and she was a teacher until she married.

I went to Simmons School on Cottage Avenue and Sumner High School and then to Sumner Teachers College, which was only two years at that time. Then I went to Howard University. But I didn't graduate from Howard. I had to come back home because of the Depression. I taught in the public schools of St. Louis until 1937. I started in 1930, and in those days, if you were a teacher and you married, you had to quit. Married teachers had to give up their jobs to the single people who were waiting for work. So, because I happened to marry a newspaperman, that's how I got into writing.

My husband owned the *St. Louis American*, and the only competition we ever had for advertising was with the *Argus*, which was the older newspaper. The Pullman porters had an office in the same building where our office was, in the old Peoples Finance Building on the corner of Jefferson and Market, and we conducted a campaign for the Pullman porters to get more pay and more respect. At the same time the *Argus* carried articles favoring the Pullman Company, and the Pullman Company paid them handsomely for ads. The porters certainly didn't have any money to pay us. We just knew that Pullman porters deserved better pay and the fledgling union was fighting a great big company. It was a long, hard fight, but the union finally won out.

Before I married, a friend and I started writing a column. We just did it for fun. We never got any money. We called our column *We're Telling*. It was a simple little social column, which told what young people were doing. That was all. We wrote about big dances and parties and who was going with whom and stuff like that. We wrote about social affairs, but on the other hand, we also would urge people to go to this or that, tell them what plays to see and what books to read.

A high point of my life was knowing Paul Robeson. I went to a concert where Paul Robeson was singing for a benefit, and my husband told me the FBI would put my name on their list as a Communist. But I went, and I was so impressed with Paul Robeson that I went to the party for him afterward. The woman who was giving the party took us to her bedroom so I could interview him. He was eager to talk about his political position. And we talked and talked. I should have saved that column. As I grew older I also wrote news stories, and I guess the most important one I wrote was on the death of Paul Robeson.

Another important story I did was about an actress who appeared at the American Theater. Back then we couldn't go to the American Theater unless we climbed all those stairs and sat way up at the top. Most blacks didn't go at all. Henry Winfield Wheeler picketed the theater for years, even if it rained, to draw attention to the segregation. A famous actress was in a play at the American, and I had heard that she opposed segregation. So I took a tape recorder and I did an interview with her, and put her picture on the front page of the paper. Our headline read "Never Again." She said, "Never again will I perform at that theater."

When I was growing up, my father was great on books. He loved Negro history. When he didn't have money for anything else, he'd come home with books. And that really influenced me. I read all the great black writers: Paul Laurence Dunbar, W. E. B. Du Bois, Frederick Douglass, Alain Locke, all those people who wrote during the Harlem Renaissance. My husband and I knew Langston Hughes. One of the nicest things that ever happened to me was when Langston Hughes wrote about St. Louis and he said our newspaper column, *We're Telling*, was the best column he had ever read.

Black newspapers have become pretty good newspapers. I was in the newspaper business because I really loved to do it. All that I ever did was fun. I mean, I didn't have any training. I like to write, and I like people. And then in 1977 and 1978 I was on the jury for the Pulitzer Prize. I was the second black person to serve on the Pulitzer Prize jury. I judged photographs one year, and then political cartoons. That was one of the high points of my life. My life has been fun.

Theodore McMillian

Judge, U.S. Court of Appeals for the Eighth Circuit

My mother and my natural father had two children. I had a sister. They were divorced about 1925 or '26. My mother remarried. She married a man who had two children, and from that marriage she had five more children. I remember one day my stepfather came home and he called to my mother, "Joy, come in here! Your children and my children are beating the hell out of our children!" My stepfather always reminded me of the father in *A Tree Grows in Brooklyn*. When the rent was not paid or the lights were about ready to be turned out, he'd bring home candy and flowers. He was quite a person. He was a waiter by trade, but at that time he worked for the WPA, the Works Progress Administration. I can remember how proud he was when he brought home his first government paycheck. Many people worked for those programs.

I started at Lincoln Elementary School and moved from there over to Banneker on Lucas, and then to Wayman Crow on Leonard. We were constantly moving because at that time we were trying to stay one step ahead of the rent man. I can remember many times coming home from school, running ahead of my friends to see if we had been set out.

My first job was in the NYA, one of Roosevelt's alphabet programs. The National Youth Administration was a tutoring program to keep students from dropping out and going to work. I tutored students who were behind in Latin and mathematics. The head of the NYA was Lyndon Baines Johnson, the representative out of Texas. I think that was one of his first big jobs.

After I graduated I went to Stowe for two years, and then I went to Lincoln University. I worked the first year in the kitchen washing pots and pans, and then I got a job tutoring and teaching physics. It took care of tuition and room and board. When the war started I was drafted. I stayed in the army, the Ninety-third Division, in the Signal Corps, till November of 1946. After the war I went to St. Louis University Law School, and I graduated first in my class in 1949.

When I got out of law school I went into practice with Alphonse J. Lynch, and we sat around waiting for clients. Benny Gordon and others from Webster Groves came and asked me if I would help them sue the city of Webster Groves for keeping blacks out of the new city swimming pool. The Fairgrounds Park swimming pool was integrating, but not

without some trouble. They said they didn't have much money, but I didn't have any clients, so I took the case. A professor at Vanderbilt was publishing articles about segregation and public accommodations in the *Vanderbilt Law Review*, and in those days that was the only place I could go for help. Anyway, I sued the city to allow black residents to use the pool. I said that the city was denying their rights to equal protection provided under the Fourteenth Amendment to the Constitution. The judge decreed that the city council was exercising governmental power in violation of the rights of the plaintiffs and told them to open the pool to everyone. The intransigent city officials refused to open the pool to anyone for three hot summers, before they were finally thrown out of office. But that case launched my career.

I worked as an assistant circuit attorney for the city of St. Louis from 1953 to 1956. Ed Dowd was the circuit attorney. Up to that time Dave Grant had been in the circuit attorney's office, but there was a rule that blacks only prosecuted blacks, they never prosecuted white people. Dowd changed that practice. If you were an assistant circuit attorney you prosecuted people.

In 1952 I ran in the Nineteenth Ward against Jordan Chambers. I carried Phil Donnelly on my ticket to run for governor. He was successful; I, of course, was not. A few years later, in 1956, I had had a regular string of victories in the circuit attorney's office, and the nonpartisan commission nominated me for the Circuit Court. The commission sent three names to the governor, and Governor Donnelly selected me to be a circuit judge for the Circuit Court of the city of St. Louis. I served on that bench until 1972, when Warren Hearnes appointed me to the Missouri Court of Appeals for the Eastern District of Missouri. Then in the fall of 1978, Jimmy Carter appointed me to the United States Court of Appeals.

Most of the cases that I hear involving civil rights are school cases. Those are some of the biggest civil rights cases. But I also hear a lot of employment discrimination cases.

When you study the options, law is a profession in which you can make changes in society for the good. History shows it is the lawyer who possesses the tools to enforce the law, to preserve the life and liberty of others, and to guarantee the equal protection of the law for all. No other career can be so fulfilling.

Carl N. Thomas

Mechanical Superintendent, *St. Louis Argus*

I grew up in the country down in Alabama. I had five sisters and one brother. We went to a country school, a county training school. My oldest sister married and my brother married and I went to find a job. That was back in 1935. I went to Kentucky and worked in the coal mines for three weeks. I went to work one morning and the whole top had fallen in. And I just left, and I told my daddy I would let him know where I was.

I had an uncle in Oklahoma who told me if I came out there he would help me learn embalming and go into business with his son. On my way, I stopped here to see my aunt who lived in St. Louis. When I told her husband where I was going, he said, "You might like it here." And I said, "What do you suppose I could do?" He said, "Well, come to work with me tomorrow. You might like it down there." J. E. Mitchell owned the *Argus*. He married my daddy's older sister, and I was visiting his wife out in Webster Groves, and he talked me into staying. So I came on down, and he showed me around, and I've been here ever since. That was in April 1935. He thought I would be an asset to them, and I tried.

I didn't know anything about printing, but the guys showed me how. Lloyd Johnson taught me how to use the Linotype, how to do make-up. I came out of an old-fashioned family. My people always told me, "If you want to do something, just try hard, and you can do it." I learned how to operate the Linotype and how to run the presses. We had the presses downstairs. I tried to learn anything down there.

The *Argus* was started by two brothers in 1912. J. E. and W. M. Mitchell started the *Argus* in March of 1912. They started out writing insurance, and they were writing a little newsletter about insurance, and people were more interested in the newsletter and wouldn't buy the insurance. So they started writing the paper. They used to have to take it to the post office in a wheelbarrow. Frank was J. E.'s son. He went to Chicago in 1936, and he came back in 1942, and they put Frank in charge. W. M. died in 1945, and J. E. died in 1952. The *Argus* is the oldest black-owned business west of the Mississippi.

When I started working in 1935, I did Linotype, I did make-up, I wrote stories. I've never been an investigative reporter, but sometimes when J. E. couldn't go somewhere he would ask me to go and I'd write about it. I'd just sit down and take notes, and then I'd write a story. I've always stayed in the background. I've never sought publicity. It doesn't mean anything to me. Mostly I repaired the machines. I'd read everything I picked up. We had books about the Linotype, and I read those books. Once I read it, I could apply it to the machine, and if a machine broke down I could fix it. We had four Linotypes in the late thirties, early forties, and I was the chief repair man.

Then in 1937 we bought a new press, and I worked on that. When the war broke out, I was working on the press. I was the only one who could work the press, so I got an occupational deferment. From 1940 to 1966 we didn't have a white man in the shop. We did all our own repairs. We had a big old press back then, and we could fix it.

We were at 2312 Market until the early part of the sixties when the Mill Creek Redevelopment Authority ran us out. We could have stayed, but you had to repair the building and bring it up to code. And Frank said that if all the Negroes were moving out anyway, why stay?

In 1948, Howard Woods became editor. I started him out at the *Argus*. When he came to the *Argus* he was selling cigarettes. He stayed here until 1968 or 1969, when he founded the *Sentinel*. One thing about Howard Woods, he didn't have much formal education, but he could do anything in writing. He was aggressive. When President Johnson came here he offered Howard a job in the government, but he didn't take it because he'd be traveling too much.

So the *Argus* has had some good times, and we've had some tough times. Now they depend on me for everything. My daughter, Carolyn, works here, and my wife, Roberta, works here. They set the type. We're the mainstay. If we walked out of here tomorrow, there wouldn't be any *Argus*.

The National Newspaper Publishers' Association offered to give me an award for longevity. See, I've been here since 1935. But I refuse to accept awards. I've never sought the limelight. It just doesn't mean anything to me to be well known. And another thing about it, once you get some recognition, once you get known, everybody wants this and wants that.

Elizabeth W. Garlington

Clinical Social Worker, St. Louis Provident Association

I grew up in Abbeville, South Carolina, and I went to school through the tenth grade there. But, at that time, the schools in South Carolina were not accredited, so my parents sent me to a boarding school to get a good preparation, Atlanta University Preparatory High School. I graduated from there, and I graduated from Atlanta University School of Social Work. I got my master's degree in social work.

When I graduated from Atlanta University there was a need in St. Louis for professionally trained social workers. There were jobs at that time in Chicago, Pittsburgh, Baltimore, St. Louis, and Philadelphia. I chose St. Louis, because I felt it was a challenge, and I thought I might get lost in a bigger city. The agency that was looking for social workers was the Provident Association. The Provident Association was later called Family and Children's Service, and now I see it has gone back to the name of Provident Counseling.

I worked primarily with families. At that time many families were moving to St. Louis and were being urbanized. I worked with families where there were children and an adult making an adjustment to widowhood, divorce, or desertion. My primary interest in social work has been working with families, strengthening families. And I have found that by working with families I have been able to make a difference.

When I was at Provident I worked up through the ranks. I was a supervisor and then district director and I did academic work while I was doing counseling. I started what we call family therapy, working with the total family, rather than individuals. We have found that when one person in a family is in trouble, it impacts the total family. I pioneered in that. I also did pioneering work in marital counseling. When I came here in the late thirties, we always separated the husband and wife for marital counseling. I was having a conflict with my coworker, who was counseling the husband while I was counseling the wife. I suggested that we experiment by working with the two of them together. So I did, and it made me become more objective. I wasn't trying to protect one and blame the other. I wrote some papers on that which were published in social work magazines, and the idea took hold with the Family Services Association of America. But that was difficult. At that time you couldn't get articles about blacks published unless they were pejorative articles about the pathology of the family. I have always focused on the strength of the family. As a social worker I prefer to

strengthen the ego rather than working with an illness. That's for the psychiatrists.

I became interested in working with adoptions. If you remember, from about 1960 to 1970, we began to place black children with white families. At that time white girls who had babies out of wedlock would keep them or arrange for private adoptions. This made fewer white babies available for adoption, so whites who wanted to adopt began to adopt black children. And we thought that they saw black babies as second best. So black social workers made an extra effort to find black families for black children. Many of the black social workers got together to work on preserving the black family, preserving our heritage. It wasn't the community that we worked on about this, we worked on the agencies who were allowing it, who were placing these children for adoption. Whites paid a large amount of money to adopt. And we saw it as selling the baby to the highest bidder. We made a national effort to discourage that.

I got involved in the civil rights movement way before the sixties. It didn't just start with Rosa Parks. Back in Atlanta in the thirties we had the League for Economic Democracy, L.E.D. I have always been involved in things like that.

During the Depression I got into the Marcus Garvey Movement. I got fired from my job for that, but they took me back. I believed in Marcus Garvey. I thought he was a great leader. He wanted blacks to go back to Africa. I didn't want to go back to Africa, I wasn't that loyal. I wanted to be a missionary in Africa, but I didn't want to stay there. But at that time, our people were struggling. That was during the Depression, and we really didn't see the light of day until 1942, until we went into the Second World War. Families were struggling. They didn't have any spokesmen. And Marcus Garvey was out there speaking for us. I was working at the welfare office in the daytime, and in the evening I was at the Marcus Garvey meetings. I lost my job, and I lost my husband. He was a court clerk, and he was a good Republican. And you know, he couldn't say, "My wife is at a Marcus Garvey meeting." Now why I married a Republican, I'll never know.

I was brought up with the idea that if you have a gift, you should share it. Of him who has much, much is expected. My family shared with others. I feel very strongly that I owe something to others. I feel compelled to help people. Wealth I do not have. Social workers will never be wealthy. But we do have talent and time and energy, and I can share that.

Everett Agnew

Director of Promotions, Regal Sports

I came to St. Louis in 1926, when I was sixteen years old. I went to the Urban League and got a job working at the Triple A Golf Club in Forest Park. I took care of the shower room, cleaned golf shoes, and things like that. At that time it was a golf club for the rich. But Wayman Smith Sr. went to court and said that a St. Louis city park should not be used as a private club. After that the city let everybody play golf out there.

My father and mother separated when I was fourteen years old. So I came to St. Louis to make more money. I had been making five dollars a week in Little Rock. When I got off work at the golf club I came down to Grand and Washington to a little store where I cleaned up in the afternoon. I worked two jobs, and I sent Mama ten dollars a week.

After that I started working at the University Drug Store in the University Club Building on Grand. That's how I met Alice Faye and Barbara Stanwyck and Al Jolson. Across the street the Missouri Building had an auditorium where they booked all those acts. I made money from tips from people like Al Jolson. I took medicine from the University Drug Store over to him, and he was blacking his face. Al Jolson was a blackfaced performer. He was the first one to make a talking movie. And that's where I got the idea I wanted to be a promoter.

My brother Claude organized Regal Sports. It started out as a social club, in 1937. It was at the Saum Hotel. We gave a show every Tuesday night with Eddie Randle, a local orchestra. One day I asked Claude, "Why don't you try to get Count Basie or Jimmie Lunceford?" He said, "I don't know where to find them." I said, "Get one of Lunceford's records and call and have the record company tell you where he is." He found out you could get him through the William Morris Booking Agency in Chicago. He wrote them, and they told him Lunceford was available for Monday night, March 31, five hundred dollars down and 50 percent of the gross. We pawned our bicycles and sent half of the money, two hundred and fifty dollars. Lunceford grossed two thousand dollars, a thousand dollars for us and a thousand dollars for him. That was in 1941. After that, everybody in New York sent us letters offering us acts.

Then we approached Kiel Opera House, but they wouldn't rent to us. So we asked Emma Bob, who was living at the Saum Hotel, to call for us. Miss Bob was a white lady with the coroner's office. We got Miss Bob to rent the Opera House for us. We started out with Billy Eckstine and a blind singer, playing the piano. We charged a dollar in advance and a dollar and a quarter at the door. We brought in Erskine Hawkins, then Louis Armstrong. We brought Duke Ellington in, and he made seventeen hundred dollars. He came in for a guarantee plus a percentage. The next time we had Earl Hines. He came in with Billy Eckstine and Sarah Vaughan. Then we had the Ink Spots, and then the Mills Brothers. We had the Platters and the Jesters and three other singing groups. Singing groups were taking over from big bands. We brought Erroll Garner to the West End Waiters Club on Vandeventer.

There were fifteen of us in Regal Sports. I was the director of promotions. We stayed in the promoting business until we closed in '86. We started as a nonprofit social club, but we got so big we formed a corporation in 1954. That's when we went to the Riviera. When we went to the Riviera we had Stan Kenton, a white fellow. And we had Duke Ellington and Ella Fitzgerald. We had Glenn Miller all signed up for Kiel Auditorium before he went overseas and got killed. And Regal Sports promoted the Dorsey brothers.

We started bringing in Motor Town entertainers in 1955. We brought in Sam Cooke, Jackie Wilson, Aretha Franklin, and Marvin Gaye. I would go to Detroit to buy the acts from Berry Gordy Jr. before he organized Motown Records. Motown was the first organization to sell tickets to whites and blacks.

Then we got hooked up with Dick Clark. Dick Clark used to send in a show with three whites and three black performers. We advertised in white papers in little towns, and we sold out that Opera House with Dick Clark. Dick Clark was the guy who actually put blacks and whites together. He started Patti LaBelle. He started a whole lot of acts.

Then I was in New York at the Music Corporation of America, and someone said, "Everett, you bought Johnny Mathis and Herb Alpert and the Tijuana Brass, what about the Beatles? They are available on August 21." So by the first of July we had sold over a hundred thousand dollars in tickets. And then John Lennon made the statement that the Beatles were more popular than Jesus Christ. When his statement hit the Bible Belt everybody wanted their money back. St. Louis sales dropped. Radio stations said, "Break all the Beatles' records! Don't buy the Beatles!" They gave us hell. I had to advertise in newspapers out of town: Denver, Oklahoma City, South Dakota, Nebraska. People sent in mail orders. We sold tickets all over. We didn't sell out the stadium, but we could have if Lennon hadn't made that statement.

John E. Ware

Pullman Porter; Tuskegee Airman; Postal Clerk, U.S. Post Office

I came to St. Louis in 1922, when I was two years old. My stepfather worked for the International Shoe Company. My father and mother separated when I was quite young. My mother was always a homemaker. I have four brothers and four sisters. There are nine of us, altogether.

At first we lived in the 1400 block of Morgan. Then it was Morgan, but now it's Delmar. Then I lived on Lucky and attended John Marshall Elementary School. I grew up in the area called the Ville. It was a very nice place to live. We moved to Kennerly Avenue, which is across the street from Tandy Park. And that's where I spent most of my time during the summer, playing ball. In fact, during those times, that's all there was to do. There were very few places we could go. We had a small branch of the YMCA, called the Elleardsville Y, at St. Ferdinand and Pendleton. It was more or less a storefront. And then we had the Pine Street Y, which was the big one, down on Pine Street. We went there during the winter months. We had basketball teams, mostly sponsored by churches. And we had football teams, sponsored by grocery stores and white businesses and black businesses. That's about all there was to do.

I finished Sumner in 1938. It was a fine school. I played football, and Mr. Beckett was the football coach. My favorite subject was sociology. In fact, I wrote a thesis on sociology. I attended Alabama State University for two years, but I quit to come home and get a job. A friend of mine told me about a job at the small-arms plant. We called it "the bullet plant." Then my friend told me about the Pullman Company. So I left the bullet plant and went to the Pullman Company. That was November 9, 1942.

I worked for the Pullman Company on all the railroads. I worked the bedrooms and the dining cars. My job was to receive the passengers, help with their luggage, wait on them, make up their beds. We were paid for twenty hours out of twenty-four. In other words, we slept four hours a night. At night, we would connect the buzzers for two of the cars, so that if a passenger in the other car rang, I would hear it and go back and see what they wanted, while the other porter slept, say from ten to two. Then I would sleep from two to six.

We had good days and bad days. The tips were what made the job so good, because the salary was nothing. When I started out, it was forty-nine and a half cents an hour. That's not a lot of money. See, we had to bear our expenses while we were out of town. In some places the railroad had quarters, but in some places we had to rent a room to sleep.

There were even times when we would go hungry, because mostly during that time we were transporting the military throughout the country. I remember one time, we were dead-heading through Arizona. See, we weren't working, because the train was empty. But the engineer could only drive that train so many hours before he had to stop and be relieved. So, we stopped out in the desert, and there was nowhere to get anything to eat. Finally, we saw a shack, about a mile and a half away. A couple of us walked to it, and it was a little grocery store owned by a Mexican. He said he wasn't going to serve us. So I said, "What do you mean, you aren't going to serve us?" "I'm not going to serve you." So I threw twenty dollars on the counter and took some candy and walked out. There was nothing around, no houses, nothing. To this day I don't know why he didn't want to serve us.

So there were good times and bad times. And I met some famous people. I met Eleanor Roosevelt, the Nicholas Brothers, Dorothy Dandridge, President Truman. Mrs. Roosevelt was on her way to Fayetteville, Arkansas. She was going down to make a speech at a school there. I met Truman before he was president. He was on his way to the Kentucky Derby, with a bunch from Kansas City. Another time, I heard him give a speech from the back of a train at Union Station. I met A. Philip Randolph. He would come through St. Louis, but I didn't know him personally. Theodore McNeal was our big man for the Brotherhood of Sleeping Car Porters. He was the field organizer here in St. Louis. He became the first black state senator in Missouri.

August Busch took a train out of here in 1953 to open up a brewery in California. He and Anheuser were on the Santa Fe private car, at the end of the train. My car was next to the private car. My car was an all-room Pullman, and I had some of the Busch family, the Orthweins, the Flannigans, and Vierheller, the head of the St. Louis Zoo. Busch had a valet, a black man, who I knew from around the city. His valet said to me, "You know, Mr. Busch is having a private car built in Decatur, Illinois. He's going to need some help on it. Would you like a job?" He said I would have to spend three months in Florida, when the baseball team was there, and three months in Connecticut. I said, "No, my wife is unhappy when I go from here to New York and back. That would be a long time to be away from my family."

I think the most important things are to spend time with your family and to get an education.

James M. Whittico

Chief of Staff, Peoples Hospital and St. Mary's Infirmary;
Surgeon, Homer G. Phillips Hospital

I was born in a little coal mining town in the mountains of West Virginia. Williamson had a small population and was located on the southern border of West Virginia, separated from Kentucky by the Tug River. My father grew up on a farm in Ridgeway, Virginia, and he went to a small college in Virginia and then to Meharry Medical College. He had to work in the coal mines and on the railroad to make enough money to establish his office in Williamson. He was the first black doctor in that area, and he had a pretty hard time in the beginning, because the atmosphere was full of prejudice. But he became prominent in West Virginia, partly because of his friendship with the Hatfield family, the ones who fought with the McCoys. After that famous feud ended, the Hatfields went on to hold prominent positions throughout the state, even the governorship.

I left home to go to college in 1932, when I was fifteen. I went to Lincoln University in Pennsylvania and then to Meharry Medical College in Nashville, Tennessee, where my father had gone. I came to St. Louis to do my internship at Homer G. Phillips Hospital, and in 1942 I went into the medical corps as a first lieutenant. I served with the Ninety-third Infantry Division for four years, and I rose to commanding officer of the hospital for the Ninety-third Infantry Division in the South Pacific. I came back from overseas in 1946 and resumed my training in surgery at Homer Phillips.

My mentor, Dr. Arthur N. Vaughn, was very proper. He wore glasses, and he always wore very proper clothes. He spoke meticulously correct English. Dr. Vaughn was over the surgery department at Homer G. Phillips as a visiting physician. He had a private practice in surgery. And he was, to some degree, a self-trained surgeon. He read a lot, on top of his basic medical education. When he came along, there were very few programs for training black surgeons. Dr. Vaughn worked in surgery at the old City Hospital No. 2, located on Lawton Avenue. That was before the days of Homer G. Phillips Hospital. He got some training in surgery there, even though it was not bona fide medical school training.

When I was studying for the board in surgery, Dr. Vaughn invited me to spend every Sunday afternoon with him, getting ready for the exam. I spent every Sunday, from one o'clock to five o'clock, for four solid months in Dr. Vaughn's home, reviewing subjects and answering questions with Dr. Vaughn. It was amazing that this man gave up every Sunday, for four months, in my interest. You know, you're not going to find very many people who will do that.

When I passed my board, the American Board of Surgery, I became a fellow of the American College of Surgeons, and I worked with Dr. William Sinkler for a while. His office was at Taylor and Page, and we were operating at only two private hospitals then, Peoples Hospital and St. Mary's Infirmary. My responsibilities were to prepare patients for surgery: examine them, write the histories, get them ready for surgery, and write the pre-op orders. Dr. Sinkler had his own set of surgical instruments, and I had to see that the instruments were at the hospital where we were going to operate. The hospitals had their own instruments, but he wanted the best instruments. There was a certain amount of pride in those days.

I also made house calls until one or two o'clock at night. Those were the days when I didn't mind making house calls anywhere in St. Louis. I went down to Russell and Gamble and places like that. You entered a lot of those houses from behind. You had to go to the back of the house, through those little alleys, and up the steps to the second floor. I never thought anything about it. I didn't worry about crime. Now, the brothers were out there cutting each other, having their own fights, but they didn't molest strangers. I didn't fear to go anyplace in the city in those days.

So then the time came to open my office, down on the Hodiamont tracks, on the corner, over Speckart Drug Store. Old man Speckart, he was a likable person, a very nice white person. At any rate, while I was in there unpacking boxes, I didn't have any chairs or desks or anything like that yet, somebody knocked on the door. I opened the door, and he said, "Is Dr. Whittico in?" I said, "Yes, I'm Dr. Whittico." He said, "Well, I'm looking for you because I need an operation." I hadn't sent out any notices, hadn't sent any cards. I never did send out any cards. Just think, there I was, I hadn't even opened my office, and somebody came looking for me to operate on him. I never will forget that.

Lawrence Nicholson

Chairman of the Department of Psychology, Harris-Stowe State College; President, St. Louis Board of Education

I am a product of the St. Louis public schools, entering racially segregated Banneker Elementary School and graduating from Vashon High School. After one semester at the University of Chicago, I went to Lincoln University in Jefferson City, Missouri, encouraged by N. A. Sweets, business manager of the *St. Louis American* newspaper, enthusiastic recruiter for Lincoln. While there, I was profoundly influenced by two sets of experiences. One of these was the YMCA's Fellowship of Reconciliation. Its wonderful magazine, the *Intercollegian,* was very much interested in the desegregation of Missouri's colleges. I met a number of white youngsters from the University of Missouri who shared this interest. The second great influence was the student-teacher relationship with Dr. Lorenzo Greene, who had collaborated with Carter G. Woodson to create the classic *Negro in Our History.*

But on the horizon was the Lloyd Gaines case. Lloyd Gaines had been my classmate at Vashon. The YMCA was particularly interested in getting black students integrated onto the campus at Columbia, and so I became involved with Lucille Bluford and the staff of the YMCA. The Gaines case was up in the air, and we thought that two students were going to get into the University of Missouri, including me. But of course we didn't. It wasn't until ten years later that black students were admitted.

In the meantime, the state of Missouri paid my out-of-state graduate school tuition, and I graduated from the University of Chicago School of Social Work. After teaching a year at Sumner and a year at Vashon, I decided I wanted to teach at a university. So I went to Columbia University in New York, where I got hooked on education, and I got a doctorate.

Returning to St. Louis in the 1950s, a handful of us started a movement to desegregate the Board of Education. We got our first black person on the board somewhere in the 1950s. He was a reverend from the church on Enright and Newstead. He was bright, but one person out of twelve doesn't cut the mustard. I discovered that twenty-five years later, when I came on the board with Mrs. Anita Bond.

After World War II, the leadership of the black community was involved with groups like the Urban League and the NAACP, which were not moving fast enough for the returning servicemen. Those servicemen had been sprawled out all over the world. They had a broader perspective of what our requirements ought to be in a democratic society. They wanted a more active approach to change. Consequently, new groups, like CORE (the Congress of Racial Equality) and the Student Nonviolent Committee, gave rise to new leadership. I was active in the Congress of Racial Equality because it was working for change in housing and in jobs in this community.

Things really began to change under the remarkable laws that came along in the 1960s. That whole series of civil rights laws had tremendous impact on job and housing opportunities. However, I don't think that the black schools dealt with what was happening. The changes in our environment were not integrated into the curriculum. We were having our own problems in the institutionalized education profession. We were slow to initiate practices and policies that reflected the federal legislation. We had separate professional teacher organizations until well into the 1970s. Missouri is a conservative state. As a leader in the state teachers association, to take a stand advocating desegregation was to court censure. But it was a responsibility.

In the 1970s, I worked to make sure that Harris-Stowe Teachers College did not go out of existence and remained a source of competent city teachers, a continuing challenge to Harris-Stowe and the St. Louis Public Schools. Between World War I and well after World War II, Stowe was responsible for the middle class in this town. The black middle class was largely teachers. Harris-Stowe was one of the last institutions in the country committed to eliciting from students the kinds of attitudes and values that make good teachers. I think teachers are terribly important. We need teachers today who are effective with our little urchins, you know, teaching citizenship skills, communication, literacy skills, and helping with the transition from school to work or school to college. There is a need for just plain old teaching. As African Americans we must constantly "Lift Every Voice" on behalf of education.

George H. Carper

Owner, Carper Casket Company; Tuskegee Airman

I lived in Kirkwood as a child. My mother and father had a little delicatessen. The store was in the front, and we lived in the rear. In the wintertime the water pipes would freeze up and we would take baths in tin tubs, No. 3. Growing up I had a constant companion, and when we were about nine or ten, my mother told him that we were going to move to St. Louis. And he said, "Can I go?" And my mother said, "Yeah." You know, she was just kidding. So when moving day came, he came up and saw us moving and said, "Hey, I'm ready to go." So my mother said, "Well, what does your mother say about it?" So she called his mother, and she said, "Take him." And we have been brothers ever since.

I started at Booker Washington, in Kirkwood. It only went to about the fourth grade. I graduated from James Milton Turner in Meacham Park, and from there I went to Sumner and from Sumner to Tuskegee. I was eighteen when I went to Tuskegee to take aircraft engine mechanics and pilot training. The first order of business was to become a licensed aircraft engine mechanic, then after that I took pilot training. My brother and I were Tuskegee Airmen. They kept me in Alabama, training airmen, until 1945. But my brother, he was one of those that flew the escort for the bombers into Germany, and he stayed in the service twenty years.

I had no other interest than flying and working on airplanes. We lived on Finney Avenue, a block from Hadley Tech, and the whole top floor of Hadley Tech was airplanes and engines and parts. And there was a certain custodian.... The only way blacks got into Hadley Tech was with a mop or a broom. But every evening at about six o'clock, this custodian would let me in Hadley Tech, and I would go up and tinker with the airplanes and engines. And I knew that the only place I wanted to go was Tuskegee.

We started this business long before I left for Tuskegee. We go back to 1938 or 1939. I used to nail the outside of boxes together and put in the cloth covers. When I came back in 1946, I put the shelves together. Originally, we were at 1039 North Vandeventer, and from there we went to 3615 Easton. And at that time we were manufacturing. We manufactured until some time in 1948. We had a lot of union trouble and had a strike. When they walked out, we went into distributing, and we have been distributors ever since. We have sold to all of the funeral homes at one time or another. Of our total sales, about 65 percent is to whites. We're not prejudiced. We're just trying to give service and quality merchandise. We supply funeral homes with the caskets, and at present we are the only black company in Missouri. And in the United States, volume-wise, we're about third.

For many years a lot of the smaller funeral directors used to bring families in to us, and we would make funeral arrangements for them. That gave us an edge on the white casket companies, because they weren't as familiar with how to do it. In the meantime, I got my funeral director's license, my son is a licensed funeral director, and my wife is a funeral director. And some white casket companies made a trip to the state board in Jefferson City to complain that there was a casket company in the city of St. Louis making funeral arrangements, when only licensed funeral directors are supposed to make funeral arrangements. And when they got up there they found out that my son, my wife, and myself were all licensed funeral directors.

So many things like that happen that I just take it in stride. Down in Alabama I had a white sergeant, Sergeant Cook, and he felt that blacks were incapable. And it was my challenge to prove him wrong. It was tough, because, after all, we were supposed to be porters, floor sweepers. But it was my challenge, and in the long run we ended up good friends.

There are so many things that I never associate with being history, and here I was a part of it.

Ora Lee Malone

National Business Representative, Amalgamated
Clothing and Textile Workers Union

I attended school in Mississippi and Alabama. We went to segregated schools where we didn't have any books. We didn't have any transportation. It was a struggle. It was just like South Africa. I didn't go to college. I couldn't go. There were too many of us. Somebody had to work, and I was the oldest one.

I got started in the labor movement when I was working at the California Manufacturing Company. I was a pieceworker. The company had a black prima donna who snitched. And the child who got fired said, "Seems to me we could get a union." I didn't know anything about who represented the garment industry or anything. In the meantime, the Amalgamated Clothing and Textile Workers were having a jurisdictional dispute with the Garment Workers Union. And they had never worried about organizing a predominantly black shop. So they decided that they would come out and start leafleting the shop where I worked. While they were passing out leaflets, the company would come out and say, "Throw those leaflets down. Don't pick them up." I said, "In this country you have a right to read anything you want." And I persuaded the people to keep the literature and read it. The company would keep us there till night, telling us what they were going to do to us if we organized a union. One of the bosses said that he was going to lay off a woman, and we didn't even have a contract or anything.

The union came out and asked if they could talk with us. And the company put us in this huge building. And the union man said, "Let me explain to them what they're joining." And the company said, "No, you can't talk to them. If they want to sign the card, let them sign." And I said, "I'm not signing anything if I don't know what I'm signing." And I turned to the man representing the union and I said, "Sir, do you have anyplace where we can meet, and you can explain it to us?" And he said, "Sure." And he told us where to come. So we went down to the union hall, and he explained, and we all signed the cards at the union hall. And I was elected shop steward. I was shop steward for nineteen years.

After that I was a business representative for the Amalgamated Clothing Workers Union for nineteen years. They didn't have any black representatives in the union until then.

I would go to all the meetings, and I would be the only black representative there from the joint board. No other blacks but I would be there. I was there to do a job for the people, and that's all. One of the shops that I was serving didn't have any blacks doing piecework—most of them were time workers. And time workers only got a raise when the minimum wage went up. And so my fight with the union was to reclassify these people. But the company and the union were determined not to give these black workers that kind of break. So I fought the union, and I fought the company. I told them these people were going to start going to other organizations to get justice. And they were scared to death. They had heard of Percy Green. And they thought that Percy would be down there picketing the union, if they didn't do the right thing. So they called a meeting at the union hall. I was asking for back pay, but the workers said, "We don't want back pay, we just want them to start paying us right." That was hard for me to take, but I couldn't say anything because that's what they agreed to. But it brought them up to scale.

I represented about twenty-seven stores, and I had three factories. I had Modern Jacket Company, Admiral, and the Novelty Jacket Company. And I represented the Raskas Tie Shop. Then they sent me out of town for five years, after the factories started closing in St. Louis.

You must have the courage to stand up for what's right, what you believe in. If we don't get our act together, we're going to be right back where we came from. We have to stand up and vote and be involved in politics. We have to be able to look a politician in the eye and say, "I don't want anything for myself, I just want you to do right by the masses." Because they'll be glad to give you a few crumbs to shut you up.

Look at A. Philip Randolph. He didn't take a backseat to anybody. When he was organizing the Pullman porters' union, George Meany sent him a check and said, "Take this check, fill it in, and don't worry about the union." But he wouldn't do it. If you don't take anything from them, you can always be independent and honest. That's what Randolph said. He said, "Daughter, you have to fight and be honest, and don't ever sell out."

John H. Gladney

Supervisor, Ear, Nose, and Throat Surgery, Homer G. Phillips Hospital; Interim Department Chairman, Ear, Nose, and Throat Surgery, St. Louis University Hospital

I have very little personal memories of my real mother. There are only a couple of incidents that I really remember. One was that she loved music. We did not have an instrument in our home, but she sang, and she had a lovely voice. And I remember walking up the street about three or four blocks with her one day, and we were holding hands, and we went up to a lady's home who was coaching my mother in voice. The other thing that I remember about her was that I went to see her when she was terminally ill, in the basement of a white hospital, Arkansas Baptist Hospital. I hated the thought that my mother was lying there in the midst of all that disarray. There were men and children, all on the same ward. And of course, it had odors that one associates with older people dying. It probably was that negative experience that helped me to decide that medicine was my future.

I went to Talladega College, in Talladega, Alabama, one of those six or eight black colleges and universities founded by the American Missionary Association of the Congregational Churches of America. Talladega was founded right after the Civil War, in 1867. My high school science teacher, Herbert Denton, had gone to Talladega, and I admired him. There were several other teachers at Dunbar High School who had gone to Talladega who inspired me.

One of my mentors at Talladega was the director of the college choir. He was well educated, inspiring, and we had an outstanding choir. I remember my freshman year, the college choir went to Birmingham, Alabama. At that time, in the state of Alabama, it was against the law for white folks and black folks to gather under the same roof. But Eleanor Roosevelt, the president's wife, and Mary McLeod Bethune were on the stage, and we gave a recital on their behalf. It was glorious! That was the first time I'd heard the Fisk Choir sing, and the Tuskegee Choir, and the Alabama A&M College Choir. And I was aware that it was a great event, to sing in a program with those great choirs, before the president's wife and Mary McLeod Bethune.

I went to Meharry Medical College. Dr. Carl Gaffney and I were classmates, and we both came to St. Louis to Homer G. Phillips in 1946, because we wanted to do our internships at a first-class hospital. When I got here, the late Dr. Sinkler was head of Homer Phillips, and he was very demanding. He sat all the incoming interns down and said, "You know, fellows, this is a charity hospital for 'Colored' people. If you can't deal with the fact that these patients are your bosses, you may be dismissed. You are here to learn off of people who have no

other place to seek medical care. I don't ever want to hear of your treating any of them in any way except with respect, or else you have my word that you will be dismissed." And I thought that was a good start.

Dr. Gaffney and I received our medical training under the auspices of the U.S. Armed Forces. We received commissions as first lieutenants in the army at the same time that we received our M.D.s, in 1947, and we fully expected to be used by the military. But during that year we received letters from the army stating: "We do not need any more colored doctors in the United States Army at this time. If you care to resign your commission, your request will be tendered with favor." After letters that blunt and that racist, we both promptly resigned.

So I took a job in Decatur, Illinois, practicing family medicine. We stayed there for three years. I was the "colored doctor," and that was the atmosphere that was there. The schools were not segregated by law, but we're talking about the middle of Illinois, where black people did not stray from the categories in which white people classified them. Decatur had about five thousand blacks, and few of them aspired to do anything. They were preparing themselves to work in the white folks' kitchens. Blacks "knew their place" more so than if they had been in Arkansas, or Alabama, or Mississippi.

I came back to St. Louis in 1956, and I opened a private practice at Euclid and Easton. I was board certified, and I was the supervisor of the ear, nose, and throat service at Homer G. Phillips. I became a fellow of the Academy of Otolaryngologists in 1962, and around that time I went to see if I could get a staff appointment at Washington University, so that I would have a place to take my private patients. The chairman of the ear, nose, and throat department told me that there would be no place for me in his department, ever. So I went over to St. Louis University, where they were glad for help in the clinic at Cardinal Glennon. I worked in the clinic a couple of afternoons a week, and after several months I got on the staff and on the faculty.

There isn't anything more important in youth than to prepare for the rest of your life, and the best way to do that is to get an education. Nobody appreciated that more than the slaves did. The first thing they wanted to do was to learn how to read. Young people must not let others get in the way of their dreams. They should dream about what they want to become, and do it. Life entails discipline. Just as football is a discipline, you can be a disciplined scholar if you choose. Don't let anybody else define you.

Frank O. Richards

General Surgeon, Homer G. Phillips Hospital,
Barnes-Jewish Hospital, Deaconess Hospital

I was born in Asheville, North Carolina, where I stayed until I finished high school. I went to Talladega College in Alabama for four years, and then I went to Howard University Medical School in Washington for four years. I came to St. Louis in 1947 to do my internship and residency at Homer G. Phillips Hospital.

In college I thought I wanted to be a physicist. My physics professor, Dr. Knox, had a Ph.D. from MIT, and after teaching at Talladega he worked on the Manhattan Project, building the atom bomb. He was always available, like a private tutor, so he was a great influence on me. The reason we were lucky enough to have him at Talladega was because he could not teach at any of the large white universities. I realized that there were very few positions available for black physicists, and my brother, who was a physician, influenced me to go into medicine.

When I finished medical school there were very few facilities where you could go to get advanced training. There were the two black universities, Howard and Meharry, of course. There were several smaller institutions like Provident Hospital in Chicago, Provident in Baltimore, Tuskegee, Harlem Hospital in New York, where you could get training. Homer G. Phillips was the outstanding institution outside of the two medical schools. In fact, it trained more physicians than the medical schools did. When I came to Homer G. Phillips Hospital, there were about thirty black doctors in training. They came primarily from Howard or Meharry. Others came from white institutions that happened to train one or two black physicians. Most of them came here to Homer G. Phillips.

We had a very interesting relationship for training; Homer G. Phillips was affiliated with Washington University. You have to go back a ways to understand how that came about. Originally St. Louis took care of black patients at the old City Hospital. After that, they went to a facility that was separate and black, located down on Garrison and Lawton, called City Hospital No. 2. At that time white physicians from St. Louis University and Washington University were responsible for training and for supervision of the patients. They were the doctors who practiced. The black doctors were on the periphery. They had no real input, as far as policy. When Homer G. Phillips Hospital opened, all of that changed. Mayor Dickmann put blacks in charge of the hospital for blacks. From that time on, we had our own service of black surgeons and physicians. We had a slew of outstanding black physicians and surgeons at Homer Phillips, including Dr. William Sinkler,

probably the biggest influence during my training; Dr. A. N. Vaughn; Dr. J. J. Thomas; and Dr. Hampton, the first medical director at Homer Phillips.

Washington University took over the training program at Homer G. Phillips. They sent attending surgeons to work with black surgeons to train new surgeons and physicians. It was unbelievable. From Washington University, physicians came to make rounds and to teach. I spent four years in that integrated teaching program dedicated to a black populace. It was very unique. The Rosenwald Foundation also sent several doctors away to white institutions to receive advanced training in their specialty. The Rosenwald Foundation was established by Julius Rosenwald, the president of Sears, Roebuck and Company, to provide education and advancement for black people. They sent several physicians away to get advanced training and then come back and head up the department and take over the responsibility of training in their specialty.

The caliber of training at Homer G. Phillips was unbelievable. The physicians from Washington University who came to Homer Phillips to make rounds and to teach were some of the most outstanding physicians in the world. Dr. Evarts A. Graham, the chief of surgery, came and lectured. Dr. Robert Elman, a world authority on burns and fluids, did his most important work at Homer G. Phillips. The same goes for Dr. Park White, an internationally known pediatrician. They were all instrumental in training young doctors like myself. We spent four years in that integrated teaching program, dedicated to serving black patients.

Peoples Hospital predates Homer G. Phillips. It was a small hospital run by black physicians to take care of private black patients. Private patients went to Peoples Hospital on Locust Street or to St. Mary's Infirmary, a Catholic hospital, located down on Papin. That's another interesting story. A sister went all the way to the pope and said, "We need a hospital to take care of black people in St. Louis." And the Catholics opened St. Mary's Infirmary in 1922. Peoples Hospital began in 1894, and it was called Provident Hospital at first. Those two hospitals are where black doctors treated their private black patients.

Medicine is a very gratifying profession. It's a long hard trek, and it is changing. If you want to be a physician for income, you can forget it. That won't happen. But if you're in it because you want to be a doctor, because you want to help people, I don't think there is any field that is more gratifying.

Marion J. Brooks

Social Studies Teacher, James Milton Turner School
and Kirkwood High School

I have been colored; I've been Negro; I've been black; now I'm African American. What will I be in five years? So I just say our people are sun-kissed.

I grew up in Kirkwood. My parents moved here in 1905, and I was born here. I remember we used to have a Lion's Carnival—we still do. When I was little, it was on the islands down on the main street, and there was a Ferris wheel and horses. I had a dime, and I wanted to ride on that Ferris wheel. But they wouldn't let me ride because I was sun-kissed. I was very unhappy, and I talked to my mother about it. And she said, "You know sometimes people have a toy and they don't want to share it. You've had a toy that you didn't want to share." That made sense, but I was still hurt because I could not ride the Ferris wheel. We couldn't go to the show, and we couldn't go in the drugstore to buy a soda.

I graduated from Sumner in June 1932. Now this going to high school in the city was because in 1919 my mother, along with Gus Ewing and Frank Stone from Webster, paid a lawyer to go to Jefferson City and lobby for a law that would compel school districts in the state of Missouri that did not provide a high school education for sun-kissed boys and girls to pay the tuition for them to go to a district that did. So when I went to Sumner High School, the Kirkwood Board of Education paid my tuition. At the time that the law was passed, the first year that they paid, the Kirkwood Board of Education appropriated four hundred dollars for fourteen eighth-grade graduates to go to high school. The tuition was $27.50 a quarter, and you had to get extra money yourself. My sister did baby-sitting, and our mother took in an extra bundle. She was a laundress. My sister graduated from Sumner High School, and I graduated in 1932. I attended Stowe Teachers College and graduated from there in June of 1937.

After I graduated I taught at Riverview Gardens School, a small school for sun-kissed boys and girls whose parents worked at the Missouri Portland Cement Plant. There were thirty-five boys and girls in the school, and two teachers, Mrs. Alma Patterson and I. She taught the first three grades, and I alternated the grades that I taught. One year I taught grades four, six, and eight; and the next year I taught grades three, five, and seven. I was there for five years, and then the cement plant needed to dynamite for shale in the area where some of the houses were. So the people who lived in those company houses had to move. The population went down, and the school board decided that they only needed one teacher.

I didn't work during the war, because my husband worked for the city. Then I helped establish a playground for sun-kissed boys and girls at Booker Washington School in Kirkwood. I was the director of the playground, and our playground won a silver cup from the American Legion for three consecutive years. Then the superintendent of schools hired me as a permanent substitute at Booker Washington School. I taught for two years as a permanent substitute, until he made me acting principal, in 1949. At that time the school board decided to close the Booker Washington School and send all the sun-kissed boys and girls who lived in Kirkwood to Meacham Park to the James Milton Turner School. That school had grades kindergarten through junior high. The board of education did not tell any of the parents that they were going to close the school, they did it like a midnight ride, one night. But the parents protested, and the school board moved the furniture and the piano back to Booker Washington School, for one year. After that, they closed the school. I was sent to Turner School, where I taught sixth grade and geography to seventh graders for five years.

In 1954 the Supreme Court decided that all schools were to be desegregated with all deliberate speed. So, as a consequence, Kirkwood desegregated its schools. You went to your neighborhood school. Sun-kissed people in Kirkwood are not colonized, they're scattered all over. So the sun-kissed boys and girls went to their neighborhood school, except those at the high school level. They did not desegregate the high school boys and girls until 1955, when the new Kirkwood High School building was near completion. I taught geography at the new high school, and later economics, government, and sociology. At first I experienced plenty of mischief, but I liked my students, and they liked me.

Anyway, in 1976, the Kirkwood School District elected me Teacher of the Year. The next year I won the State Teacher of the Year honor, and then I was chosen one of four National Honorary Teachers of the Year.

Sylvester LeClaire Smith

Superintendent, Kinloch Public Schools;
Secretary-Treasurer, Royal Vagabond Club

My family consisted of about sixteen members, twelve boys and four girls. We left Macon, Mississippi, and came to good old St. Louis and landed on Morgan Street, which is now Delmar. We had to get out of Mississippi. My dad had to leave because of racial tension. He could read and write, and he had quite a following. The racial people didn't like to have a smart fellow leading others. It was a threat. The white sheets and the cone heads were after my dad. They caught my brother and beat him up pretty good. And my dad said, "We better move on out." So we came to St. Louis. And I'm glad we did.

After we lived in St. Louis for a while, we moved to Kinloch. Naturally, coming from the South, my dad loved the dirt. He loved raising vegetables and hogs and chickens. Kinloch was surrounded by the white community of Ferguson. There was no Berkeley. Kinloch extended into the Florissant Commons and included the airport. That's where President Theodore Roosevelt came and had his first plane ride, at the airport.

There was a dog kennel near Ramona Lake on Hanley Road, and we used to have a dog track, a racetrack, in that area. Kinloch was a resort area for whites. People who worked in St. Louis came to Kinloch for recreation. They could fish, and there was a horse racetrack. There were big white farmhouses where people raised all types of fruits and vegetables. Those Kinloch farmhouses were mansions with big porches on the front and trees all around them. They were left from earlier days when slaves worked on the farms. When we moved to Kinloch, there were a lot of orchards, even back behind Dunbar School. There were pear trees, cherry trees, and apple trees. As a young man I use to work on a farm, and I thought it was something to make seventy-five cents a day picking cherries and blackberries.

I completed my schooling at Dunbar in 1928. We had no high school in Kinloch, so I enrolled at Vashon in September 1928. I was in the second full four-year class at Vashon High School. I graduated in 1932. But at that time St. Louis University wouldn't let us enter, and Washington University wouldn't let us enter. So my pastor, the Reverend W. L. Johnson, said to my dad, "Send him to Lincoln University." I, in my short knickers, went to Lincoln University, with two hundred dollars in my pocket.

Just before I graduated from Lincoln, the principal of Dunbar School died. Reverend Johnson was a member of the school board, and he called me and asked if I would help. So when I left Lincoln University, I came back to Kinloch, and I started teaching at Dunbar School for thirty-five dollars a month. I started out teaching first grade and worked my way up to seventh and eighth grade, plus I was the assistant principal. Kinloch added high school classes at Dunbar in 1935. I became the principal of the high school in 1938, and we built a separate high school in 1939.

In 1943 they made me the superintendent of schools for Kinloch. I was the first black school superintendent in the state of Missouri. I was the principal of the high school and the school superintendent for twenty-one years, until I retired from Kinloch in 1964.

Right after I became superintendent, St. Louis University decided to begin admitting African Americans. I was the first African American to register at St. Louis University on June 6, 1944. That was D day for the Allies and D day for me. I was a graduate student. I received my master's degree in educational administration in 1947, while I was principal of the high school and school superintendent.

Kinloch built a second elementary school in 1960, and they named it after me, Sylvester LeClaire Smith Elementary School. We really needed that second elementary school. Dunbar had an enrollment of 934 pupils, and some of the classes had thirty-five or forty students.

When I left Kinloch, I became the first vocational adjustment coordinator in St. Louis. In those days some students only attended high school for two years. They called that Terminal Education. And my job was to find jobs for T.E. students when they were in their last year. Later on I found jobs for four-year students. I visited Barnes Hospital, Jewish Hospital, hotels and motels, and private clubs, recruiting jobs for the students. I would take kids out to these big private clubs, you know, and to state institutions, like out on Arsenal, and I found jobs for them.

I worked for sixty years, and I was only absent half a day. My dad taught me to be industrious. He taught me that you can do whatever you set your mind to. You can make bricks out of straw if you have a mind to do it.

Ida O. Scott

Assistant Director, Rent and Occupancy, St. Louis County Housing
Authority; President, Concerned Citizens of Elmwood Park

Blacks began to move to Elmwood Park in the late 1800s—I guess it was 1893. This was kind of a sharecropping place. Blacks started buying lots and building little houses and raising their own food. They had gardens, they had chickens and pigs, and some had cows and horses. They had everything they needed to live. Some ladies did domestic work, but most of the women did not work—they were homemakers. The men farmed, and at one time a lot of men worked at the Volks Clay Mine down on Page Avenue, and some of them worked at the brickyard in Maryland Heights. But most of them did farmwork.

My father was a janitor in the West End, down around Page and Union. My parents had ten children. My father died when I was thirteen years old, but we had a good life. We were poor, but we didn't know it. At that time there was no electricity out here. We had lamp lights. We had to wash and clean the chimneys when we came home from school. We had coal stoves, and wood stoves, and my brothers would chop wood. We did not have any water system out here, and the neighbors got together and dug wells. The people who didn't have a well got water from the ones who did.

Later, when I was a young woman, people still had outdoor toilets and everything, and there was a polio epidemic. We started petitioning the county to get water on our streets. It was just open sewage, you know, ditches and all, and that's really what started the urban renewal, this polio epidemic.

Mr. Harvey J. Simms was the principal out here at Elmwood School. Every Friday, after lunch, we would all come together for an assembly. We would sing school songs and hymns and army songs and all kinds of stuff. Mr. Simms was a philosopher. He told us things like "A stitch in time saves nine," or "If you take care of a problem when it's small, then it never gets to be a big problem." Things like that. Even now, I remember the things that he told us. He was like a father. He was a great man.

The schools were segregated, so Ritenour paid tuition for us to go to Sumner. We would walk from Elmwood to Overland and catch the streetcar and ride it all the way downtown. It was dark in the morning when we left, and it was dark in the evening when we came back home. Going to high school was really a chore. Mr. Walton was the music teacher, and there was one song that he taught us, "Go down, Moses, way down in Egypt-land. Tell old Pharaoh to let my people go." I don't know what it was about, that song, but it would just stir me.

We've always had some kind of a community organization here. Concerned Citizens is about twenty or thirty years old. Before that my mother belonged to the Elmwood Park Improvement Association. At that time we didn't have sidewalks, and the men made boardwalks down the street for us to walk on. We didn't have roads, and the men who had trucks and hauled ashes and cinders made the roads and filled them in with cinders and ashes. They made the roads, they dug the wells, they did everything that was necessary.

They had to petition Union Electric to get electric lights, and Union Electric sent a salesman out to sell electric stoves. Only three or four people were able to buy electric stoves, but once the lines got out here, we began to get electric lights. To get water out here we had a water club. The water company charged so much to run the water so far up the street, and each person who was in the water club paid to get the water lines run. They ran them up one block one year, and people would carry water from there, and then the next year the water club would carry it up a little further until we got water in the area.

Mr. Cohen had a big hog farm down where the Government Records Center is now. All that land was his hog farm, and he had three or four trucks. He hired men on the trucks and he hired men on his hog farm. He had a grocery store out here too. He was one of the more affluent people out here.

Elmwood Park is just a little stop in the road now. You see, at one time Elmwood went from Page Avenue all the way to Olive. Then, as the county began to be annexed, Olivette annexed all the way down to the Rock Island Railroad track, and then Overland annexed as far as Meeks. So that just left us right here in a little huddle. Olivette and Overland did not want to annex Elmwood Park because we had no tax base. In the next fifty years or so, Elmwood Park might be forgotten. So I want to get something on record that we've been here.

Clifford H. Frazier

Overhead Crane Operator, Mississippi Valley
Structural Steel and Nooter Corporation

My mother had a limited education, but she knew about history. My brothers and sisters and I sat and listened while she told us stories that her mother and her grandmother had told. She told us about our background and about Civil War soldiers riding through the area. We must pass those stories on to our children.

Our land came from my mother's grandfather. He came to Chesterfield in 1797 with Daniel Boone and Lawrence Long. They brought fifty slave families from Kentucky and Virginia. They came up the Missouri River, and Daniel Boone took his slaves into St. Charles County. Lawrence Long stayed on this side of the river with his slaves, and that's how my ancestors came to this area.

After my great-grandfather William West was freed from slavery, he purchased 343 acres from his slave owner. Polly Ellis, my great-grandmother on my father's side, was only eighteen years old when she was freed from slavery, and she purchased 80 acres from her slave owner. There used to be a beautiful creek on her property where we all swam and fished. We called it Aunt Polly's Hole. We had something unique, growing up in Chesterfield. Few blacks can trace their heritage back as far as we can.

I remember my first school. I was not enrolled, but in a little area like that, I could just go. I must have been around five years old when I started tagging along with my brothers and sisters. Our first school was called the Chesterfield School, and it was about five miles from where we lived. The whites had their Chesterfield School a little distance past ours. Then they started sending us to Glencoe School, eleven miles away, and we had to walk. My dad kept asking the school board to provide transportation, because the white children had a bus. Finally, Charlie Schaeffer's daughter, Pearl, began driving us back and forth to school. About eleven or twelve kids would crowd into that automobile. The Schaeffers owned a lot of land out in this area, plus a tavern and a picnic area.

My dad's name was Henry J. Frazier. He did a lot of farmwork, because that was the only work that blacks could get out here. During the Depression he had two trucks, and he hauled rock for the WPA. He hauled rock for the construction of Babler State Park. All of that beautiful rock work in Babler Park was done by the guys of the WPA. A lot of blacks owned land where Babler Park is.

Our little church, Union Baptist Church, sits on a hill. There was always a lot going on at our church. We even sponsored fireworks on the Fourth of July. The men shot off skyrockets. It was gorgeous. And the older people put on great plays.

The whites had their things too. Madam Defoe owned a lot of land, and a lot of blacks lived on her property. They were servants. She held the Bridlespur Hunt. Everyone wore red coats, and they turned a fox loose and chased him on horseback. They had that every year, and blacks were included. We didn't hunt, but we enjoyed the food.

My father was a great man. He enjoyed his children. He took us to things in the city: the Annie Malone celebrations, ball games, and the fights. He played games with us until the wee hours of the night. My mother would say, "Henry, you let those children go to sleep. They've got to go to school in the morning." My brother Harold was another inspiration. He was the leader of our little gang. He suggested all the games we played. And when we built our own sleds, or whatever we did, he was the ringleader.

When the WPA ended, people were looking for jobs. One of our white friends asked my dad if he would like a job in a factory. My dad said yes, so our friend got him a job at Mississippi Valley Structural Steel in Maplewood. My dad got me a job there, and I worked there for two summers, and then I was drafted when I turned eighteen.

When I went in the service, there were no black leaders. All of the officers were white. All of my leaders in the past had been African Americans. It was hard for me to comprehend whites telling that many blacks what to do. But I accepted it.

When I got out of the service I wanted to get my job back at Mississippi Valley Structural Steel, but they wouldn't hire me. So I went to Tom Curtis, our Second District congressman, and he was very helpful in getting my job back. I think that was in 1950. I had been an operating engineer in the service, so I knew how to operate anything. I wanted to use the skills I had learned in the service. I kept asking the plant manager, "When is my time going to come?" After about seven or eight months he said, "Oh, God damn, Cliff. Come on!" and he made me the first black operator of an overhead crane. From then on, I instructed every operator who came into that plant. Mississippi Valley Structural Steel was bought out by Bristol Steel, and when our plant closed, the Nooter Corporation asked three of us to come down there to work. We were the best operators in St. Louis. We could handle anything. I supervised the loading of all the railroad cars going out to San Francisco.

Life has been good to me.

Doris A. Frazier

Gospel Singer; Music Educator

I grew up in Maplewood, Missouri. My dad was the pastor of Mount Zion Missionary Baptist Church in Richmond Heights for thirty-two years. His name was James E. Fiddmont. My mother is Lucy Barnett Fiddmont. They came to St. Louis about 1926, from Arkansas. They lived in St. Louis for a while, but then they bought a house in the Maplewood area. The family house is still there. My mother and father had twelve children, and I'm the ninth child born to that union.

My father was active in the community. He interacted with City Hall when people wanted to buy up land in the black neighborhood for a city park. They wanted to make a park where Mount Zion Church is. Now that my dad is gone, the city of Richmond Heights is accomplishing some of their urban renewal. They are building a community center and a park on the north side of Dale where black families lived, and they are planning a city works building on Elinor near Hanley, near the church.

My dad was relatively quiet. My mother did most of the disciplining. But we could talk to my dad. He gave wonderful advice. Even in church, when there was adversity, he was always calm. I never saw my dad get angry.

My mother was a believer in grace and mercy from God. But she worked herself to the bone. Just doing the washing for eight boys with a washboard was exhausting. She wanted her children to have a good education. She wanted us to do better than she had done.

We went to Lincoln School, part of the Maplewood–Richmond Heights School District. And when we graduated from the eighth grade, we went to Douglass High School in Webster Groves. My brothers and sisters played ball together and marbles and jacks. We had a big yard, about an acre. We all worked in the garden, and we had a cow and a barn. Sometimes my mother would gather the children around to sing. She taught us harmony. And we performed in little churches around the area. Four of my brothers grew up to be ministers.

I just love the piano, and when my mom and I were around a piano I would say, "Look Mom, I can play this, I can play that." My parents were poor, but my mom went home and said, "Honey, I think this girl really needs to take some lessons." And my dad told her, "Well, honey, if you can squeeze twenty-five cents out of the budget, give it to her." That's what I started on, twenty-five cents a lesson. I took piano from Bertha Black, a very prominent lady in St. Louis. I mean, she carries a lot of history. She did a lot for the city of St. Louis and the county. She lived in the city, and she taught seventh or eighth grade at Lincoln School. On Saturdays she came out and taught piano at a neighbor's house for twenty-five cents a lesson. She wanted to give kids something extra, because there was not much music at our school. Her enthusiasm was contagious. She wanted children to have the best. She fought for the betterment of black people.

When I started taking piano from Miss Black, we did not have a piano. I got a piece of cardboard and drew the piano keys on it, and that's how I practiced. Then someone in the church was moving, and they told my dad that if he could get their piano from the third floor he could have it. And that's how we got our first piano.

My fondest memory of high school would be Kenneth Billups, who was in the music department at Douglass. He gave me the opportunity to play for the choir, and he taught me to direct the choir. I credit him with giving me exposure. There was an important competition between music students from the St. Louis area at Berea Presbyterian Church, and Mr. Billups taught me to sing "Pace, Pace Mio Dio!" by Giuseppe Verdi for that competition. And I won the voice competition.

So that's how I got started with music. And I love it. I went to Lincoln University and majored in music. I tell you what, I've had other jobs, but music was always my heart. I had a professional singing group, called the Fiddmont Singers, made up of my younger brother and a sister and myself. We traveled all over the United States, singing. When my brother went on to become a preacher we got another guy to sing with us. His name is Richard Hollins. We have recorded four albums, and we have about twelve original songs that my husband and I wrote. We've been to a lot of colleges, and we've participated in black festivals all over. We sing gospel music, of course.

I started playing at my first church when I was fifteen years old. I played for the Old Community Baptist Church in Webster Groves. And that's how my music got started. I played for my dad's church, Mount Zion, until he died in 1973. After that, I came out to play and be a part of Union Baptist Church, and I love it. When I retired from the IRS I started teaching piano. I've got about twenty-five students. And I'm still church musician, and I still train the choir at church. I knew what I wanted to do when I was ten years old. I wanted to teach music. I love music to this day.

I hold my head up high and reach for the stars.

Colleen McCaine Johnson

Nurse's Assistant, Barnes Hospital, Missouri Baptist Hospital, and St. Luke's Hospital

I grew up in Clayton. My parents died when I was quite young, and my grandfather, who was my mother's father, brought us to Clayton. I had an older sister and two older brothers. I was raised by my grandfather and everybody else.

Clayton was just a low-level place. It was very quiet and very secluded. Everything was right there. We walked everywhere, unless we were going into the city—then we took the streetcar. Streetcars were the most common form of transportation. If we wanted to go to the movies, we went into St. Louis to the Comet Theater. It was a black theater. If we wanted to do any shopping we took the streetcar into the city to Famous or whatever other store. There was nowhere in Clayton to buy clothes. I don't remember any black families owning businesses in Clayton. But I remember my grandfather, Harrison Pitts, had a Model T Ford which he drove all around. We would chuckle through Clayton in that Model T Ford.

Most of the black families owned their own homes along Hanley Road, south from Forsyth. It was very quiet and tucked away. Everybody was safe. My grandfather owned his home on Brentwood Boulevard. The church was next door, where Reverend Rhodes was pastor, ever since I can remember. South of Forsyth was black, and north of Forsyth, toward University City, was white. The black homes were torn down when the high-rise buildings were built. People griped and moved out.

My grandfather had a huge home, and he rented rooms for an income. I guess we were there because he had enough space for us. I can remember, he would send me to the store every day for a pack of Camel cigarettes. He wouldn't buy a carton. Today you would buy a carton so you wouldn't have to go to the store every day. But not him.

My brothers went to school for a little while, but I'm the only one who went all the way through. Our school was named Crispus Attucks. It was a one-room school on Hanley and Bonhomme in Clayton. We had one teacher, Mrs. Clorine Bodine Thomas. She was an all-around teacher. She taught kindergarten through eighth grade. I started school when I was five years old. We walked to school, and I seem to remember walking by myself. My two brothers went infrequently, because everybody had a job to do on the farm. Since I was the baby I was the only one who went all the way through school.

As a child I stuttered. And I think I received more attention and love from the schoolteacher than I received from my family, because they didn't have time. They were all working. The teacher had a lot of patience with me. After I graduated and

went to high school I didn't stutter anymore. I went to Douglass High School in Webster Groves. We had a choice: we could either go to Sumner in the city for high school, or go to Webster Groves. My grandparents decided that I should go to Douglass since it was in the county.

My brothers left and went to New York because we had distant cousins there. My sister had a job where she stayed at the place, so she only came home on the weekends. I stayed at home with my grandfather.

I always enjoyed taking care of people, helping the underprivileged, and so that's what I did. I went into nursing when I was nineteen years old. I was a nurse's aide. I learned much of my nursing skills and knowledge from experience. My first job was at Barnes Hospital. I was probably there a year and a half, and then I moved to Pennsylvania. I had a cousin from Pennsylvania who came here, and I went there and stayed for a while.

I came back to St. Louis and worked at Missouri Baptist, in intensive care, for about ten or twelve years. I could always find a job in nursing. I worked at St. Luke's Hospital on Delmar for a while. Nursing is what I wanted to do, and that's what I did. I moved to Florida, and I came back here in 1966. This is where I married my husband.

When I came back home to Clayton, things were beginning to integrate. Instead of having to go in the back door we were able to go in the front door. When I came back I went into a restaurant in Clayton, and when the waitress brought my order, she had it in a bag. I said, "I want to eat it here." And she said I couldn't. Before, we didn't pay much attention to segregation, because we always had our own businesses, our own taverns or whatever, all black. As a child I would not have dared go into that restaurant. But things were supposed to be changing, and now I resented it. I had grown up in Clayton, and she was telling me I couldn't eat in her restaurant. I told her to eat it!

But things changed for the better. I think the Lord works out the bad things and turns them into good. As a child we had to go to church. My grandfather never went to church, but regardless, we always had to go. The church was right next door, so we didn't have to go far. In those days we went from Sunday school, to church, to BYPU, and then to church again. That foundation has always provided me with the protection I need when I am alone. I don't worry, because the Lord protects me. Whatever I need, it's always provided. I don't worry about anything.

Henrietta Ambrose

Councilwoman, City of Webster Groves; Author

I grew up in Webster Groves on Kirkham Avenue. My mother and her two sisters were widows. One sister had a daughter who was asthmatic, and in the twenties the coal and soot in St. Louis would discourage anyone from breathing. My mother visited friends in Webster Groves, and she thought it seemed like a good place to raise a family. It was like the country. The Kirkwood-Ferguson streetcar ran from Ferguson to Kirkwood, and went down the middle of Kirkham. The three sisters bought a little house on Kirkham Avenue, and that's where I grew up. I watched those three women struggle. This was during the Depression. I used to hear my mother pray out loud, "Lord, please let me live till my daughter is grown and she can take care of herself." It's amazing what those women went through, and they still made it.

My cousin who had asthma died early, but not from asthma. There was a spring that bubbled up behind our house. It was clear and cold and beautiful, and it had watercress in it. Webster Groves did not have water pipes that far north, so our water came from wells or from that spring. We didn't know the water was not pure, and my cousin drank the water and got typhoid.

My mother had a garden every year: carrots, tomatoes, turnip greens, and mustard greens. Along the back of our property were grapevines, those big purple grapes. We had a plum tree in our yard; the people next door had a pear tree; and the folks next to them had a cherry tree. The women exchanged fruit to make jelly, or they exchanged jelly. The Johnson family, behind us, had eight kids. Mama used to make jelly and give them some. And when their boys went hunting, they always brought Mama something back, rabbits or whatever.

We had a strong sense of community. I went to Douglass School from kindergarten all the way through twelfth grade. It was all in one building, and it was the only accredited high school for blacks in St. Louis County at that time. We had movies at Douglass School. I walked to school, and I picked up friends as I walked along. We walked to church and to Webster, to the shopping area. The adults looked out for all the kids in the neighborhood. We didn't realize that we were discriminated against because we had everything we needed: church, school, and home. We have lost that sense of community.

I don't have a college degree. I went to Tucker Business College. Mrs. Tucker had learned her skills in Indianapolis. She was the secretary to Madame C. J. Walker. When she came to St. Louis, she opened a secretarial school, a business school. When she sent me on my first interview, she told me to wear a suit, a hat, simple shoes, and white gloves. Before I went on the interview I had to go have her look at me to make sure everything was in place. All of my graduating class got good jobs. The students came from all over the country, from Illinois, Mississippi, Texas, Arkansas. There were three of us from Webster Groves, and we caught the streetcar every morning. Mrs. Tucker had day classes and night classes. When World War II was over, she accepted young men, because they had veterans' benefits. A lot of places wanted Tucker graduates. We worked at City Hall downtown, St. Mary's Infirmary, the St. Louis School Board. The Peoples Finance Building on the corner of Jefferson and Market had a lot of lawyers and doctors and receptionists. Those were the places that hired black secretaries.

When I left Tucker I got a job with Family and Children's Service. I was the first black to work in the Clayton office. Then I had a temporary job with the IRS during tax season. I worked from December until June for three or four years. I quit to be home with my children. Later, I worked for the army at the Mart Building, the VA Hospital on Grand, and I worked for Social Security from 1964 until I retired in 1985.

I became involved in the community in the late fifties, early sixties, when the city of Webster Groves was planning to annex North Webster. The city had a Land Clearance Authority which was targeting homes to be torn down. We had just built a little home on Eldridge, and I thought they were going to take that area. When I stopped working I told my husband, Walter, I would like to get involved. And he said, "Go for it!" So I went to City Hall and asked questions.

When Glenn Sheffield was elected mayor, I was appointed to fill her vacant seat on the city council. Then I was elected to the council in 1988 and again in 1992. For ten years the white community thought I favored North Webster, and North Webster residents didn't think I did enough. But I am proud of the North Webster housing venture. We built fifteen new houses on the vacant lots where houses were torn down by the Land Clearance Authority.

My advice to young people is: Stay busy. Know what is going on. Get involved! You'll never know what's going on, unless you're on the inside.

Walter S. Lathen

Instrumental Music Teacher, Douglass School;
String Bass, George Hudson's Orchestra

I grew up in the city of St. Louis. I attended West Bell School, Marshall School, and Sumner High School. I took violin lessons from Carl Tolle, who was a violinist in the St. Louis Symphony. That's how my music career started. I took lessons from him until I left Sumner. I went to Sumner for two years, and then I went to Monterey, California, and spent two years at Union High School, where I graduated. While I was at Union High School I learned how to play the bass horn, so I played the violin in the school orchestra and the bass horn in the band.

I came back to St. Louis, and I enrolled at Lincoln University. I wanted to pursue a music education degree, but unfortunately Lincoln University's music department was not capable of providing a full degree in music. As a matter of fact, I did more playing in the prison band than I did at the university, because the university did not have a band. While I was a student at Lincoln, I stayed with C. G. Williams, who taught the prisoners at the institution in Jefferson City. The black prisoners had a band. And I would go with Mr. Williams when he taught the band on Tuesday or Wednesday night, and I played in the band. On Sundays the prisoners gave a concert in the park, and I played with them. After a year of this I realized I was not getting what I wanted from Lincoln University, so I transferred to the University of Illinois. I spent four years there, and I got a degree in music education.

After graduation I got a job in Cairo, Illinois, as the music supervisor for the black schools. I visited the elementary schools, the junior high, and the high school. I taught all the choral music, and I started a band. I stayed there for two years, and when I left Cairo, I left them with a forty-piece band. My salary at Cairo was eighty-five dollars a month. I came to Webster Groves to teach music at Douglass School, where my salary was fourteen hundred dollars a year.

I taught in Webster for about forty years, and in that forty years, I saw the schools integrate in 1956. At that time, I started playing with George Hudson's Orchestra. We played for every top black entertainer that was on the black nightclub circuit. I came to George Hudson's Orchestra when George Hudson's bass player left his band to go to Count Basie. I stayed with George twenty-seven years.

George Hudson's Orchestra was well done. It was known all over the East. It was the most popular band in St. Louis. They called it the society band. When fraternities or sororities wanted to have some sort of pageantry or processional marches, we could play those things. It made the affairs very fine. We played at Tan Tara, Notre Dame University; we played at Sangamon University; we played the Military Ball at Lincoln University; we played a lot of political events; we played for the opening of the Hawks professional basketball season; we played the All-Star game in St. Louis. George had an excellent bunch of musicians. About half of them were instrumental music teachers in the St. Louis school system. Others worked in the post office, and one or two worked out at McDonnell Douglas. His musicians did St. Louis proud.

I played with Jeter Pillars, and I played with Eddie Randle. Eddie had an excellent band, six or seven pieces. We would leave of Friday and play a town in Illinois Friday night and another little town in Illinois Saturday night and another one Sunday night. Then we would come back. Miles Davis was his trumpet player. I played with Count Basie and some of the other big-time musicians that came in and needed a bass player. They would call the black musicians' union and request a bass player who knew how to read music. I played with Nancy Wilson, Lou Rawls, the Mills Brothers.

When I was teaching, music teachers visited other schools to see what they were doing. So, on my way from Cairo to St. Louis for the weekend, I stopped by the junior high school in East St. Louis. A good friend of mine, an alumni of the University of Illinois, Ellwood Buchanan, taught instrumental music there. So I sat in on his rehearsal. After he got through, he said, "I want you to hear a little fellow play." So he calls this fellow, and he says, "Go get your trumpet, I want you to play for Mr. Lathen." So this little fellow, junior high school age and small in size, went and got his trumpet. And he put his trumpet up to his mouth, put the mute in there, and played the trumpet solo to "Tuxedo Junction," by Erskine Hawkins. Didn't miss a note. I said, "Who is this?" He said, "This is Miles Davis." That's when I first met Miles.

I enjoyed teaching very much. I could see that I was doing something to help the youngsters, and that was my primary object. In those days, the black youngsters responded. I can sit back now, and see some of the former students that I had at Douglass High School. They're judges, they're Ph.D.s, they are prominent in the community. So it means that we were doing something right. Those black teachers at Douglass High School got out into the community; they were more than teachers—they were mothers and fathers to the students. I remember when I had students who didn't have the right clothes to wear, and I took them shirts and ties. And they appreciated it.

Benny W. Gordon Jr.

Real Estate Developer

I started growing up in Brooklyn, Illinois, and then I came to Webster Groves when I was about nine years old. My mother was a guiding force. When we moved to Webster Groves she married Reverend Blackburn, but he traveled, so she was like a single parent. I have one brother. Originally there were the two of us, but my aunt expired, and my mother adopted her two children, and they moved in with us.

I attended Douglass School in Webster Groves and graduated from Douglass High School. Then I attended Stowe Teachers College. It's now Harris-Stowe State College. After the war I studied business law at St. Louis University, until I was drafted during the Korean conflict.

After World War II, I worked for the government at 4300 Goodfellow. We did audits. This was during the McCarthy era. One of the white guys who worked for me accused me of being a Communist, and I lost my job. I finally got another job with the Universal Life Insurance Company in the city. I had never sold insurance before, but I was given the accounts in the Ville. Then the Korean conflict broke out, and since I was a reservist I was drafted. I didn't think I should go, if the government thought I was a Communist, but I went back in and served as the first black sergeant major at Fort Leonard Wood. While I was there I requested an investigation of myself, and I received the results of the investigation after I was discharged. The newspapers wrote about it with a headline that read "Vindicated After Five Years."

Then I went to work in real estate. I started building houses. I figured somebody should be building houses for African Americans. I built houses in Kirkwood, South St. Louis, and on Kirkham Avenue in Webster. Then I decided I would build a subdivision, Marvin Court, named after one of my sons. I did it on my own, and Roosevelt Federal was my lender. They gave me enough money to build a display house, and we put the utilities in. But the people who lived on Newport and backed up to the property did not want blacks that close to them. They sold their houses and threatened to boycott Roosevelt Federal if they continued to make loans to us. With that, I didn't have the money to pave the street or anything else. I had to practically give the display house away. It was demoralizing. But after a while I got back into real estate. I've been in the real estate business for about forty-two years.

But getting to the swimming pool. When I got back from the army in 1949, I was up at the drugstore, and I ran into one of the Webster Groves councilmen, and we were talking. He told me about the progress the city had made on the municipal swimming pool during my absence. I said I was looking forward to taking a dip. "Oh no!" he said. "We'll have to build a separate pool for the black community." I said, "Don't do me any favors." The swimming pool opened on May 30, 1949. My mother telephoned me and said, "Lord have mercy, Benny, don't go up to that swimming pool, son, or trouble is going to happen." I hadn't thought about it, but they weren't going to get away with worrying my mother. Finally, on a hot Sunday afternoon in August, I got Frank Witt, who was the only one with a car, and Evalee Wilkerson and Erma Calvin to go up to the pool. I called the *Star Times,* which was the most liberal of the three daily newspapers, and told them what was going on. A reporter met us at the pool at two o'clock, and we got in line to buy tickets. The ticket girl said she was sorry but she had instructions not to sell us tickets. The reporter asked by who's orders, and she said the city council. In the meantime, here came the police with sirens going. The mayor was there and all the city council. The reporter asked us what we planned to do, and I said we were going to sue. We asked George Vaughn to be our lawyer. He had just won the *Shelley v. Kraemer* restrictive covenant case before the Supreme Court. Vaughn wanted five hundred dollars to take the case, and that was a lot of money in those days. We were going to have fish fries and barbecues to raise the money, but before we could raise the money, Vaughn died. In the meantime, I knew Ted McMillian from Stowe Teachers College and St. Louis University. He had just graduated from law school, and I asked him if he would take us as his first case. He was starting a law firm with Alfonse Lynch and working at the post office. He took the case for a hundred dollars. The judge told the city council they would have to give us equal time in the pool, but the council claimed it would be too expensive because they would have to change the water each time we used it. So they closed the pool! It was closed for three years until we elected a new city council. I didn't know how to swim, but they didn't know that. It was the principle! My children and my grandchildren enjoy the fruits of what we fought for.

Today I am concerned about the number of young black people in jail. It would be cheaper to educate them than to incarcerate them. When our youngsters say they have nothing to do, it hurts me. I would like to build a community center in North Webster that would provide job training, day care, elderly care, health care, home economics, a multipurpose room, a place for young people to get theatrical experience, facilities for banquets, dancing. I'd like to make a joyful noise in this community.

Hutcher L. Dixon

Letter Carrier, U.S. Post Office; Real Estate Appraiser

I have been working since I was eleven years old. It was part of real life. My father left my mother when I was six years old, and I helped my mother raise my three sisters. My mother worked at a pecan factory, shelling nuts, when she first came to St. Louis when she was seventeen. But most of the time she did day work for a private family. How did my mother manage? With goodwill, perseverance, and prayer. We grew up in poverty, but she gave us discipline. She spanked us until we had welts, because she wanted to teach us respect, and she wanted to raise us to be independent citizens. I do not regret those spankings. Discipline is love.

When I went to my grandfather's grocery store for my mother, if the store was crowded, I had to get behind the candy counter and get all the kids out before I left. Those were my grandfather's instructions. My grandfather died when I was fifteen, and my uncle took over the store. My uncle was like a father figure to me. He taught me the grocery business. I delivered groceries in my uncle's truck, I picked up the wholesale goods, I ordered the supplies, I even learned to butcher. I could bring a side of beef all the way down to the skillet; same with pork.

When I was nineteen or twenty years old I was earning thirty-five dollars a week at my uncle's store, and my uncle saw a sign at the grocery supply company on Manchester Road where we bought our supplies that said: "Warehouse Man Needed, $85 a week." My uncle asked the man to hire me because I knew the grocery business. But the man said he couldn't because his customers would all leave.

When I was young, the most important community institution was our church, the United Methodist Church in North Webster. We had Sunday school and summer Bible school and other youth programs, but more important was the support. Families sometimes helped each other out financially, but it was the moral support, the encouragement about school, the father figures, that meant the most to me. C. L. Thomas was our Boy Scout leader, and he made sure I got a Boy Scout uniform.

Another important institution was the North Webster Volunteer Fire Association. My uncle and my grandfather helped organize it. Mr. Witt, Rosco James, Mr. Goins (the principal of Douglass School), Walter Rusan, Mr. Jenkins, J. C. Dixon, and Will Dixon organized it in 1939, because the Webster Groves Fire Department wouldn't fight fires in the unincorporated area. We also organized the Rock Hill Fire Department.

I worked for the post office for twenty-nine winters: twenty-eight years, three months, one week, and one day. I

was a letter carrier in Kirkwood, in the business district along Kirkwood Road. It was unusual for a black man to have the business district. But it was pleasant being outdoors and walking and getting to know the people.

My grandfather was in real estate, and I got the desire to go into real estate from him. He owned several pieces of property. I took my first real estate sales license test in 1961, and I took my first appraisal course in 1975. I kept working at it, and now I'm a state-certified appraiser.

I ran into discrimination in the St. Louis real estate market when I had my first salesman's license under Mr. Benny Gordon. We ran across the problem with a property on Swon Avenue in Webster Groves and one up on Fairlawn. The neighbors begged us not to put up a For Sale sign, but Mr. Gordon did anyway. Sometimes the neighbors got together and bought the property themselves, and then turned around and sold it to whites. That's what they did on Swon Avenue. I wasn't directly involved, but Gordon Real Estate Company was. In 1967, Mr. Gordon had to go to New York to finance a house in Crestwood, where a black bought. None of the local lenders would loan the money for the mortgage so the people could buy the house. They would not finance that house. So Mr. Gordon went to New York and sold it with a package. We had numerous encounters with redlining.

Over the years I have helped solicit loans and housing for minorities. I was able to get minorities into housing that they would not have been aware of otherwise. I educated some of them about the procedures you have to go through, step by step, in order to buy a home.

My real estate broker and I formed the first black chapter of the National Society of Real Estate Appraisers in 1984. We saw a need for blacks in St. Louis to have a chapter for unity. Any time you have a problem in any industry, you need a national organization with support behind you. That way you can get some help.

Hopefully our history will teach us where we came from and give us insight into where we are going. Wherever I walk in Webster Groves, Kirkwood, or St. Louis, I study the people. And I still feel hostility because I am black. Things are not really better than they were when I was growing up. There is as much prejudice in Chicago and St. Louis as there ever was in Mississippi. And I always think of what Jesus said: "What you do to the least of my brothers, you do to me."

Kennard O. Whitfield

Cartographer, Aeronautical Chart and Information Center;
Mayor, City of Rock Hill

I grew up in Kirkwood, the Queen of the Suburbs. I went to Booker T. Washington Grade School and James Milton Turner Junior High. That was during the time when schoolchildren were segregated, so students from Kirkwood went to Douglass High School in Webster Groves.

My father was from Amory, Mississippi, and my mother was from Little Rock, Arkansas. They met in St. Louis. My father was the oldest of twelve, so he had to leave school in the fourth grade to help his mother and father. When he came to St. Louis he went to night school, and he got to eighth or ninth grade. My mother went to Philander Smith College in Little Rock. She died when I was eleven and my brother was six. My father raised us by himself for six or seven years, and then he married my stepmother, from Memphis, Tennessee. My father was a custodian for forty-seven years at the Liggett and Myers Tobacco Co. My stepmother did day work until she was about eighty-one or eighty-two.

In the old days teachers could provide corporal punishment. Being a somewhat mischievous boy, I met up with that kind of punishment. When I went to Turner School, Llewellyn Smith had a tremendous impact on my life, because he was a disciplinarian. He was the boys' gym teacher and the baseball and basketball coach. He taught us a tap dance routine, and we put on a review for our parents in the gymnasium at the end of every year.

I graduated in 1951 and went off to college. I had a basketball and baseball scholarship to Xavier University in New Orleans, but I didn't graduate from Xavier, because I was drafted. I served in the army for two years, stationed in San Francisco. When I came out I went to St. Louis University and finished in 1958. I majored in physics and minored in math. Then I was hired by the Aeronautical Chart and Information Center, now called the National Imagery and Mapping Agency. I was a cartographer there for thirty-seven years. We made maps for weapons systems in case of war. We provided the maps for Desert Storm.

The Aeronautical Chart and Information Center sent us to a six-months school to learn how to be cartographers. After I had worked there about five years, they sent me to Yale University to get a master's degree in astronomy. We supported the space program with maps and charts. When I first started at the Aeronautical Chart and Information Center there were about a thousand employees, and diversity was not a buzzword. There were few African Americans. When I retired we had about four thousand employees, and we had made an effort to hire minorities. We recruited at the historically black colleges—Tougaloo, Jackson State, Alcorn, those kinds of schools. When I retired in 1993 I was a division chief, supervising a hundred and fifty people.

Being mayor of Rock Hill is not a career, it's a community service. I enjoy it. When I moved to Rock Hill in 1968, I decided to go to city council meetings and just watch. I said to myself, I can help, you know what I mean? Friends of mine from school said, "Why don't you run for alderman?" The alderman for my ward had decided not to run. And if you ever want to win an election, the best time to do it is when an incumbent is not running. I won the election in 1973, and I was an alderman until 1994. In 1989 I was president of the St. Louis County Municipal League, an organization of city officials who share knowledge and lobby the state on behalf of their cities. I was president of the Missouri Municipal League in 1990.

When I campaigned for mayor four years ago, economic development was the big issue. People in Rock Hill pay substantial property taxes, and most of that goes to the school district instead of the city. We just finished a commercial development called McKnight Crossings, at McKnight and Manchester. We moved one of the oldest buildings in St. Louis County from that site across Manchester Road to the property of the Rock Hill Presbyterian Church. It was the home of James Marshall, built in 1839. Marshall gave the land for the church, and his slaves built the old rock portion of the church.

I'm concerned about black kids today. So many are killed as a result of drugs. Parents, particularly black parents, need to know what their children are all about. They need to be more strict with them. It is not the school's responsibility to raise our children. My father told my teachers, "Call me if he does something wrong, and I'll straighten him out when he gets home." It wasn't harsh for him to tell me I couldn't have this or that. It is absurd to buy a kid a hundred-dollar pair of Nikes. I see four year olds negotiating with thirty-five year olds, and the four year old is winning! Older kids come home and their parents don't have any idea what is on their breath, if they're smoking, if they're shooting drugs. What I wonder is: who's paying the bills around here? I mean, who's in charge? Parents ought to make their children take responsibility for their actions. I think it's child abuse when you don't raise children properly.

I'm through soapboxing.

Mae F. Wheeler

Jazz Singer

I was raised by my mom. My mom and my dad were divorced, and I lived with my mom. We moved to St. Louis in 1940, when I was about six. We had relatives here, and my mom hoped that things would be better for us.

The first school I attended was Lincoln Elementary School in Richmond Heights, and from there I went to Douglass High School in Webster Groves. The teachers were something really special. Their profession was respected. Music class was almost like going to Juilliard. We listened to classical music, and we had to identify what instruments were playing, woodwinds and so forth. We had to know whether we were listening to an overture, or what, you know? We were taught all this. You see, we didn't just learn a song and sing it. It was taken apart for us and taught to us. Art was the same way. We had great teachers. We gave an appreciation dinner for our teachers a while ago, and most of them were still living. One of the teachers that inspired me the most was Marthenia Bates; she taught me about telling the truth, and she taught me about blackness, about black history. We were taught well.

If our children were taught by the teachers that taught us, we would not be in the fix that we're in today. But then there was a difference in the upbringing at home, too. Okay? The teachers were like parents, and parents were parents, you know? School was special. We put on school plays. We had cantatas. And they were productions! I mean, I think back about that now, and I realize I've been entertaining all my life.

I sang with the Sunshine Band, and there was more music learning. As I got older I sang with a gospel group called the Gospel Harmoneers, the Original Gospel Harmoneers. And when I was fourteen, we toured all the way to New York. I was the youngest one there. I went on the *Ted Mack Amateur Hour*, and we went to the Apollo Theater, and we went to the RKO Palace, and Times Square. The day that Bill "Bojangles" Robinson's funeral came down Times Square, I was there, and I saw it. It was memorable. We sang at Adam Clayton Powell's church in Harlem, the Abyssinian Baptist Church. The churches are huge in New York. It was just fun. I really had a good life.

When I was sixteen, I won a St. Louis talent show three weeks in a row. Chick Finney produced a talent show called "Stars of Tomorrow" where kids could come and exhibit their talents. That was exciting.

I began singing professionally in the 1950s. I started at the black social clubs, such as the Hawaiians, Cosmopolitan Ladies, and the Club Riviera on Delmar. I sang at Peacock Alley, at Fats States on Easton, at the Toast of the Town on Taylor Avenue, at the Hawaiian Roma Room at Vandeventer and Finney, at the Sportman Lounge at Finney and Sarah, and at Spider Burks's Palace Garden on Finney. Those small, black-owned lounges were instrumental in keeping music alive in St. Louis.

In the early sixties I sang in Gaslight Square. I sang at the Dark Side Night Club, the Black Horse, and the Crystal Palace. After Gaslight Square, I sang on the riverboats, the *River Queen* and the *Becky Thatcher.* Then I sang at Laclede's Landing, at Pupillo's Club, at the Typists' Club, at Chapin's Club, and at Lucius Boomer's Jazz Club. Hannegan's was one of the highlights. I loved working at Hannegan's. It was brand new in 1979. Al Hirt was playing there, and I went in and got a job. I was the first local entertainer hired there, and I was there from 1979 to 1985.

I've sung at the Fox, at Gene Lynn's, at Al Baker's, at the Moose. I sing the blues. And it's frustrating, because even though I'm able to sing at clubs where blacks didn't sing before, I'm still not recognized as I deserve. I'm still not paid what I'm worth. But I'll always be striving for success, and in that striving I'll do anything I can to help someone who is trying to overcome obstacles that I have overcome. I will tell young girls who want to become singers not to get tied down with boys and babies. It's a hard road when you try to have a career and some babies.

Singing has always been the most important thing in my life. I remember, as a little girl, going to the movies and seeing Jeanette MacDonald sing, and Ethel Waters and Lena Horne and Dorothy Dandridge, Pearl Bailey and Ella Fitzgerald. All of these people instilled in me a deep-rooted desire to be an artist.

My mom said that my grandmother sang. I never knew my grandmother. But my mom said my grandmother had a beautiful voice, and she said that I look just like my grandmother. To me, I look like my mother.

But the music thing has been there forever. It's always been a part of me. I wish I could feel that I'm a great singer. There are days when I feel that I'm a good singer, but not necessarily a great singer. Then there are days when I feel I did a good job. I'm pleased with myself and the music, with the totalness, not just with me. The musicians, the people in the audience, everything, just come together. I don't have those days often, but when they happen, boy, they're something else. It gives me that something that I need to keep on keeping on.

Julius K. Hunter

Senior News Anchor, KMOV-TV, Channel 4; Author

I grew up in midtown St. Louis. My first home was upstairs over a barbershop at 722a North Vandeventer. The first school that I went to, Cole Elementary School, was a half block from my house. And everything else that a person could want—grocery shopping, cleaner's—was right there in the neighborhood. There was no need to leave that neighborhood, and many of us kids never did.

My father was a custodian of a large apartment complex, and my mother was a domestic for many years. She later went to work at Jewish Hospital, where she kept the lab tidy. My parents were divorced when I was six or seven, so I did not have much contact with my father after that, except maybe three or four times a year for dinner. I have three younger sisters, and I was not only a brother but a father to those sisters.

I also took on the job of Sunday school teacher at my church at age twelve, which makes a person grow up quickly. By the time I was sixteen I was organist and choirmaster of the little church that I grew up in, and then by age twenty-four I was president of the congregation.

Eventually we moved around the corner to a street called Windsor Place. Windsor Place was built back in the 1890s for the servants who worked on Vandeventer Place. Vandeventer Place was a plush, luxurious private street, one of St. Louis's most beautiful. Windsor Place was a street of little shotgun houses for the servants. My mother was able to convince the landlord to allow her to bring four children and my grandmother into that house.

My grandmother raised us, while my mother worked every day. My grandmother got us off to school in the morning and was there when we came home at lunchtime and in the evening. She was a great inspiration to us, a born-again Christian, the pillar of the Westside Baptist Church. She was wonderful to us. But she was also very strict. When we did something wrong we would have to go out to the peach tree in the backyard and get a switch and bring it to her, and she would whip us with that switch. We would always get the smallest switch that we could find, and she would send us back until she was satisfied with the size. It never did any harm, but it certainly was a deterrent to us being bad.

We had a lot of chores to do around the house in those days, and I was never very athletic. While other guys were out shooting hoops, I was practicing the piano or reading. I was a bookworm. I never played basketball. I hate basketball.

There were four men teachers at Cole School who had a profound effect on my life. They were always neat and well dressed. They were also very articulate. All the people in my neighborhood were blue-collar folks. And I think more than anything else, when I was a kid, I wanted to dress in a suit and tie. Edgar Burnett, John Hartfield, Leonard Evans, and Rufus Young—all of them were dashing young men. I wanted to grow up to be like them.

In school I was interested in music, the dramatic club, and the political stuff. I was president of my sophomore, junior, and senior class at Sumner High. And I was president of my classes in college. In high school I was a student accompanist and student director for the Sumner High School a cappella choir, under the direction of Kenneth Billups, who was a giant in his own right. In college I put together my own choir. And at church I played the organ every Sunday and had weekly choir rehearsals from the time I was sixteen.

In the sixties, I was involved with CORE and civil rights organizations that were picketing places. I remember picketing White Castle and wondering why would I want to eat those things and work there anyway. I remember picketing the Howard Johnson's on Kingshighway, because they didn't serve blacks. Then when I moved to Chicago in 1968, I started going to Jesse Jackson's Saturday morning programs, Operation Breadbasket. We met at a church, then we moved into a theater in Chicago. It was a great inspiration, listening to Jesse preach. I not only listened to the message, I listened to Jesse's style of speaking, which was reminiscent of the Baptist preachers I had heard as a child. I was interested in the poetry that he used, all the rhyming words, phrases like: "Those who are blessed must take care of the rest." You can remember that the rest of your life. And I remember being impressed by his cadence and rhythm, his use of volume, from a whisper to outright screaming. I borrow from Jesse's style, especially when I do graduation speeches. I've delivered graduation speeches at most of the high schools and colleges in this area.

I tell young people they have to work hard for the things they want in life. The elevator to success is broken, so you have to take the stairs. I believe in an assertive, aggressive approach to getting what you want in life. I also tell young people to be true to themselves. They must not try to achieve things that they are not capable of achieving. Figure out what you are good at doing, and then pursue that. And then, as my grandmother always taught me, "If you ever need a helping hand, there is a perfectly good one at the end of your arm." That's my little lesson for the day.

Margaret Bush Wilson

Attorney; Chairman of the Board, National NAACP

Dorothy Freeman is responsible for my becoming a lawyer. She had just finished her freshman year at Lincoln University Law School, and she was recruiting for the law school. She came to my house one day, and we had a good visit, and then she said this fateful comment, "Why don't you go to law school? Everybody can use a little law." Well, she was very persistent. She even made an appointment for me to talk to the dean. So I walked over to Poro College where the law school was, and I walked in and introduced myself to Dean William E. Taylor. He was a former professor of law at Howard University, and he came here to be the dean when the school opened. You probably know the story about Lincoln Law School being opened so that Lloyd Gaines would not have to be admitted to the University of Missouri Law School. So it was a controversial law school. But at any rate, after the amenities, I said to the dean, "I'll consider going to your law school, if you will provide me with a scholarship to pay for my tuition and fees, and a part-time job to pay for my books and spending money." He hardly paused, and he said, "Young lady, if you're bold enough to ask me for it, I'm bold enough to give it to you."

So I started law school, and I loved it! It was different from anything I had ever experienced in a classroom. Law schools don't have textbooks, they have casebooks. A casebook is nothing but cases, law cases that have actually happened. And they're organized by subject matter. If you're studying constitutional law, they'll have cases that have to do with due process or cases that have to do with equal protection. The reality of it intrigued me.

In my third year of law school we were deep into World War II, and some of my classmates were drafted before they finished, including my future husband. Well, it got to be such a sweeping draft that the bar examiners decided to let seniors take the bar before they left. There were three or four fellows being drafted from my class who took the bar early, and I decided to take it with them. I took the bar and I passed, so I was a lawyer before I finished law school.

About 1954 I walked into the local NAACP office where Ernest Calloway was president, and I said to him, "My name is Margaret Wilson and I'm here to volunteer. What would you like me to do?" And I'll always remember his answer:

"We need jobs." Here we are forty years later and we still need jobs. So I went home and thought about it, and I suggested we organize a job opportunities council, do an analysis of what jobs are available, and then meet with the people who have the jobs. So I got this going, and Ted McNeal was the chairman. We had a three-person team—Ted McNeal, Ernest Calloway, and myself—that visited these companies. And it was fascinating, some of the responses. Some of them were not nice. Others said, "Nobody asked us." And I would say, "Well, now we've asked." And in due course they opened up the jobs. A&P did this. Woolworth's was hard, as I remember.

When I became state president of the NAACP, we had at least fifteen branches around the state. They didn't have much money, and they didn't have many members, and it was kind of pitiful. So I proposed that each branch should have a Freedom Fund dinner and the state office would do all the work: get the speaker, get out the invitations, get the meeting place. We had our first Freedom Fund dinner at the Holiday Inn in Sikeston, Missouri. Have you heard of Sikeston? That's where the last lynching in Missouri took place, right in Sikeston. I never will forget it. Roy Wilkins was the speaker. I drove down and arranged everything. Fortunately, the manager of the Sikeston Holiday Inn was new; he had come from someplace like Ohio, and he knew nothing about the foolishness down here. He was very gracious. We had a packed house, standing room only, a salt-and-pepper audience, black and white. Roy was great! The event was perfect. And I never thought anything about it. But I understand the place was crawling with FBI and plainclothes police, because they didn't know what the Klan was going to do. This was 1957 or 1958, and I was completely oblivious. But I learned after it was all over that they had people guarding Mr. Wilkins. The security must have been wild. But the program was outstanding. It raised a bundle of money and triggered Freedom Fund dinners in all of the branches. And we got on with the business of civil rights.

From the beginning I made a decision to give my time and talent to you know what: the NAACP. I did that very deliberately. I had certain strengths, certain qualities, and I wanted to give them to the organization that belongs to my people. We need the NAACP more than ever. It should be leading this nation.

Ira M. Young

Attorney

I was born in St. Louis in 1929. I was raised right here, in the central part of the city. I spent many years on Enright Avenue, the block between Vandeventer and Sarah. And then I spent a number of years on Page, the 4200 block of Page. I knew a great number of families in the Ville. There seemed to be a feeling of caring among the people there. Families looked out for other families and for the young people who were growing up there. It was a close-knit community, and black businesses were located there.

I started off at Cole School, and I went there until we moved from Enright onto Page. Then I went to Riddick School on Whittier and Evans Avenues. Riddick was an old school, a white school that was in an area that was changing, on the fringe of the Ville area. When I first started going there in 1939, it had just changed from a white school to a black school. Integration was a long way off. St. Louis schools were strictly segregated. As the whites moved out, and the area became predominantly black, they turned that school over to blacks. It was kindergarten through eighth grade. And that's where I was assigned when we moved onto Page Avenue.

I entered Sumner High School in 1943. Sumner was one of the two high schools for blacks in the city at that time. If you lived west of Grand you went to Sumner, and if you lived east of Grand you went to Vashon. Of course, there was rivalry between Sumner and Vashon, in athletics and in other ways. I was on the football team. I played tackle. Pop Beckett was in his final years as a coach at Sumner when I started, and he was a legend. But Lamar Smith took over. In 1946 our team was one of the best teams in the history of Sumner High School. We were undefeated that year, and only one team scored anything against us. Vincent Reed was the captain of our team, and now he is a vice president with the *Washington Post*. As I look back at the positive influence that those teachers at Sumner had on us, and at the education we received, I really appreciate who they were and what they gave us.

In 1947 I went to Oberlin College in Ohio, and I finished in 1951. When I finished college I was drafted, and I spent a couple of years in the army. When I came out of the army I entered Washington University Law School. At that time only three other blacks had gone to Washington University. My father was instrumental in getting me enrolled at Washington University. He knew I was coming back from the service, and he inquired at the registrar's office whether they would enroll me. They said they would. So I got out of the army on Monday, and I was going to class on Friday. I had planned to kick

back and relax for six months, but I appreciate what my father did for me. My father was a story in himself. He graduated from Yale University Law School in 1918.

Of course, law school was different from anything that I had experienced, educationally. It was a whole new process of learning and of discipline. It was rough. There were no other blacks in the school to communicate with, to exchange thoughts with. So in terms of having a study group with other students or picking their brains, I was pretty much on my own.

During high school and college I had little jobs after school and over the summer vacation. Jobs weren't very plentiful for blacks then. Service jobs and maintenance work were about the only avenues open to us. During my first year of law school I worked as a streetcar operator. The Public Service Company, the transportation company here in St. Louis, was just beginning to hire blacks as operators. That was in the early fifties. Prior to that the operators were all white. I was a streetcar operator when they took the Broadway streetcar out. I made one of the last runs on the Broadway streetcar before they converted over to buses. I worked the Grand, and the Jefferson, and the Broadway streetcars.

A job I had during the summer after I finished high school stands out in my memory. I was working as a porter at the Mercantile Bank, downtown. One of the veterans' organizations had a convention here, and they had a big parade downtown during the day. Some of the other guys and I went outside the bank and stood there watching the parade. A group of southern veterans came by and saw us standing there and made disparaging remarks about us. We were only seconds away from starting what could have become a riot. We were incensed that those guys would come from out of town and make those gratuitous remarks to us. We started to follow the guy down the street, responding in kind, until some of his buddies took the drunken veteran in tow and quieted him down. I still think about that and the possible consequences that could have occurred.

That was back in 1948. Twenty years later I returned to that bank, where I used to mop floors, with a client for whom I had drafted a trust agreement. The bank was to be the trustee, and so the bank officers of the trust department invited my client and myself to have lunch with them in the executive dining room. That was quite an experience. It let me know that I can never know what to expect. Everything is within reach. If you prepare yourself, the opportunities will come.

Anita L. Bond

Guidance Counselor, St. Louis Public Schools; President, St. Louis Board of Education;
Member, Citizens Advisory Committee on School Desegregation

When I graduated from high school, my elementary school principal, Mr. Clarence Hunter, and a friend of his, Mr. Creamus Evans, came to speak with me and my parents about entering as the first black undergraduate student at St. Louis University. They offered to take care of the tuition and everything. You see, history hasn't told the fact that black Catholics in St. Louis were advocating the admissions of black Catholics to St. Louis University. They were saying, "You have students from all over the world, but none from the black community." But the Jesuits warned them that they couldn't find a black student who could compete academically.

I developed a strong relationship with St. Malachy's Church. Now, St. Malachy's has been torn down. I remember Mr. Charles Anderson—every Sunday he would stand and pass out pamphlets to the people going into the church. Many black Catholics were involved in the struggle to open the university, and there were several Jesuits helping in the fight for admission. Father Heithaus gave the sermon which began the real opening of the university.

But people should know that our conditions were very much like they would have been at a southern white university. I mean, Father Holloran said that black students would be admitted for academics only. They could not participate in any of the social affairs. We did not take gym because they didn't know how the whites would react. When I was a freshman I could not take gym, and then when I was a senior they told me I needed gym in order to get my teaching certificate. But I did have friends at the university. Dr. Everhart, the head of the health department, was one who helped with the burden as I went along.

We couldn't swim in the swimming pool. So a girlfriend and I went to the gym for free swim, and the first person to jump out of the pool was a Filipino whose name was Flora Belanic. I'll never forget it, never. Also, at that time, the university did not have a cafeteria. Everybody ate at a Filipino restaurant across the street from the university on Grand Avenue. All the other students could go there and eat, but we were not allowed. One day, one of my friends said, "Anita do you want me to bring you a hamburger?" I said, "Absolutely not." That was more insulting to me, even though she was a caring person. I brought my lunch from home, because I didn't have time to fight everything.

I was surrounded by strong people. My family knew that I was on a mission, and they were too. Sometimes I would study until three and four o'clock in the morning. They let me sleep, and they reinforced whatever feelings I had. And then Father Markoe, who was the parish priest at St. Malachy's, stayed in touch with me. He was moved to Creighton University in Omaha, to teach mathematics, but his heart was with the African Americans in this community. The Jesuits sent Father Markoe to Omaha because he bucked the leadership. But Father Markoe wrote me single-spaced letters, two- and three-page letters, to encourage me to keep on, and to know that God was with me. I didn't save those letters, because I didn't have any idea that we were part of history.

I've been on about twenty different boards here in St. Louis. Ernest Calloway taught us to be on these boards. He was the research man for the Teamsters, and there were about twelve of us who were his disciples. We went to his house on Sunday afternoon, and he taught us how to identify the power structure, who's in charge, and what boards are important. So I was put on the City Plan Commission, and when we would have discussions, they would just ignore me altogether. I would make a suggestion and they'd listen to it, and then they would go right around it. Then someone who was white would repeat the same suggestion…but anyway. I was on the Zoo Commission with Cervantes when they were considering making people pay to go to the zoo. We couldn't do that to a family with four or five children.

The reason that I'm telling you these things is that you must never let yourself be intimidated or ignored in matters that come before you. You must confront them and fight them, as far as you can, so that in your soul and in your mind you know that you did the best you could. If you feel that things should be changed, go as a committee of one, and let yourself be heard. We are voices crying in the wilderness. We must do the best that we can and not give up.

Leslie F. Bond

Family Practitioner and Surgeon, People's Health Center

I was born in Louisville, Kentucky, and when I was about ten we moved to Galesburg, Illinois, which is in central Illinois, near Peoria. I graduated from Galesburg High School. My father was a physician. My mother was a schoolteacher. My father was from Kentucky, and my mother was from Oberlin, Ohio. My father went to Meharry Medical College and came to Homer G. Phillips Hospital as an intern. I'm proud of my parents, and I'm proud of the fact that I was able to follow in my father's footsteps.

My childhood was happy. We were not rich, by any means. In those days, my father got twenty-five cents a house call. He was also paid with eggs or bacon, pies or cakes, in place of money. He taught me to look at people with compassion. When I went into practice he told me there are two things I must do. Number one: If a lady is in labor, I must be willing to get up in the middle of the night and deliver her out of her pain. And number two: When it comes to charging a fee, have a heart.

I finished Galesburg High School at age sixteen and went to the University of Illinois at Champagne-Urbana. It was a formative stage of my life. My favorite course was cellular physiology. It is the basis of the treatment of many diseases. It just fascinated me. We studied the biochemical changes going on inside the cells, the intake of different ions and the output, what enhanced the intake and what did not. We wrote formulas and put arrows on top of the "catalysts." We have subsequently learned what those catalysts are and whether they cause or prevent the uptake of things. Little did we know that the catalysts were the important parts of the equations. Just as in life, catalysts are the things or the people that make things happen.

I stayed at the Kappa House. Fraternities and sororities were the only social outlet for blacks on the campus. If it had not been for those organizations we would not have had any social life. We mixed with white students at the Student Union, but no blacks lived in the dormitories on campus, and we could not be served anyplace off campus. We could go to the theater, but we had to sit in the balcony. And I remember, at home in Galesburg, I couldn't sit at a lunch counter. I had to get my lunch in a sack, while my white friends who sold newspapers with me ate right there. That made a deep impression on me, but it was business as usual in the days of Jim Crow. In 1945 we had sit-ins at the Steak & Shake in Champagne-Urbana. We sat there every Sunday for about four hours. It was the first sit-in that I knew of. To me it was a case of speaking out against injustice.

My grandfather was a lawyer from the hills of Kentucky. His brother founded the first college for blacks in the state of Kentucky. I remember my father going to city council meetings in Galesburg and sitting in the back of the room, and every so often he would say, "I object to you spending any money on anything until you pave the streets of West Galesburg where blacks live." He spoke up when he was the only black there. I am not an innovator, but I have a long heritage of people who have made contributions to civil rights. I am proud of that heritage, and I try to make a difference. I want to raise the awareness of rich young people who will be the movers and shakers of society, so we have established the Eric Bond Scholarship Fund at Country Day School. We also bring a lecturer to Country Day every year, someone like Julian Bond or Bill Clay. It is raising awareness.

I went to Meharry Medical College, and I came to St. Louis to be an intern at Homer Phillips in 1952. Homer G. Phillips Hospital was the epitome of black graduate training in the world, for all surgery; internal medicine; ear, nose, and throat; ob-gyn; and ophthalmology. Dr. William Sinkler, the medical director, was a perfectionist. He told us, "These patients may be poor, but you will treat them with dignity." We were affiliated with Washington University, and we did a lot of research. We had a large number of patients, and with those numbers, Dr. Sinkler expected us to write papers. That gave us a good feeling about ourselves. When I finished my training, white hospitals were just beginning to admit black doctors to their staffs, and I was proud to see that our general surgeons were as good as those from Washington U.

Medicine is still a good profession; however, there are more professions open now. Blacks need to know that they have an opportunity, because if they have an opportunity they can perform. There has been progress in race relations, but there is a lot to be done.

I'm proud to say that if I had to do it all over again, I would have the same mother and father, the same brothers and sister. I would marry the same girl, and I would have the same children. I do a hard day's work, and I sleep at night. I am a liberal, compassionate man. I look at my fellow people with compassion and love, and I am proud of the fact that I have tried to make a difference.

Dorothy Thomas Matlock

English Teacher, Sumner High School

I was born in St. Louis. My father died when I was three, so I was raised by my mother and grandmother and grandfather. I had a wonderful childhood. My mother was a nurse at Homer G. Phillips Hospital, and she worked at night. My grandmother and grandfather provided me with all the little things you remember as a child.

My grandfather could not read or write, but every Tuesday we walked from Jefferson and Market to Thirteenth and Olive Streets to the library, where I was exposed to books. The librarians found out that he could not read, and while I was getting books, they would read to him. It got to be kind of a soul journey for us. Every Tuesday, rain, shine, sleet, or snow, unless the library was closed, we were there.

Young people must learn to read. That is the most crucial thing. If you learn to read, you have an avenue to get into any other subject you're interested in. Reading does something else. You may not have money to travel all over the world, but you can go anywhere in a book. You'll spend many, many enjoyable hours. And it is something that you can do alone or something that you can share with someone.

I went to Lincoln Elementary School and Vashon High School, where I was valedictorian of my class. I went to Stowe Teachers College, and I've done additional work at St. Louis University and Webster University. I taught English at Sumner High School, where I was the head of the English department for twenty-two years. I served as a consultant for Project Stay, at Soldan High School. And when Kenneth Billups, the great music educator at Sumner, had a TV program called *God's Musical World,* I frequently appeared as a guest and read poetry or discussed literature.

Then, in the late sixties, after the Watts Riot, there was a national emphasis on integration, and African American studies became popular. The Los Angeles School System chose me as one of seven people throughout the United States to write teacher's guides for an Afro-American Literature Series. They liked the teacher's guide that I did for the textbook called *The Scene,* and they asked me to create a black humanities program. So I wrote the teacher's guide for the Scholastics Black Culture Program. It is a humanities program that includes black art, black music, black dance, black poetry, and black religion, and it has film strips and tapes to accompany the teacher's guide. You can find it in the St. Louis public high school libraries.

I became president of the Greater St. Louis Council of Teachers of English, and I had a difficult time getting inner-city people to come to meetings. I told Dr. Beckwith, a school principal and a former student of mine, about my problem. And he said, "Where will the meeting be?" On the day of the meeting, Dr. Beckwith showed up with his whole staff! That was, to me, one of the highlights of my career. The greatest compliment a teacher can receive is to be thought of and honored by the students you have taught.

I served as a consultant to the St. Louis Public Schools Division of State and Federal Programs, and I gave a series of lectures on the Harlem Renaissance for their staff-development unit. My first lesson was on Harlem Renaissance publications, including *The Brownie's Book* and the magazines *Fire* and *The Crisis. The Brownie's Book* was a magazine for children. It was only published for two years, and it was written by W. E. B. Du Bois and a lady named Jessie Fauset. I discussed major writers: James Weldon Johnson, Claude McKay, Countee Cullen, Jean Toomer. I really enjoyed discussing women writers. I spent an entire meeting on Georgia Douglas Johnson. During this period, if you know anything about the Harlem Renaissance, the men writers were the only ones that were really considered. The women were, as usual, in the background. But some of the best writers of this period were women: Jessie Fauset, Angelina Grimké, Helene Johnson, Gwendolyn Bennett, Nella Larsen, and Anne Spencer. I lectured on Langston Hughes. Most of the teachers were familiar with him. And then I did a book review of *Their Eyes Were Watching God,* by Zora Neale Hurston, who is my favorite writer. I'm a fanatic for the Harlem Renaissance.

Another source of our cultural heritage is the church. I belonged to St. Paul A.M.E. Church for over thirty years. I spent many hours there, and, believe it or not, there I got a sense of pride. I remember that at every church meeting, other than the regular service, we sang "Lift Every Voice and Sing." We learned about James Weldon Johnson and much of our black history from the church.

Young people must get an education, find out what they're good at, and do it well. When I came along, black women could be one of three things. They could be a teacher, a nurse, or a domestic worker. Today, every field is open. Women are principals, they're in politics, they're in every avenue of work. Life is what you make it. Do what you can. Be a good citizen. Be a good role model for those who follow you.

Joseph Palmer

Editor, *Proud Magazine*

I am going to give a journalist's perspective of my life—very short. I was born in St. Louis. I attended the public schools in St. Louis. I went into the United States Navy. I went to NYC in New York City, and I stayed in New York for much of my life. I came back to St. Louis to go into business. I was involved in several private ventures, and then *Proud Magazine* came along. I've been with *Proud* over twenty years.

You don't find the thing you love to do until you reach a certain age. Marketing and advertising are the most exciting things to me. Without advertising, journalism is nothing. You can't publish or broadcast anything unless you have financial support to pay for it. When you start dealing with business and advertising you meet lots of people, you get involved with people. I love business; I love people.

I worked on a business venture that went belly-up, and I was in a depressed mood, when Congressman Clay asked me to help Betty Lee put out a paper. Clay was just starting to run for Congress, and when you run for office, you put out little political papers, "Voice of the People," "The Right Way," things like that. Ever since that time I have been doing most of the congressman's PR work.

We started *Proud Magazine* back in the sixties. The whole idea behind *Proud* was to make people in the black community look at the positive things about themselves. We did stories on education, on the hospitals, on community organizations. When *Proud* first came out, large corporations thought it was fashionable to support a black publication. Remember, in the sixties there were riots. Corporations felt compelled to do something, because blacks were raising their heads. We were a threat. Putting an ad in our magazine was easy. Corporations wanted black employees, and *Proud* was a great vehicle for bringing blacks into the fold to work for them. Every major corporation in St. Louis put an ad in: Ralston Purina, Monsanto, McDonnell Douglas. Then we started writing stories that revealed things the corporations didn't want us to reveal. So they began asking us, "What is your next issue going to be about?" They looked on us as hostile. They began saying things like, "Our budget was cut. We can't buy an ad." In the past twenty years *Proud Magazine* has not been part of the advertising budget of any major corporation or advertising agency. That is a disgrace. They don't ask the *Post-Dispatch* or the *New York Times* what they are going to write about.

Now, if the black community would support the magazine, I wouldn't need corporate dollars. But reading material is the last thing on the economic agenda in the black community.

Our priorities are food and shelter. That's why most black publications have to be throwaways or giveaways. On a list of economic priorities in the black community, reading material is at the bottom of the list.

I know six Pulitzer Prize–winning writers personally. Ken Cooper is from St. Louis. The *Post-Dispatch* said he couldn't write, so he left and went to Boston, and within a year he won a Pulitzer Prize for a story in a Boston newspaper. Most of the talent leaves St. Louis, because St. Louis is a racist city. And because of that the whole town suffers.

I would love to be in a position to hire talented black writers from all over the country, find the funds to purchase every major black newspaper across the United States, put all that black talent into one hat, unleash that power, and produce a black publication that would really tell the black side of things. I think one of the things that has hurt this country is that the truth has never been told. It is always either flowered up or neglected. When we, as black people, start talking about our culture, I see some of our people withdraw and feel ashamed. That bothers me. It is because it has all been such a negative situation. I don't want to accept that. I will not accept that. I want to be a part of telling the true story.

I believe that we as a people slid backwards because of integration. Before integration we were united, we all had a common goal. Our neighbors felt a kinship. A person rarely went hungry because his neighbor looked out for him. We knew that it was our responsibility. Our schools were excellent. Black teachers weren't allowed to teach in white schools, so teachers with doctor's degrees and master's degrees taught at Sumner and Vashon. And they taught us to be the best. They taught us that we had to do better than 100 percent—we had to do 110 percent. Our common goal was to achieve excellence.

What we need is economic integration. Economics divides us. We are all scatterbrained. We are all over the place. We use excuses. We do not take the time to learn the system. Once you learn the rules of the game, you can be a star, or at least you can be a better participant, your potential is unlimited. But we fight each other. Society has broken down in the black community, because we don't hold our children accountable, we don't hold our neighbors accountable, we don't hold our police department accountable, we don't hold our grocery stores accountable. We don't hold anybody accountable for anything. I would rather for them to have kept the damn integration thing.

Jane Woods Miller

Publisher, *St. Louis Sentinel*

I was born in St. Louis. I am a third-generation St. Louisan. My mother graduated from Sumner High School in 1910, when there was only one high school for blacks. She went to the old Sumner at Fifteenth and Walnut. The new Sumner High School was built in the Ville in 1910. The auditorium was finished for her commencement. But she never actually attended school in the new building.

I started out at Waring School at Ewing and Laclede, and in 1937 my family moved west of Grand. After that I attended Cole Elementary School and Sumner High School. Then I attended Stowe Teachers College. It was not Harris-Stowe then, but Stowe Teachers College.

My life was different from today. I grew up in our own community, if you will. I grew up thinking that I did not need white folks for anything. City Hospital No. 2 was right across the street from us. I remember, my sister and I weren't allowed to go around the neighborhood, but my two brothers were. There used to be a whistle from some manufacturing company that blew at nine o'clock, and I can see my brothers now, running home to beat that whistle.

My mentor was Anna Lee Hill Scott, the director of the Wheatley Branch of the YWCA. She came to St. Louis when I was six or seven years old. I can still remember the first day she came to the Y. I was impressed with her. And throughout the years, she was my greatest mentor. I grew up in the Y.

I was interested in teaching, but I ended up working as a medical records librarian. Beginning in 1958, I worked at Jewish Hospital in the medical records department. I was supervisor of the transcription department until 1964, when my late husband, Howard Woods, received a presidential appointment and we moved to Washington. Lyndon Johnson appointed him associate director of the United States Information Agency. We went to a lot of White House dinners and parties. It was quite an experience.

Before leaving St. Louis, my husband was the editor of the *Argus.* That was during the sixties, so, of course, he was heavily involved in the civil rights movement. He worked with people like Norman Seay, and he met Dr. Martin Luther King several times. I don't think he ever actually marched, but he wrote heavily about civil rights in the paper.

My late husband started the *Sentinel* in 1968, at the end of the civil rights movement. And when he passed away in 1976, I became the publisher. My son-in-law is the editor. He is there all the time. Since I retired from the Washington University School of Medicine Library, four years ago, I have tried to spend part of every day at the *Sentinel.*

Young people don't realize the impact that individuals had in the past. For instance, my mother was one of the first black committeewomen in St. Louis. She was Elizabeth Slaughter Gamble, and she was committeewoman of the Sixth Ward. At that time we lived at 3001 Lawton, in the Sixth Ward. Vashon High School, where Harris-Stowe is presently, was scheduled to have a grade school added, and my mother fought with the Board of Education and finally ended up suing them to keep Vashon a high school. Attorney Robert Witherspoon was the lawyer.

I don't know if integration has changed things for the better. I think the schools used to be better. We received an excellent education, and there was more discipline. Back in my day, if you got in trouble at school, you just prayed that it didn't get home, because you would be in bigger trouble at home.

I think young people have lost the moral standards we used to have. I don't have a solution, but I think basically it starts at home. And I think that until that is recovered, the young people are just going to dwindle down.

William A. Pearson

Associate Superintendent, Curriculum and Programs,
St. Louis Public Schools

I was born in Starkville, Mississippi, in 1932. I was one of four boys. When I was three or four years old, an aunt brought me to St. Louis to visit my great-aunt, and I was so fascinated with electric lights, bathtubs, and things that people in the urban areas took for granted that my great-aunt asked my father if I could stay with her. He consented, so I stayed in St. Louis until 1939. That was the year my father died, and I went back to Mississippi for his funeral. I stayed in Starkville for a while. Then my great-aunt visited us and asked if I wanted to come back to St. Louis. Well, clearly my answer was yes. As a widow, my mother felt the economic pinch of trying to raise four boys, and she saw this as an opportunity for me, so she consented.

I went to Banneker School and then to Vashon High School. Following Vashon I entered Stowe Teachers College. And then I started teaching for the St. Louis Public School District. The schools were segregated, and because all of the teaching positions in black schools were filled, I had to enter the system as a substitute. I substituted for about eight months, until March of 1953, when I was inducted into the army. I spent two years in the army, and when I returned from the army, I received a teaching appointment, because now there were vacancies.

After the army I had planned to go to Yale Medical School, but my great-uncle, who had reared me, had a stroke, and I decided to stay until he got better. I was a teacher and then an administrator in an elementary school, and I entered the graduate program in education at St. Louis University. I completed my master's degree and was working on a Ph.D. when William Pollack, my former principal, asked me to help him set up teacher-training institutes in Liberia. It was important for a developing nation to have a school system and teacher-training institutes to supply teachers. We spent two years in Liberia, working with Tuskegee Institute and the U.S. State Department, and we set up three teacher-training institutes.

When I came back I went to work for the St. Louis School District again. William Kottmeyer, the superintendent of the district, wanted to revitalize Harris-Stowe Teachers College because enrollment in St. Louis schools was at its peak and there was a shortage of teachers. Kottmeyer made Dr. Richard Stumpe president of Harris-Stowe and me the academic dean. Several years passed, and Clyde Miller became superintendent. Clyde was full of energy and ideas, and he asked me to work with him in the central office. I was reluctant to leave Harris-Stowe, but he persuaded me. He had me study the budget. Everything revolves around the budget, whether you can put in new programs, hire more teachers, or build new schools.

Then we got the petition from the Liddell plaintiffs, filing suit against the board for segregating schools. Miller asked me to be the point person for the district as we went into the case, and he asked if I saw any chinks in our armor. I suggested that we develop a balanced-staff policy to insure that our faculties were integrated. "Write one," he said. I contacted friends in other districts and got copies of their balanced-staff policies, and wrote one for the St. Louis School District. It was the basic plan for integrating black and white teachers throughout the district and desegregating our schools. However the Liddell plaintiffs said the movement was too slow. And it was. They went to court in 1977, and we came out of there with a consent decree, agreeing to do certain things to move integration forward. Three years passed, and they still were not satisfied, so the case went to the federal court. Judge Meredith ruled that the school district had not engaged in segregation, so the plaintiffs appealed, and the appeals court reversed Meredith's decision. This was March of 1980, and in May we had to come back with a plan to desegregate the schools. I had major responsibility for building the plan. The big issue was where to find money to fund desegregation. The federal government had a program that allowed school districts that qualified under court-ordered desegregation to get funds for magnet schools. So I wrote a proposal for an eight-million-dollar grant to implement magnet schools as the centerpiece of our desegregation program. This put me in contact with Congressman Clay and Senator Eagleton, who were very helpful in getting us our grant.

I'm very keen on the profession of education. Education opens doors, it serves as a ladder of social mobility, it allows you to feel that you can engage in conversation with anybody, on any subject. Education links the present with the past and gives you a vision of the future and your role in it. Education enables you to be all that you can be. It enables you to help other people. Young people have got to prepare themselves to be competitive, and to win. They have to learn to reach for the stars. I once asked Leontyne Price how she got to be a star at the Metropolitan Opera, and she said, "Mr. Pearson, we have to be a little bit better." I have never forgotten that quote. It is a lesson that our young people have to learn. You have to be a little bit better.

Lou "Fatha" Thimes

Disc Jockey, KATZ Radio; Court Representative, City of St. Louis

I grew up here in St. Louis. I attended the public schools in St. Louis, and I went to Lincoln University in Jefferson City. I went to Washington Technical High School at Nineteenth and Franklin, where I played basketball. That's how I got to Lincoln, by playing basketball. That is the only way I got there. My family was poor with no money. I was born at Sixteenth and Division, and when my family got money we moved to Twenty-first Street.

I got involved in radio in the service on Okinawa. When I came back to the States, I began broadcasting at the veterans' hospitals, Cochran down on Grand and Jefferson Barracks. KATZ hired me in 1958, and I went to KXLW in 1960. I was a broadcaster there from 1960 until 1966. I started in radio in 1958, so that's about forty-two years. I guess to stay in radio and hold a fair amount of popularity for that length of time is really unique. I haven't changed my musical format much since I've been on the air.

I have a show called *Motown Thursday*. Motown was such a diverse company. It had so many great artists all at one time: Chubby Checker, Sam Cooke, the Temptations, the Four Tops, Gladys Knight and the Pips, Al Green. *Motown Thursday* is a smash with the listening audience. They love it. On the weekends I deal with blues and oldies.

The blues is something that will never die. It is a type of music that even younger people appreciate. Bobby Bland, B. B. King, Jimmy Reed, Johnny Taylor, Howlin' Wolf. It is a part of black culture. The blues is reality. You relate to the lyrics of the songs because they are everyday life. It happens to everybody. And when one of the major artists passes, like Big Joe Turner, I like to tell the background of that particular artist. Years ago when an album was released they would have liner notes on the album that gave the history of the artist. But today they don't do that, not with the blues. They don't give the history. So I like to do that out of respect for the artist.

KATZ started in 1955. I was far from being the first black disc jockey. I started working when Dave Dixon was on the air. Spider Burks was before that. But the Rockin' Mr. G., George Logan, was really my mentor. He was on KXLW, and he was talented. He did gospels on Sundays and rock 'n' roll Monday through Saturday. When he played gospel and read those poems, I tell you, the whole town stood still.

In the beginning I worked with Jack Murdock as a producer. In radio we called producers our engineers. Some days you'd have a good engineer and some days you'd have a bad engineer. But, would you believe, all of that is gone now? In black radio, there are not any engineers to produce our shows. You produce your own show. You handle the board, the records, and answer the phone. Well, I try to answer the phone. I have had people say, "I've been calling you ever since…," but I wasn't able to answer the phone. I have to do a lot of things, and I don't think folk know that. If they could see what a guy has to do to produce his show, it's not easy. You've got to grab spots, and jingles, and drop-ins. You need to be an octopus sometimes. When you are doing twelve or fifteen spots an hour, that's a lot of spots. You don't have a hell of a lot of time for music.

I was one of the first people from this city to be elected to the board of the National Association of Television and Radio Announcers. NATRA is an organization that tries to keep announcers on the air. Lots of stations were starting to do funny things to announcers. Personality is the thing that has built black radio, and some personalities were getting so big that station owners were trying to cut them back or release them. So NATRA would talk with the general managers or station owners and try to keep the personalities on the air. Personality is the salvation of black radio. To hear someone just do straight-up radio is boring. Advertisers don't care what happens as long as they can sell their product, and personalities sell products. Advertisers prefer personality-type radio, but they can't always get it, because it is slowly being phased out. To the national networks I would like to say: "Hire more black announcers." That's my complete thought.

I've worked with some of the greatest stars in show business: Dinah Washington, Cootie Williams, Erskine Hawkins, Nat King Cole. But their music is seldom played anymore. I never have anyone ask me, "When are you going to play some Cootie Williams?" Those names are from the days when you could go to sleep at night and leave your windows open. If you go to sleep now and leave the windows open, you are going to have company.

In broadcasting you've got to be able to contend with all types of personalities, your boss, the program director.… You've got to be able to communicate with those people. And you must become known outside the station, become involved in the community. Go to your sponsors and say, "Hi, I am so and so, and I want to thank you for advertising on my show." That sense of community involvement encourages sponsors. Become involved in the community and understand communication. Broadcasting is a beautiful field. I've loved every moment of it.

Billye Haley Crumpton

Director, Scott Joplin House State Historic Site

I was born in Little Rock, Arkansas, and I grew up in a small town in southeast Arkansas, called Dumas. My father, my mother, and my grandfather were all educators. My father traveled around, representing the Rosenwald Fund, to the black communities that were out in the wilderness back then. My father would open up Rosenwald Schools in the small farm communities where there were no schools. By the way, there was no electricity back then. This was back in the 1930s, the early 1930s, say around 1935. I was about four or five years old, and I would travel with my father from school to school. We had to move every two years. At each new school my father would introduce the children to other cultures, to people in other lands, and also to different cities in the United States. He showed the children how other people lived. He had a projector which ran on batteries, because there was no electricity. He would show films on the wall, and it motivated the children to want to do more with their lives than just farm. Some of the children did become farmers, but they went to agricultural schools and they became better farmers. Others went on to other careers. He showed the films and brought artifacts into the schools to broaden their horizons, make them dream of better things. He also set up sports programs. He created a miniature Olympics to bring children from different communities together. I remember basketball and high jumps and track.

We moved to St. Louis in 1941, at the beginning of World War II. By that time my father had nine children, and he could not support nine children on the salary that he was earning in Arkansas. So when we moved to St. Louis, my parents opened up a dry-cleaning and tailor shop, and my father worked for the railroad. That's how he was able to support nine children.

I went to Stowe Teachers College where my favorite classes were history, art, and theater. Dr. Dreer, Naomi Guthrie, and Dr. Smart were my mentors. I guess you can tell that I love history and art and theater by the things I'm doing now.

After my children were up some size, I substituted in the St. Louis Public Schools for about fifteen years. And then I worked for TWA. Then I became the director of the St. Louis Cultural and Recreational Center, which was upstairs in the Sheldon Memorial Building. I had workshops that involved history and creative arts. In the early seventies I had an early childhood development center in Laclede Town. It was such a large facility that I was able to set up exhibits and run a day-care center. Students from Harris-Stowe Teachers College worked with me.

I incorporated all of my interests and experience when I started working for the state of Missouri as an interpreter of historic sites. I was a tour assistant for the state at the First Capitol in St. Charles, Missouri. I was teaching Missouri history to tourists. I gave tours of the First Capital of Missouri in St. Charles, and I told tourists about what happened in the early 1800s, how Missouri became a state, and other bits of Missouri history.

When I was young I thought it was fascinating when my father used artifacts and films to teach about other cultures. That became my greatest dream from when I was five years old. When I grew up I wanted to share history, using different media, rather than just lecturing about it.

I think history is more interesting when you have what I call show-and-tell. I belonged to a little theater group, and when we used props and showed how different people lived, I thought of that as show-and-tell. I felt as if I actually became those people.

As you can tell, I'm still interested in history. I think if you have a dream, you should live it.

William G. Gillespie

Pastor, Cote Brilliante Presbyterian Church

I came to St. Louis in 1956. The purpose of my coming was to reorganize the Cote Brilliante Presbyterian Church, the church that I am now part of. This neighborhood was in change. There had been a lawsuit in the city of St. Louis against restrictive covenants, involving a house that's a block and a half away from this church. The court said that there could be no restrictive covenants as far as housing was concerned. As a result of this, a lot of whites left the community as blacks began to come in. And this church refused to welcome blacks into its membership. The Presbyterian denomination asked me to come here as the pastor to try to integrate the church. Around 255 white members left the church, because they refused to become part of this movement. After canvassing the community, we opened the church in September of 1956. Eighty-six persons, black and white, came to the first service. It was out of that context that our church began to grow and relate to the community.

In the meantime, I found that school integration was the order of the day. There was de facto segregation in the St. Louis community. We marched on the school board to do away with segregation in the public schools. I was also one of the ministers who carried signs in an effort to see people hired at Jefferson Bank. There were a number of clergy who marched daily at that bank. We would leave from the Jamieson C.M.E. Church, on Washington Boulevard, and march down to the Jefferson Bank, where we demonstrated.

I guess the most memorable thing that I participated in was the march on Selma, Alabama, with Dr. Martin Luther King. A delegation of us left St. Louis and went to Montgomery, Alabama, on the final day of that march. We joined them and marched to the state capitol, where Dr. King addressed us. I recall, vividly, the strange feeling that I had as I walked through those streets, through Selma. Little children came to the windows in their school, because they were not permitted to participate in that march. They waved at us along with their teachers. There were hotel persons who couldn't participate either because, after we left, they had to earn a livelihood there.

But they waved, giving their support. And there were people on the street who cheered us as we moved along the way. State troopers had been federalized as the national guard. There was a strange atmosphere that day. I could feel the tension. George Wallace was governor of the state at that time. I think that march helped to spearhead the civil rights bill that finally passed in the United States Congress. As minor as my roll was, I feel I had an opportunity to become a part of history.

I also had the opportunity to meet Dr. King here, in St. Louis, when he spoke at the Washington Tabernacle Baptist Church. I don't know of any communicator that I ever heard or read who could do it better than Dr. King. It seemed that God put him here, at that particular time, to do what he had to do. Dr. King was a great influence in my life.

I served on the board of trustees of the Interdenominational Theological Center in Atlanta for ten years. It is a consortium of six black seminaries that trains ministers for the Presbyterian, the Methodist, the Baptist, and the Church of God denominations. Dr. Martin Luther King Sr. served on that board with me. I mention him because he helped me to understand his son. He was deeply concerned about civil rights. He was very outspoken, and he believed that young people had to take leadership. Young people played an important role in the civil rights movement.

I read quite a bit, and one thing that bothers me is the life of Dr. George Washington Carver. He was one of the greatest scientists, but he never trained anyone to succeed him. It's tragic if we do not pass on to the younger generation what we have been able to accomplish, in order that they might build from that. Those of us who are older have got to find somebody that we can pass our experience on to.

I believe that we can be very successful people. But the role models that we have today are guys who are driving big Cadillacs and making big bucks. And it's killing us as a race. Our future generations are going to be decimated unless we get out of this vicious circle in which all of our young people want those big bucks and are totally unconcerned about mankind.

Samuel W. Hylton Jr.

Pastor, Centennial Christian Church

I grew up in Roanoke, Virginia, in the foothills of south-western Virginia. My father was a minister, and my mother was a homemaker. They had three children. I was the oldest, my sister was the second child, and my brother was the baby, as we called him. I attended school in Roanoke and graduated from Addison High School.

I went to Morehouse College in Atlanta, Georgia, where I received a degree in history and political science, with a minor in sociology. From Morehouse I went to Boston University School of Law. My brother and I entered law school together. At the end of my first year in law school I changed my mind about my life's vocation.

I received a call from God to preach the Gospel, and I went from Boston to Christian Theological Seminary in Indianapolis, Indiana, to further my education. After three years there I received a Master of Divinity in 1954. Then I became the pastor of the Cleveland Avenue Christian Church in Winston-Salem, North Carolina. I was pastor of that church for seven years, and during those years I married. My wife was a teacher of music in one of the high schools in Winston-Salem when we met. We married in 1956, and we stayed there until October of 1961. We left North Carolina to come to St. Louis, when I accepted the position of pastor of Centennial Christian Church. I recently retired after serving for thirty-five and a half years.

I had excellent teachers all through my education. Those teachers motivated me and instilled in me a desire for learning. One teacher who stands out in my memory is Sadie Lawson. She taught English, and she was difficult to please, but she knew her subject. She took a genuine interest in her students and wanted us to do well. Isn't it strange that you remember the hardest teacher? And she was probably the best.

Dr. Melvin Kennedy was my most outstanding professor in college. He was the chairman of the history department at Morehouse. He was an excellent teacher. He made history come alive. As a result, I majored in history and political science. And my sociology professor instilled in me a desire to know more about society and to do what I could to help people. But I didn't make up my mind to enter the ministry until I had finished a year in law school.

I knew Martin Luther King Jr. at Morehouse College. He was a year ahead of me. I lived on campus, and he lived at home with his mother and father, who was the minister of Ebenezer Baptist Church. Martin was an excellent student, a

warm, friendly individual. We got along fine. In later years, as we traveled, we met in different places. He came to St. Louis several times, and I saw him on those occasions. I also remember meeting him in Dallas, Texas, when he was preaching at one of our conventions. We were always glad to see each other.

When I came to St. Louis in 1961, I was involved in the Jefferson Bank demonstrations. The demonstrators met at our church. In those days CORE and other aggressive civil rights organizations were not popular. They had a difficult time finding a place to meet, so we had them meet at our church.

The civil rights leader who impressed me the most was Walter White, executive director of the NAACP. He was a scholar, a clear thinker. He was able to explain to people why the civil rights movement was important. Walter White was an impressive man and a good speaker. He was an outstanding individual.

When I was in high school and college we were exposed to outstanding educators, ministers, and civil rights leaders: people like Benjamin Mays, president of Morehouse College; Mordecai Johnson, president of Howard University; Howard Thurman, dean of the chapel at the University of Chicago and at Howard University; and men like Charles Wesley, an outstanding educator, and Vernon Johns, pastor of the Dexter Avenue Baptist Church in Montgomery, Alabama. They were great orators. Mary McLeod Bethune was another person who traveled the lecture circuit. They went to every city in the country, paying special attention to African American problems and giving special attention to young people. It was impossible to listen to people like Howard Thurman and Mary McLeod Bethune and Benjamin Mays without feeling something in your mind and in your heart. It stirred us to do something for our race and about the condition of American society. It was a very inspirational time. We grew up during the time of segregation and severe discrimination, yet these people put a torch to the lamp of learning within us. And I'm still living on some of that inspiration today.

We've come to a place in American society where, because of past evils, African Americans are economically sick, not academically sick, not morally sick, but economically sick. African Americans subsidized the building of this nation with our blood and our sweat. The nation owes us something. The nation needs to get on with some type of program that will remedy the situation. That's why I believe in affirmative action. It's necessary. It's a matter of justice, not a matter of charity.

Frankie Muse Freeman

Attorney; Member, U.S. Commission on Civil Rights

I was born in Danville, Virginia, the last capital of the Confederacy. My parents believed that all their children had to have an education, and they provided for all six of us to go to college.

I came to St. Louis because my husband, Shelby Freeman, was a St. Louisan. We met in New York. He was a graduate of Lincoln University in Missouri, and he was attending Columbia University graduate school. I was living with my aunt. We were married in New York. Then he got a job with the Department of Defense, and we moved to Washington, D.C., in 1941. While we were living in Washington, I went to Howard University Law School. I met Thurgood Marshall when I was in law school. The lawyers from the NAACP would come down to Washington to argue cases before the Supreme Court. Some of us were specializing in constitutional law. I always wanted to be a civil rights lawyer.

We moved to St. Louis in 1948, and I passed the Missouri Bar in December 1948. My first civil rights case was in 1949. When we came to St. Louis, I immediately became active in the NAACP and let them know that I was ready to become a civil rights lawyer. The NAACP had a team of lawyers who were handling cases in St. Louis: Sidney Redmond, Henry Espy, Robert Witherspoon, all of whom are now deceased. And David Grant handled some of those cases.

There was a case that came up shortly after I met them. There were two technical high schools in St. Louis. They were still segregated by law. Washington Technical High School was for blacks, and Hadley Technical High School was for whites. Hadley Technical High School had a course in airplane mechanics. Washington Technical High School had a course in automobile mechanics. The Brewton brothers wanted to become pilots. They wanted to take airplane mechanics. So their father went to the Board of Education and said, "You've got this course at Hadley Technical High School. My sons want to take it." The Board of Education said, "No." They came to the NAACP. We, of course, went through the same request to the Board of Education. The board said we couldn't do it because of segregation. So a suit was filed in the Circuit Court of the city of St. Louis against the Board of Education for the denial of this course in airplane mechanics, denial of equal protection under the law,

under the Fourteenth Amendment. And Judge Arinson of the Circuit Court decided the case in favor of the Brewton brothers. The Board of Education appealed to the Supreme Court of Missouri, but the Supreme Court said that if the Board of Education was going to provide the course in airplane mechanics to the white students, it would have to provide it to the Brewton brothers. So the Board of Education closed down the course in airplane mechanics at Hadley Technical High School. A couple of years ago in a speech to the St. Louis firemen, I was telling about the case. One of the Brewton brothers was there. He now works for the FAA.

I handled other cases on behalf of the NAACP. Robert Witherspoon and Thurgood Marshall and I filed a suit against the St. Louis Housing Authority challenging racial segregation in low-rent public housing. Constance Motley and I argued that case in 1954, and in 1955 the federal court ordered the St. Louis Housing Authority to cease segregation in all public housing. After the housing suit in 1956, the executive director of the St. Louis Housing Authority called me. He said, "Now that you've won this case, I want to offer you a job with us to help to make it work." I accepted the job as associate general counselor of the St. Louis Housing Authority.

In the meantime, I had been active in Democratic politics and civil rights. And in 1963, President Kennedy promised that he would appoint more women to high federal positions. On November 17, 1963, I went to the White House for an interview, and I was told that I had been recommended for membership on the U.S. Commission on Civil Rights. Then on November 22 President Kennedy was assassinated, so I thought nothing would come of it. However, in February, President Johnson came to St. Louis for a big party sponsored by the Democratic Committee, and he asked me come to the Chase Park Plaza. He said he wanted to appoint me to the U.S. Commission on Civil Rights.

I was the first woman on the U.S. Commission on Civil Rights. I served for sixteen years on the civil rights commission, until President Carter appointed me as the first inspector general of the Community Services Administration, the antipoverty agency. I'm still on the Citizens' Commission on Civil Rights. I believe that you cannot just acquiesce to discrimination. You've got to fight to eliminate it.

Daniel T. Tillman

Judge, Circuit Twenty-two of the Missouri Circuit Court

I was born in Wadesboro, North Carolina, a small town about twenty miles from the South Carolina border. I attended a neighborhood school, during the height of segregation. The white school was known as Wadesboro High, and the black school was known as Anson County Training School. It sounds like we were incarcerated. And that was the high school for blacks throughout the whole county.

I graduated right after the Depression, at the tail end of the war. My brother and I worked all through our school days. My mother and father had some cows, and we delivered milk every morning before we went to school. We had to help take care of the cows. My last two years in high school, I worked at a grocery store in the town. It paid very little, but I was able to save some of it. Work was an enjoyable thing.

I graduated from A&T College in North Carolina and from Georgetown University Law School in Washington, D.C. I was in an accelerated program at Georgetown, and I was working at the post office. If they had found out I was working, they would have put me out of school, but if I didn't work I couldn't go to school.

I came to St. Louis in a unique way. I was dating this girl in Washington, D.C., and when I graduated she gave me the telephone numbers of her sister and a girlfriend who lived in St. Louis. I was admitted to the North Carolina Bar, in the fall of '54, and I went to be sworn in at the courthouse. I had on a brand-new suit, I had a brand-new briefcase, I went in, and the judge said, "Boy, what do you want?" He was talking to a farmer who had his foot up on the witness chair. The judge said, "Have a seat, boy." I had a seat, and he continued to talk to that farmer for half an hour. Finally the judge said, "Come on up, boy. Let me see what you have." I went up and presented my papers, and he swore me in. I thanked him, and I left that courtroom and went straight home and started packing. I could not endure that type of indignity. I had those two girls' telephone numbers, so I headed for St. Louis.

When I came to St. Louis, I took the bar exam in January of '55, and I was admitted to the Missouri Bar in May of '55. I opened an office at Sarah, just north of Martin Luther King. It was Easton Avenue then. I opened an office with Robert Witherspoon. He took me in, and I started from there. I also started a business, a bookkeeping and tax service. And I taught business law at Hubbard Business College, on Washington Boulevard. I met a lot of people there, and that helped my practice get off the ground, as I was not from St. Louis. When I left Hubbard Business College, I went to work with Alphonse Lynch.

Alphonse Lynch and Theodore McMillian were early graduates from St. Louis University Law School. Lynch worked at the post office and practiced law at the same time. Lynch is dead now, but he was a hell of a nice guy. He had a beautiful mind.

I went from private practice to being an assistant attorney general of Missouri, an assistant prosecuting attorney, an assistant circuit attorney, and an associate city counselor for the city of St. Louis. At one time I was representing the Second Injury Fund, and I was only making a hundred dollars a month for representing that Second Injury Fund. I was associated with Jordan Chambers, and when Dan Bowles in the prosecuting attorney's office died, Jordan said, "Young man, I don't have this job, so I'm going to send you over to see Fred Weathers. Tell Fred I sent you." I got along beautifully with Jordan. He told me, "People do funny things down there. But I'm not going to ask you to do anything for me." And he never did. He never asked me to do anything but be the best that I could be.

I was active in the NAACP before I was appointed a judge, but I could not continue to be active, because a judge cannot participate in anything controversial, anything that could affect his ability to perform as a judge. I continued to be active in the Urban League after I became a judge, but for any cases involving the Urban League, I would have to disqualify myself. Over the years I've only had one case in which I had to disqualify myself.

St. Louis has been good to me, and I am happy to give some of it back. I feel that encouraging young lawyers and probation officers to excel and helping others along has been my legacy. But the person in St. Louis who deserves the most credit as far as integration is Henry Winfield Wheeler. Henry Wheeler was a soldier. He picketed the theaters when nobody else would think about picketing. He was magnificent, a little guy, quiet, unassuming, but he rendered an invaluable service. He deserves a lot of credit for what we are enjoying now.

The black revolution of the sixties changed the practice of law. When I came to St. Louis, the big law firms did not even consider any black lawyers. The first time I applied to the St. Louis Bar Association, they turned me down. Now we have a large number of black jurors serving, and that has helped black lawyers get into law firms.

Law is a difficult profession. I'm disturbed that so few black lawyers move up to become great trial lawyers. Most lawyers don't want to invest the time. But when you run across a person who has the drive and initiative, it's a joy to be in that person's presence.

Bernie Hayes

Media Professor, Webster University; Columnist, *St. Louis American*

I grew up on Chicago's south side. I had a brother who died in 1981, and I have a sister whose name is Annie. She lives in Chicago. Dinah Washington went to my high school. Nat King Cole, the Staples Singers, Lou Rawls—we all grew up in Chicago. Mahalia Jackson lived upstairs over me.

When I was in grade school, I knew I wanted to be a disc jockey. I listened to Daddy-O Daylie, Al Benson, and Jack L. Cooper on the radio, and I thought they had a nice way to make a living. It was glamorous. It wasn't working in a factory eight hours a day. And it seemed like they had lots of fun. My counselor told me to pursue journalism as a means of getting into radio, so I did. I went to the University of Illinois, where I got a degree in journalism.

Jack L. Cooper was the first African American with a radio program in Chicago. That's who everybody in Chicago listened to if they wanted to hear black music. That was in the late thirties and early forties. Al Benson was another pioneer of black radio in Chicago. I worked with him during my years at WGBS in Chicago. I was chief staff announcer at WGBS, which was *the* black station in Chicago. When I left Chicago I went to New York. I worked at WMCA for a little bit, then WNEW for a brief minute, and then WNJR over in Newark, New Jersey.

But my first job was at KDBS in Alexandria, Louisiana, in 1956. I was the only black disc jockey there, and I was the first black to do newscasts in central Louisiana. That was unheard of. People in New Orleans and Lake Charles used to listen to me, and they thought I was white. They thought anybody could be a disc jockey, including a black person, but only white guys could do the news. But I did newscasts at KDBS in 1956.

I went back to Chicago in 1959, then to San Francisco in 1963. At KSOL in San Francisco, I started using Dr. Martin Luther King Jr. at station breaks. I was the first one to do that. I used to call Dr. King when he was marching in different cities. I would call down to the sheriff's office wherever he was, and people in San Francisco would call in and give him support. In fact, I used to call the sheriff's office collect. One time Bull Connor called me back and said he would have me arrested for mischief.

I came to St. Louis in April 1965, to KETZ, where I did the afternoon drive time, from two o'clock to six o'clock, and the jazz show live from the Blue Note Club, from midnight to three in the morning. Spider Burks had just left. I did a rock 'n' roll show in the afternoon and a jazz show with an entirely different approach to music at night. In 1969 I was at KWK, and I was the first disc jockey to play long cuts from albums, five, six, seven, eight, nine minutes long. People in radio were playing two-, two-and-a-half-minute records. But artists deserved longer cuts. The Temptations, the blues artists, jazz artists, and R and B artists—they all had long cuts. So I just played them, and it caught on all across the country.

I left radio and went to MCA Records as their regional promotion director. Those were great days. I promoted R and B in Chicago, Detroit, Milwaukee, Cleveland, Pittsburgh, Cincinnati, Indianapolis, Kansas City, St. Louis, Omaha, and Minneapolis. Then I decided to start my own record company, Mission Park Records. We recorded my wife, Uvee Hayes, but the disc jockeys here in St. Louis wouldn't play her records. There's a lot of jealousy in this business. She became well known in Baltimore, Philadelphia, Chicago, Detroit, the Carolinas, Atlanta, Houston. And finally she recorded "Do You?" and "In Your Eyes," and there was such a demand for her that they had to play her in St. Louis.

I also used to produce live shows. I had a theater on Delmar near Hamilton, right across from the Palomino Lounge in the West End. It's not there anymore. I rented it from the Fox chain. I had all the big artists there—the Temptations, the Impressions, all sorts of people. It was really good. And in San Francisco I produced a show called *Soul Night at the Palace.* We charged $2.50 to get in, and we had Walter Jackson, the Temptations, the Supremes, Sonny and Cher, Jackie Ross, Solomon Burke, and Sly Stone. We sold out the Cow Palace.

The radio field is crowded. You really have to be at the right place at the right time to get in. Oftentimes you have to know somebody. I was just lucky that when I auditioned at WGBS in Chicago, they chose me.

I am proud of the efforts I have made to improve conditions for black people in radio. We shut down KWK and KKSS because of racial discrimination. KWK hired two white programmers from Tennessee, thinking they could program black radio better than black folk. We picketed and we shut them down and we got them out of town. Then KKSS was paying their white employees more than their black employees, and we sued them for racial discrimination. They changed their call letters to Magic 108 to try to make people think it was a different radio station.

African Americans can run radio stations. Black people know what they want to hear on black radio. African Americans should be in charge of their own destiny.

John A. Wright

Assistant Superintendent, Ferguson-Florissant
School District; Author

My family came to St. Louis in the 1920s and settled in the Ville, near relatives. My grandmother and grandfather and aunt all lived in walking distance. My mother worked at Homer G. Phillips Hospital. During my formative years we lived in the Ville, and then after the *Shelley v. Kraemer* decision my family moved west to the 4700 block of Labadie. I attended John Marshall Elementary, Simmons Elementary, Cote Brilliante Elementary, Cupples Elementary, and I went to Sumner High School. I received my bachelor's degree from Harris-Stowe Teachers College and my master's and doctorate from St. Louis University. My Ph.D. is in education administration.

Growing up, we may have lived in a poor community, but you never would have known it from the school we attended. We had teachers who brought out the best in all of us. They never said, "You can't do that. You can't go for that." Consequently, many have gone on to do great things, because of the influence of those teachers.

I had so many interests in school that they kept me too busy to get into trouble. I minored in art all the way through college, and I was interested in black history, in the Carter G. Woodson Club, in the theater, in gymnastics, in weight lifting, and I was in the rhythmic club as well as in the band. Those interests kept me moving. Robert James, a teacher at Sumner High School, led the Carter G. Woodson Negro History Club, and much of my interest in black history goes back to his enthusiasm for that subject. He promoted black history with programs during Black History Month and regular meetings of the Carter G. Woodson Club throughout the year.

When we moved to Labadie, two blocks from the Shelley house, on the outskirts of the Ville, things were quite segregated. But we were shielded from a lot. We programmed our life around segregation. When my mother took me downtown, we ate before we left, and we ate when we got back home. We had a movie theater in the Ville, so we didn't have to sit in the back of a white theater. We knew we couldn't go west of Grand Avenue, so all our activities—church, school, theater—were confined to the Ville. Another place we could go was the Salvation Army. I learned to play a horn with the Salvation Army. That organization provided an outlet for all the youngsters in the neighborhood.

When I got older I wanted to play music and travel with the Salvation Army Corps. That's when I found that I couldn't go in certain restaurants. When I went to camp, I couldn't leave the camp. Kids from other parts of St. Louis had a difficult time dealing with black youngsters. Through the Salvation Army I spent the summer of 1956 in Europe at a youth conference. Two hundred and fifty high school students went from the United States, and I was the only black representing this country. Having grown up in a totally segregated community, my first taste of freedom was leaving this country. In Europe I was able to go anyplace that I wanted to go, eat at whatever restaurant I wanted to, stay at whatever hotel I wanted to. That experience had an impact on me, and now I travel out of the country a lot. I try to get others to see the world beyond the local community. You can't judge the world by experiences here in St. Louis.

During my first year after college, I worked as a youth leader at the juvenile court. Then I started teaching at the St. Louis Board of Education's school at the juvenile court. I set up the program and developed the curriculum. After five years everything was running smoothly, and there was no excitement, so I went to Webster Groves as an assistant principal in charge of the federal Chapter One Program. After I'd been there three years, I became superintendent of schools for Kinloch, Missouri. I was one of the youngest superintendents in the state of Missouri. After two years, we merged with the Ferguson-Florissant School District, and I worked for them for a couple of years. Then I went back to the city of St. Louis to head the Citizens Education Task Force put together by the Board of Aldermen and the Board of Education. I have been back here, at Ferguson-Florissant, since 1979.

I was involved in landmark court cases—the one in Black Jack, for instance. As a parent, I have kids affected by desegregation. So I have been involved with education on many levels. And I don't see things getting better for black youngsters, because we don't have a good completion rate. Fewer black students are going to college than in the eighties. The bottom line is completion and careers. How do you prepare for the future? How much money will you make? How do you become a viable part of the community? I see more young people in despair, and that's disturbing. I think things will eventually turn. But how low will things go before they turn?

Betty Jean Kerr

Chief Executive Officer, People's Health Center

I grew up in a small town called Yulee, Florida, which was only about fifteen minutes from the Atlantic Ocean. I grew up on seven acres with five sisters, one brother, and my mother and father. I remember the wide-open spaces, living in that small town. There is something exciting about growing up in a small town, because you always believe that the other parts of the world are so much bigger and greater and fantastic. When I traveled to other small towns, they were not much different from the one I grew up in. And when I traveled to other cities, they were not significantly different from the cities around Yulee.

I had a very happy childhood. Almost all of the children in my community were relatives, related in one way or another. So it was just one big, happy, fun family. It was very supportive and sheltered. I attended elementary school in Yulee, and then I went to high school in a little town called Fernandina Beach, fifteen minutes away, on an island in the ocean. That's where I graduated from high school.

From there I went to nursing school and became an RN. I married a young man from Florida who was transferred to St. Louis to work. After we moved here I went to St. Louis University and received my bachelor of science in nursing. I also became a pediatric nurse practitioner. And then I went on to get my master's degree in urban health planning, all from St. Louis University.

Growing up in the South, I went to schools that were segregated. My nursing school was segregated. It was a Methodist school of nursing, run by the United Methodist Church. They had a school for the black nursing students and a school for the white nursing students. The teachers at both schools were white. When I was a senior we weren't supposed to graduate at the nursing school. We were supposed to graduate at the church. But my class was a mixed group, and we threatened violence, so we ended up graduating in the school instead of the church. I was an adult by the time I was really going to school in an integrated environment.

I think that when you grow up in a segregated environment, your parents teach you coping mechanisms. They tell you, early on, that you're not accepted over here. I think they do that to protect you. It's just a way of life. You read the sign, and you do what it says. I don't recall being bitter about it. I just did it, and then when integration came along, I just did that too.

I was a participant in the civil rights movement as a teenager and as a young adult. I used to sit in at the restaurants. I was happy to see things change from segregation to integration in the South. Where I grew up, black and white people lived in the same community; we knew everybody. But we went to different schools and different churches. And almost overnight, it was as if somebody said, "Okay folks, you can go to each other's school, you can go to each other's church." I saw it happen in my hometown.

Far away and foremost, the civil rights leader who influenced me the most was Dr. Martin Luther King Jr. He was the greatest leader I've ever known. He was compassionate. He helped us look at the movement as people learning to live together and not to hate one another or to feel that one group is superior or inferior. In his movement, he used everybody to achieve his objectives. He didn't care what color you were. If you could help us achieve integration, come on. His movement was forgiving. It was exciting. I think Dr. Martin Luther King Jr. probably would have been the first black president if he were still alive.

I went to St. Louis University and got my bachelor of science in nursing and then my master's. I taught in the Department of Community Medicine for four and a half years. After that I wanted to make a bigger impact on improving the quality of life in the community.

When this job was advertised, I thought maybe I could run a health center. It was not such a challenge. It was small. And my colleagues said, "Betty, how can you leave St. Louis University, the ivory tower, to work in this little storefront?" And I said, "That's what it is today, but that's not what it's going to be in the future. I'm going to make a big impact on this community and improve the quality of health."

Our little storefront clinic was run by volunteer medical students from Wash U. and St. Louis U. The board of directors wrote a grant and received funding from the federal government to support comprehensive primary care in this area. We provide prevention activities for everyone from the unborn to the elderly. We see a lot of pregnant women, and then we deliver them. We follow the newborn babies. Our whole goal is to improve the quality of life in the community. We involve the people that we serve, and we network with other agencies in the community.

Right now, we're sponsoring a special project for adolescent girls and boys, to teach them to delay sexual activities. I think if we can instill in young people the value of being in control of their own destiny, making informed decisions for themselves, feeling okay about themselves, then I think that we'll perpetuate a community that we can be proud of.

Lynn Beckwith Jr.

Superintendent, University City School District

I'm a native St. Louisan, one of five children. I was born to teenaged parents who did not have the benefit of a complete high school or college education. But they constantly encouraged us to read, to go to school, and to learn all that we could. From the earliest days, growing up, there were always books in the house, stories being told, and things of that sort. In my first ten years of life we lived east of Jefferson, at Leffingwell and North Market. It was a good neighborhood. We had great times. I have four sisters, and my oldest sister was our role model, because she excelled in school and helped us have high aspirations.

My parents came here from Mississippi because they had relatives here and they thought it would be a better life. They wanted to be better than they were. My father would scrounge books from wherever he could. He brought home books about everything, and he would just lay them around. My mother bought us cards, not regular playing cards, but author cards where you matched up famous authors, and she read fairy tales to us. Every day was get-an-education day.

I went to seven different elementary schools, and it always seemed that I got to a new school right after my class had learned what I needed to know. When we finally moved to 4615 Cornell, across from the Cote Brilliante School, I was able to finish my elementary school career in one place, where there were dynamic teachers up and down the hall. Then I attended Sumner High School, a member of the class of '57. I'm very proud of Sumner. I was blessed to be a student at Sumner High School. We had very learned teachers who had been educated all over the United States.

I have been out of high school for a long time, and every month members of my class, a planning committee of twelve of us, meet to develop activities for our class. When we have a reunion, folks come from all over the country. It's like a church reunion. There has always been something, a pride of school and togetherness. When you say that you are a Sumnerite, you know you are carrying on a legacy, and it means something. Mr. Brantley, our principal, used to get us in the auditorium and say, "Young people, you have a bright opportunity before you. You must educate yourselves to take advantage of it."

I knew I wanted to go to college, but I couldn't afford to go away. We had two teachers' colleges here in St. Louis—Harris Teachers College was for whites, and Stowe Teachers College was for blacks. At the time when I was thinking about college *Brown v. Board of Education of Topeka* was only two years old, and Harris and Stowe had recently integrated. So I decided to go to Harris, not because I wanted to be a teacher, but because I wanted to get a college education. And my twelfth-grade counselor called me in and asked me where I was going to college. I told her "Harris Teachers College." And she attempted to discourage me from going to Harris Teachers College because she said that there were white students there, and she wasn't sure that I could compete against them. I was respectful, and I smiled, but when I left her office I thought, "Nobody's going to deny me this opportunity that I have to go to college." So I went to Harris because that's what I could afford. And I worked as a Western Union messenger, riding a bicycle in all kinds of weather, at a dollar an hour, to pay my tuition and buy my books.

When I was going to college in St. Louis, I would go to the store, and folks sitting on their front porch on my block would say, "Junior, you hang in there now, and you continue to study!" I'd be in the store and they'd say, "Junior, we're praying for you, at the church. We're praying for you." So the whole neighborhood was boosting me up. "You can do it! We're behind you." I'll always remember that. My church sent me three dollars a month because I was going to college, and that three dollars a month helped.

At Sumner's hundredth anniversary, my eighth-grade teacher said, "Lynn Beckwith, I never dreamed that you would turn out to be one of our best principals." I simply smiled, but in my mind I said, "That's because you didn't see what was up here, in my head. You only saw a ragged, skinny little thirteen-year-old boy. You didn't look within to see the potential that I had." And that's why I constantly tell people, "Don't judge the book by its cover. You don't know what these kids can be, so give them all the same. Some of them are going to fool you, they're going to do great things. They have the potential to be whatever they want to be, if they work hard at it and put forth the effort and educate themselves." Don't look at yourself now. Look at yourself as how you want to be, and you can be that.

Henry Givens Jr.

President, Harris-Stowe State College

When I grew up St. Louis was very segregated—the schools, the neighborhoods, the restaurants, everything. We may have been poor, but we didn't know it, because everybody was about the same. We all were eating three squares, we all had clean clothes, and we all had disciplined homes.

I attended Simmons Elementary School, the best elementary school in the city of St. Louis, particularly among black schools. I had great, great teachers. Mrs. Julia Davis was my father's teacher, she was my teacher, she was my sister's and brother's teacher. And she lived on our street, so she monitored us all day and all evening. Many of our teachers worked for the Y as Y Boosters and could send kids to Camp Rivercliff during the summer. That's an advantage that I had every summer.

After Simmons it was Sumner High School. Now I tell you, Sumner was one of the greatest high schools in the nation! That school had black teachers who had graduated from Harvard, Yale, and Princeton. If they had Ph.D.s the only places in Missouri they could get jobs were Lincoln University, Stowe Teachers College, or Sumner. We had scholars teaching us in high school!

I went to Lincoln University, and then, right out of college, I started off as a classroom teacher at Douglass School in Webster Groves. I loved it. I taught fifth and sixth grade, and since I was the only man in the building, I ended up teaching all the physical education. In the fifties and sixties it was still segregated. Douglass had all black teachers and all black students, because it served the community of North Webster. It was a wonderful school. H. B. Goins, the principal, was a great man, a great mentor of mine.

But I became impatient. I wanted to be principal. And you know, timing is everything. Life is not going to change just because you think you're ready. You've got to be patient, and you've got to be prepared. That's what the superintendent said. "If you can hold on two years, Mr. Goins is going to retire, and we want to make you principal."

They needed to integrate, so when the time came, they said, "We want you to design a program that will be unlike anything in the nation. We want you to come up with a program that will draw whites from all over this district into this all-black school." So we took down all the walls. We carpeted the floors. We integrated most of the black teachers all over the district. I kept five. We needed thirty white teachers and we got eighty-five applications, so I was able to pick the cream of the crop. And then we designed a curriculum that was different from any in the nation. We had team teaching, we had multiage grouping of youngsters, first and second graders together. And we went to the community and sold it. The first year we had students from every school in that district begging to come to this new school. The black students stayed there, and we integrated. And in two years it was fifty-fifty, black-white, and we had a waiting list of two years to get in. Achievement hit the top of the charts, nationally. It was called a demonstration school. It was the prototype for a magnet school.

In 1979 I became president of Harris-Stowe. Then seven or eight years ago the governor called me and told me Lincoln University was in trouble and asked me to take over Lincoln. They had a deficit, they had personnel problems, it was in disarray. I went up there, pulled a team together, and straightened the place up in eight months. We hired a new president, and I came on back to Harris-Stowe. But I was the president of Lincoln and Harris-Stowe at the same time, working at Lincoln three days a week, Harris-Stowe three days a week, and Sunday I didn't even know where I was. The greatest challenge, the greatest accomplishment, that I've had in my career was serving as president of two historically black colleges at the same time and having a hand in saving both of them.

I was successful in getting the legislature to change the mission of Harris-Stowe. It used to be only teacher training. Now we have business and criminal justice and secondary education. This is an inner-city college. If this place closed down, 98 percent of our students wouldn't be able to go to college.

It's a pleasure to work in my own town, among the friends that I grew up with. The only disappointment that I have is that St. Louis is still divided. There is a lack of integration in our housing, in education. This city is polarized economically and racially. I would like to see us eliminate the polarization and do a better job in employment and in taking care of the poor. We're doing a lot of good, but St. Louis is not going to be a great city until racism is wiped out.

Norman R. Seay

Director, Office of Equal Opportunity,
University of Missouri–St. Louis

I was born and reared in the city of St. Louis, on Dixon Street, now named James Cool Papa Bell Avenue. When we moved onto that street there were only a few African American families. Most of the residents were Jewish. My sister and brother and I were raised by my mother and grandmother and grandfather.

I went to Vashon High School, and during those years right after the Depression, although the schools were segregated, I participated in integrated activities at the People's Art Center on Delmar, which was an art facility started by the WPA and supported by the Urban League.

Also while I was in high school I helped to organize a group called CORE, the Committee of Racial Equality. That's how I became active in the civil rights movement. CORE fought against racism using the philosophy of direct action without any violence. We demonstrated against places of public accommodation, such as hotels and restaurants, seeking admission. We demonstrated against Stix, Baer, and Fuller for eighteen months just to get the opportunity to eat in their restaurant. We sat in at Famous, and Scruggs, at the Chippewa Drug Store, Walgreens, Katz Drug Store, Howard Johnson's.

After we were successful, we began working on employment. We did a survey, and we found that there were five or six banks in the African American community, and none of them employed African Americans in white-collar positions except Jefferson Bank. Jefferson Bank employed African Americans as tellers while the bank was located on Jefferson and Franklin. Then when the bank moved farther out to Washington and Jefferson those African Americans were terminated. We decided to zero in on the Jefferson Bank. I shall never forget that. It was in 1963, when A. Philip Randolph and Martin Luther King were going to have the March on Washington. I was in a dilemma, whether I wanted to participate in the March on Washington, or participate in the demonstration at the Jefferson Bank. I decided to stay here in the city and demonstrate.

So on August 30, 1963, about two hundred to three hundred blacks and whites demonstrated in front of the bank, because the bank had refused to honor our request to hire four African Americans in white-collar positions. Our attorney, Ray Howard, had contacted the bank. And Jefferson Bank went to the courts and got an injunction that said we were not to interfere with the business of the bank. We planned to obey the injunction. We didn't want to violate any laws. When we got there, everything was peaceful until the factory across the street, Gulf Electric Company, closed. The employees came out, and many of them wanted to do business in the bank. And we told them that they couldn't go into the bank across our picket line. We were in front of the doors. But the employees went into the bank, and when they went in, some of our people followed them and then there was pandemonium in the bank. People were yelling and singing and standing in front of the tellers' cages. The bank maintained its operation until the closing time, which was six o' clock. We walked away; there was no violence or anything. We thought everything was fine. But later that evening, the sheriff enforced the injunction and came to our homes to pick us up. Marian Oldham was the first person who was picked up, and before she left she called some of us and told us to hide. So we were able to meet, and we decided to surrender to the jail on Sunday.

There were many demonstrations for about three or four months, trying to get the city to withdraw its money from Jefferson Bank. Fortunately there was no riot, but we were able to get the African American community on our side. Everybody could see there was discrimination. As a result of that major demonstration, we now have African Americans working in many financial institutions and other institutions in white-collar positions. And it had an effect on many other things in the community. One of the outcomes was that Bill Clay became a congressman. Ray Howard became a state senator. They had a platform. People began to know them.

But we had to pay a penalty. I stayed in jail ninety days, the city jail and the workhouse. There were people there who could not read and write, and I had my degree in elementary education, so we established a school. And I'm pleased to say that school continues today.

I began as an elementary school teacher. I left teaching and worked for the antipoverty program, the Human Development Corporation, and then the Health and Welfare Council. I lost my job because of my involvement in civil rights. Then I worked for the federal government in Washington for eight years. During that time I reactivated the NAACP chapter in Montgomery County, Maryland. I helped to establish the St. Louis Police Ethical Society and the Black Police Association for the nation. I worked to make Dr. Martin Luther King Jr.'s birthday a national holiday and to name a street and a bridge for him. I hope that one day there will be no discrimination, just respect for the dignity of each human being.

William L. Clay

U.S. Representative, District One, United States Congress

I grew up in downtown St. Louis, around what's now the Columbus Square Housing Development. I was born in that neighborhood. I went to a public school for the first six years, Jefferson School, and then I transferred to St. Nicholas, where I graduated from St. Nicholas Elementary and also from St. Nicholas High School.

I worked as a bartender during my college days. I worked as a cartographic aide for the federal government at Aeronautical Chart and Information Center here in St. Louis for a little over a year, and I left that and went to drive a bus for the old St. Louis Public Service Company. And from that I went to sell insurance for about four or five years. I worked up to assistant manager and then to manager.

My interest in politics flowed naturally out of my interest in civil rights. I got involved in the civil rights struggle when I was in the service, stationed at Fort McClellan, Alabama. St. Louis was no different from any of the cities in the South. We had rigid segregation—not by law, but by custom. The only things segregated by law were the public schools. But we couldn't eat in any of the restaurants. We couldn't go to any of the downtown theaters or to theaters in white neighborhoods. We couldn't use the recreational facilities. We couldn't go to the hotels. People like Norman Seay, Charlie Oldham, Marian Oldham, and myself fought this for many years. We had sit-ins in restaurants and department stores and picket lines and other peaceful protests. Restaurants opened up, one at a time. When I got elected to the Board of Aldermen, in 1959, there had been several votes on public accommodations bills, but they had failed. Lawrence Woodson and I were elected at the same time—again, that was 1959—and we thought we had enough votes to pass the public accommodations bill. But some of the people who had supported it prior to that changed their votes. It took another two years, but we finally passed the public accommodations bill in 1961.

My other main interest on the Board of Aldermen was fair employment. I introduced a resolution to set up a committee to investigate job discrimination at the Plaza Apartments, under construction between Fourteenth Street and Eighteenth Street at Olive. There were only six blacks on the Board of Aldermen, out of twenty-nine members, but we passed the resolution by one vote. A. J. Cervantes, president of the Board of Aldermen, appointed me chairman of the committee to investigate job discrimination. All summer we worked hard having hearings, and before the term was over, we had blacks working as bricklayers and carpenters and painters. That was the first breakthrough in the trade union movement, getting blacks hired on these job sites. Republican Alderman Harold Elbert and I wrote the fair employment bill for St. Louis. You must remember this was before we had all of the national laws. We abolished job discrimination in employment in the city of St. Louis.

My thirty years in Congress have been spent on the House Education Committee and the Workforce Committee. My two main interests are education and labor. Education is the key to most successful careers. Without an education you're handicapped from the start. I chaired the Post Office and Civil Service Committee, which gave me a direct relationship with federal employees and postal workers. I introduced some landmark legislation on behalf of federal employees and postal workers that has become law. For instance, I worked for twenty years to revise the Hatch Act, which prohibited federal employees from participating in politics.

As I said before, St. Louis was as segregated as anyplace in America. It was rigid in its polarization. My impression was that we had a problem here. That's why I got involved in the civil rights movement, to challenge those who dictated policy and to force them to change.

Martin L. Mathews

President, CEO, and Cofounder, Mathews-Dickey Boys' Club

I grew up in the small town of Poplar Bluff, Missouri. Blacks and whites went to separate schools, and I didn't know that the white school was superior. We kids socialized in other things, like sports. We played baseball together, blacks and whites. And I think competing in sports prepared me for the big city. I never realized until I came to St. Louis that segregation made such a big difference.

I had teachers who encouraged me in elementary school and in high school. I spent a lot of time with my high school principal, talking with him. He was a big influence on me. I also looked up to various people in the community, especially in my church. The deacon, the assistant deacon, the minister, a member of the choir—all were mentors. I was president of my 4-H Club when I was twelve years old, and that was a valuable experience that taught me how to organize and be successful leading a group.

When I came to St. Louis I worked for Burkart Manufacturing Company, a division of Textron. I worked in the engineering department, where we developed things for General Motors and Chrysler and Ford. We made all the padding that went inside the automobile.

I got involved with a group of young men who met at A. C. Anderson's house, where I happened to be living while I was saving to buy a home. These young men wanted to do something with their lives, but they had no leader. I came to admire Mr. Anderson and those eager young men, so I got involved with them. I started a baseball team with about thirty boys. That was about 1959. At first when we played baseball the white teams always beat us. The white teams had uniforms and dozens of balls and bats and three or four adults with them. Our team had one bat, one ball, and one adult—me. The young men were twelve and thirteen then, and they had a lot of hard work to do to catch up. But I wanted to give them the chance to prove that they were as good as, or better than, those other boys. We worked hard for two years. We worked and worked. And the third year we were the best in Missouri and Illinois and Kentucky. Those kids were champions. And they would take that championship experience with them the rest of their lives. Dickey

Ballentine and I formed the boys' club so that we could give that same pride to other young men.

When you are young, you don't actually realize much about racism. You look for opportunities to compete. When I came to St. Louis, I looked around and saw things that other people weren't able to do. I was fortunate when I went to Burkart Manufacturing Company, because I was able to compete with white Americans. I didn't look at racism; I looked at opportunity. I tried to make every opportunity available to me, to make it work for me. And I do that for other African Americans. I say, "Make the system work for you. Work hard. Do the right thing. Take advantage of what America has to offer."

We need to look at people like Jackie Robinson, who broke the color line in baseball. He grew up in Los Angeles, California, and went to UCLA. He was always at the top of the line there, at whatever he competed in. Then you look at Martin Luther King, a scholar, a well-read man. He graduated from good universities. He was well equipped to lead black America out of segregation and give us an opportunity to be first-class citizens. You look at Thurgood Marshall, on the Supreme Court. He was a man who fought hard to change the laws in order for people to have an opportunity to become contributing citizens. Those three people made a difference. They accomplished the goals they set out to accomplish. We all worked hard on the change, but those three people led us in the struggle. And now everybody has more of an opportunity to be whatever they want to be in life.

At Mathews-Dickey we hope that we have made a difference in the lives of the people we serve. We hope to continue to do that. Mathews-Dickey is people helping people. I would like to say to young people today that you are living in the greatest country in the world, the greatest state in the world, in the greatest city in the world. So why not take advantage of it? Take the opportunities that are offered to you and do something with them. Try to get the best education that you can get, because you are going to need it. All of us are pulling for you. We are here for you. But you have to be ready for the challenge when it confronts you. It will come one day. Your opportunity will come. Be ready to take advantage of it.

Oliver Sain

Musician

I grew up around Memphis and West Memphis. I spent a lot of that time fooling around with music and instruments. My mother was married to one of the great blues musicians, Willie Love. Willie Love worked with a guy named Sonny Boy Williamson. They were both well-known blues artists. Willie Love was my stepfather. My real father was a baseball player. He was not into music, but his father was a musician. My grandfather was Dan Sain. He worked with a guy named Frank Stokes. In fact, I have a new CD, a reissue of Dan Sain playing.

I got started in music after I dropped out of school in the eleventh grade. I picked up music from hanging around, seeing guys play. I met people like Howlin' Wolf. He was around West Memphis. Howlin' Wolf was a unique man. He was imposing, looked big, a mean-looking man. But he was a very gentle man. I started playing with Wolf when I was about eighteen or nineteen years old. I was playing drums at the time. I was just kind of picking up on the music. I didn't really know very much. I was a kid really.

I knew Ike Turner down south, before he came here. As a matter of fact, I left Mississippi and went to Chicago before he did. Before Ike or Little Milton ever left Mississippi, I was in Chicago. Then I heard the rumor that Ike Turner had gone to St. Louis and the whole band with him. After about a year or so, I heard that Little Milton had done the same thing. I thought, "Those guys must have found something in St. Louis." About a year later, Little Milton called me and asked me to come down here and play the weekend. He needed a saxophone. I never went back. That was about 1959.

I work all over the world, but I live here. I had a hit with Bobby McClure and Fontella Bass, a song I wrote called "Don't Mess Up a Good Thing." With the first royalty check I got, I built the recording studio, right here where I am now. We record all kinds of stuff—rap, gospel, you name it. We recorded Tina Turner here. We cut Zella Jackson Price, Cleophus Robinson, and the Montclairs here. My studio was down in a storefront for a while, but I moved back up here because this is a bigger studio, and everything is digital and computerized now.

I have written several other songs that were recorded by different artists. I had the flip side of "Rescue Me," by Fontella Bass, called "Soul of the Man." That was a million seller. I had a hit, myself, called "Bus Stop," which was a big dance record in the seventies. And I had another hit called "Feel Like Dancing," where I sang, but to me I'm not a good singer.

But before that, I played with a lot of people, mostly blues artists. I played with Elmore James, Howlin' Wolf, Sonny Boy Williamson, Willie Love, Little Milton, B. B. King, you know, years ago in Memphis. Most of my career, people have associated me with the blues. I do play blues, and I really love blues. But that's not all I play. How could I play a saxophone and not play jazz?

But what happens is, the style I play is kind of bluesy. It's how I play. It's my style. I try to find the attitude of a song. You know what I'm saying? I get into the attitude of whatever song I'm playing, but I still sound like me. I can't do anything about that. My playing is kind of patterned after Louis Jordan. Louis Jordan's music includes some of the greatest songs in the world. Some of them are original songs by Louis Jordan, even though you know them by somebody else. "Let the Good Times Roll," for example—that's Louis Jordan. A lot of other people did it, like Ray Charles. Then you've got "Caledonia" and "Five Guys Named Moe." Some of his songs are so famous I've seen them used in cartoons, like "Ain't Nobody Here but Us Chickens." I've seen Felix the Cat use that tune. Louis Jordan was really a jazz saxophone player. A lot of my playing is patterned after Louis Jordan. Then there's Hank Crawford, who came along much later, but with that same intensity.

There have been many musicians from St. Louis in all fields of music. Oliver Nelson and Clark Terry came from St. Louis. Jimmy Forrest had one of the classic jazz-bluesy kind of saxophone things, the "Night Train." Then you have rock 'n' roller Chuck Berry, and Johnnie Johnson, the piano player for Chuck Berry. So a lot of people have come out of St. Louis.

Many times young people who want to be musicians say, "Man, I think I'll go to somewhere, L.A. or somewhere, go to Atlanta. Yeah, man, the whole thing is in Atlanta." So I tell them that they're talking geography. Geography has absolutely nothing to do with it. What they should do is try to make records. That's the only way to get into music nationally. And if you're going to make records, this tape recorder is going to sound the same in St. Louis as it does in L.A. You know what I'm saying?

But anyway, in this business, you've got to persevere. Hang in there and try to do what you're doing. If you do it, you do it. I play just as good for fifty dollars a week as I do for five hundred. You do what you do.

Pearlie I. Evans

Administrative Assistant to Congressman William L. Clay

My dad was a brickmaker. He came to St. Louis to work for a company called Laclede-Christy Clay Products, and he stayed there until he died. We came to St. Louis when I was eight or nine years old. So I grew up in St. Louis. I grew up in the south of the city. We lived at 1520 Papin, right next to St. Mary's Infirmary. I went to Lincoln Grade School.

When I think of the people who helped me know that I was important, I remember Mrs. Hazel Evans, one of my elementary schoolteachers. She told us, "Now, if you will study hard, like I know you can, then we are going to do some exciting things." Those exciting things were trips to places like Grant's Farm. In those years, of course, St. Louis was a very segregated city. We couldn't go to the Highlands in Forest Park. And so she took us to Chicago, to Hull House. It was a settlement house, but around it was this big amusement park, just like the Highlands. So we got a chance to see Hull House, where Jane Addams worked, and we went to the amusement park. We had a great time. Mrs. Evans was a lady who had a tremendous impact on my life.

Anna Lee Scott, the director of the YWCA, was another lady who had a great impact on my life. I didn't realize that the area where I grew up was supposed to be poor, but that is what my peers told me when I got to high school. In grade school, it didn't make much difference. Mrs. Scott told us that we were very important people. And she told us to develop our magnificent potentials. And from that time on, I have gone through my life talking about that to young people. When I finished my education, I became Mrs. Scott's Y girl. She sent me around the country for the YWCA, to help raise money and develop initiatives for the Y. Anna Lee Scott was extremely important in my growing-up years.

I went to Lincoln University in Jefferson City. I went in and came out in four years. I enjoyed my years at Lincoln. Then I was a settlement-house worker. I worked at Carver House as a junior leader for Mr. Ralph Young. He was a great influence in my life, too. Ralph Young and Ruth Green. It was Ruth who told me that I have a knack for serving people. She convinced me to go to Washington University. So I went there and got a master's degree in social work.

After that I was a commissioner in the Welfare Department in the city. Then I came to work for Mr. Clay. That was twenty-five years ago. I haven't worked anywhere that long.

I worked on civil rights with Bill Clay when we were high school teenagers. Norman Seay, Bill Clay, and myself worked to open up places around St. Louis for blacks. I remember the Howard Johnson's, up on Natural Bridge and Kingshighway. And then there was White Castle. We held marches in St. Louis at the Jefferson Bank, and we went to Alabama, and we went to Georgia.

I worked with Bill Clay before he was an alderman. First Bill was a committeeman. Then he got Norman Seay to be the committeeman, and he went on the Board of Aldermen. In those years we were involved in almost everything. We considered ourselves change agents. When Bill Clay went on the Board of Aldermen in 1959, he introduced the public accommodations bill. The public accommodations bill grew out of our protesting at Howard Johnson's and White Castle, but it didn't become law until 1961. We could not even eat in restaurants.

I've been involved in civil rights quite a bit, and I have felt good about every moment, including when Betty Lee and I were in the city jail. Prisoners in the city jail were protesting, setting things on fire, and they put together a list of people who could negotiate for them. Betty Lee and I were the only two women on the list. John Bass was my boss at City Hall, and he asked me to go down there. And the police department sprayed us, they hosed us down, they did pepper. They did all of those things. I have never gotten over what the police department did. But we got it settled. We got the men to stop burning the mattresses. It took a lot of courage. The newspaper called it "The Courage of Women."

We who were on the front line in St. Louis must encourage and push those behind us to the front line. I hope that young people will continue to try to make St. Louis a better place, make St. Louis a more harmonious community and more economically sound. We walked through the years of social justice, fighting to be treated with respect and dignity, and now it is time to develop our young people, politically and economically. Young people must define themselves. They should not let others define them, as people, as human beings. As Mrs. Scott told me so many moons ago, "Develop your own magnificent potential."

Stanley Newsome

Deputy Chief, St. Louis Fire Department

I came into the fire department when they were integrating the fire department, around 1962 or '63. Prior to that, they had three companies that were black. They had Engine No. 28, Hook and Ladder No. 9. They were on Enright across from Cole School. Then came Engine No. 10, which was over by Homer G. Phillips Hospital. Those two stations served the blacks. They had black firefighters, and some of them had black captains. Originally, blacks came on the fire department about 1921. They had black firemen with a white driver and a white captain.

So anyway, I came into the department in 1962. And they sent me to a fire station with thirty white men and told me what I had to do to get along with thirty white men. It was a little Jackie Robinson speech about things might happen that you might not like. Looking back over it now, the problem was the administration of the fire department. The people who ran the department did not prepare the people for the change, or tell them why it was changing. The leadership of the fire service should have gone to the firemen and explained to them that we're going to have an integrated department because it is time to do this.

Later, I was transferred. They sent me down to the fire station at Enright, across from Cole School. It was a very busy fire station. I really liked it. Then they closed that station and I went out on Shawmut and Ridge to No. 13, which was the busiest fire station in the city at the time. There was a black fireman there who was set up to be fired. And I knew they did the guy wrong.

I realized that the only reason people do what they do to black people on this job is because we let them. In other words, we were not organized. We let these people do these things to us. What happens, in the fire department, we've got shifts. We have three twenty-four-hour shifts. I'm on the A shift now. I'll work Sunday, Tuesday, and Thursday of next week. In between time, the B and C shifts work the days in there. Well, if you're on a different shift, you don't see the other people. They're in the fire department, but you don't meet them because of the way we work shifts. So most of the blacks didn't even know each other on the job. We had no type of networking.

Me and a guy got together, and I told him that we needed to form some kind of organization to do something about the way they were doing the brothers. There were a lot of things that blacks were excluded from. For example, when we're going to have a potluck dinner, everybody puts in so much and a guy goes to the store, gets some food, and cooks. They have this dinner, and we're excluded. They didn't invite us. This is what happened in the fire department, up until 1965.

So I called a meeting. Not knowing who the black firemen were, I just called the firehouse and said, "Let me speak to the colored fireman." And they called the guy to the phone. And that's how I got the people to come to the meetings. I had them come up with ten valid things that we thought were unfair: no blacks drove, no black chiefs, the supper club was separate, and other valid things. I was elected to take them down to the fire chief's office, a nice old man. So anyway, I went down, and we talked about what the problems were in the fire service. In the conversation, the chief asked me, "Newsome, what do you really think the problem is with the fire department?" So I said, "Well, now that you ask me, you're the problem." He said, "Why would you say that I was the problem?" I said, "Because you call us niggers in front of your battalion chiefs, and they call us niggers in front of the captains, and the captains call us niggers in front of the men." I said, "If you had the right attitude about this problem with race in the fire service it would be solved in nothing flat."

Anyway, I gave him my list of ten things, but instead of looking at what the suggestions were, they went around from fire station to fire station and asked the black firemen, "Are you part of this black fireman thing?" And the black firemen were all afraid for their jobs.

I ended up going to Ina Boone and Joseph Clark, at the NAACP. They didn't have a really good cause going, so they took up our cause, and the Justice Department joined in. We sued the city and the fire department. The court found that the city was guilty of discrimination in hiring, and they ordered the city to hire one black for every white they hire. Since that time, half the people they hire in the fire department are blacks.

Being in the fire service is a very honorable profession. We have a lot of job satisfaction. We have an opportunity to help other people and to serve the community. And with that attitude you can go a long way in life.

Clarence Harmon

Mayor, City of St. Louis; Chief, St. Louis Police Department

I grew up in the middle of the city of St. Louis for most of my formative years, in the 4200 block of Evans, in the neighborhood just south of the Ville. Then when my parents bought their first home, we moved to the 1800 block of Papin. We lived there about eight years, and then when I was in my teens we moved to the 5100 block of Cabanne Avenue.

I have one sister who is still living. Two sisters passed away. I was the only son. My father worked for the Wabash Railroad as a cook, and later he worked on the Union Pacific Railroad. I recall traveling on the train with my father and watching how hard he worked in that small kitchen, doing all the things he had to do, with the train moving back and forth. I had not imagined how difficult it was for him to earn a living. I came away from that experience with a very great respect for, and love for, my father.

I liked to read a lot as a child. Reading opened up new worlds for me. I imagined myself in the places I read about. I always had my nose in a book. Also I liked science and chemistry. And I did ordinary things like playing ball and taking piano lessons. I did the things that every kid does, including getting into trouble. One Christmas my parents gave me a chemistry set. And I did some disastrous experiments. My father said, "Don't you buy that boy any more of that stuff, or we will all be killed in this house."

My sisters and I attended parochial schools. I started at Visitation School on Taylor and then went to Holy Angels, when we moved south. My sister Alice went to St. Mark's High School, and I went to McBride High School. I will always remember my eighth-grade teacher, Sister Mary Grace. She was compassionate and stern in a way that brought out the best in us. Even then we had a lot of excuses for not doing our best. She believed, as my parents did, that education would gain us access to the better things in life. I carry her lessons of humility and respect and attentiveness with me today.

I have had a long and varied career. I had ten jobs before I became a police officer. I spent three years in the army airborne at Fort Campbell, Kentucky, where I learned skills in radio communications. Then I worked at Homer G. Phillips as a hospital attendant. I worked for the post office and then Emerson Electric, McDonnell Douglas, the Federal Aviation Administration, Air Route Traffic Control Center. I went to the Federal Records Center, where I became the head of the Communications Division for the United States Army Administration Center.

And then there was that fateful event, the death of Martin Luther King. I was traumatized by his death. I felt that I had somehow only witnessed most of the civil rights movement. Although I was a member of CORE and the NAACP, I had watched most of the civil rights movement unfold on my television set as a panorama of events I knew very little about. So in the summer of 1968 I quit my job, grew a large Afro and a Fu Manchu mustache, and I took to the streets to change the world. I worked for an antipoverty program called the BYU Jobs Project.

I was always impressed by the way Martin Luther King could express love for people who spat on him, people who sicced dogs on him, and people who beat him and the others who were merely trying to gain rights that everyone else expected to have. I was impressed by his ability to be stoic in those circumstances. He was such a good person. Malcolm X began to interest me after his historic trip to Mecca, when he came back and amended his vision of what we all can become. Martin Luther King and Malcolm X are my heroes.

I went into the police department in 1969, and after twenty-one years I made police chief. The police department was a great learning experience. I had a great time. There is nothing about it I would take back.

All of us find ourselves in difficult times now and then. What often seems difficult later seems to have prepared us for an important experience later on in life. Sometimes, when I think about it in the dead of night, I am grateful that I had some experience, that I met someone, or that I did something that was important.

Jean King Chavis

Management Training Consultant, Jean King and Associates, Inc.

I grew up partly in Osceola, Arkansas, where I was born, and then in Memphis, Tennessee. In 1947 I migrated to this big city, and I've been here ever since. I started school in Osceola, attended elementary school in Memphis, and went to Cole Elementary School in St. Louis. I attended Washington Tech High School, and I took courses at various business colleges in the St. Louis area.

I worked for the old Aeronautical Chart and Information Center for a number of years, but I was not able to advance. I got tired of training white children out of high school who became my supervisors, so I quit. I got married and played housewife for a while. In 1969, we were living in public housing, raising one child, when my husband and I decided that we could do better. We decided to move to Laclede Town. My husband made arrangements with Jerry Berger, who was the manager of Laclede Town.

At that time there was talk throughout public housing of residents engaging in a rent strike, because we had received notices for the third rent increase in a year. On a snowy day, I was waiting for a taxi to take me to sign the Laclede Town lease, and I saw a child pick up a piece of soggy bread from underneath the snow. I went out and grabbed him by the hand and took him upstairs to his mother. She started to cry and said, "Mrs. King, we don't have any food. I get $134 a month welfare, and my rent just increased to $165 a month."

I went to the rent strike meeting at Blumeyer and stood up front. I knew no one in that room. As I listened to the stories being told by residents from all over public housing, I don't know what I said, I don't know what happened, but when I walked out of that meeting, I had been elected president of the Citywide Rent Strike Committee to lead the rent strike against the St. Louis Housing Authority. My husband said, "What about Laclede Town?" I said, "I don't have time for that. People need help."

All of the St. Louis public housing developments were part of the Citywide Rent Strike Committee except for Carr Square and Vaughn. They had their own leader, the Reverend Buck Jones. But our needs were the same, and we met frequently to map out strategy. We created a list of demands, opened bank accounts, collected rent from the residents, and held the rents in escrow. Our main objective was to get the St. Louis Housing Authority to base the residents' rents on their ability to pay. We wanted public housing rents to be 25 percent of a family's income. We wanted a tenant affairs board to become the official voice of public housing residents. We wanted two residents

appointed to the Board of Commissioners of the St. Louis Housing Authority. And we wanted tenant management corporations to manage their own developments. We started the rent strike on February 3, 1969, and we ended it on October 29, 1969. All our demands were met.

I worked with Senator Edward Brooke on the Brooke Amendment, which required residents to pay 25 percent of their income for rent, regardless of the amount of space they occupied. It paved the way for the Department of Housing and Urban Development to give Section Eight subsidies to housing authorities to make up the difference. It touched everybody all over the country who lived in public housing. I'm very proud of that.

After working in public housing as a rent-strike leader, I learned housing management from McCormick Realty. Then in 1973 the Ford Foundation funded our first resident management corporations. Carr Square, where I was, and the Darst development became the first resident management corporations in the city. At the end of a year, both developments were doing better than the Housing Authority, so in 1974 the Ford Foundation funded two more tenant management corporations: Clinton-Peabody and Webbe on Chouteau. Cochran Gardens became a tenant management corporation in 1976.

Because of the success of the St. Louis public housing rent strike, the first national convention of the National Tenants Organization was held in St. Louis. At that convention I was elected vice president of the National Tenants Organization.

In 1993 the residents of Blumeyer hired me to train them to manage their own development. I trained the residents to take charge of their destiny. I took people off welfare and trained them to work at meaningful jobs with benefits.

Developers build new and shining homes, but nobody builds people to occupy those homes. My motto is, "We build people for housing." People have to have responsibilities if they're going to live in this kind of housing. Rules and regulations must be established and followed if public housing is going to work. Bad elements must be removed from public housing.

I came to save this development for the good people who wish to remain here. I like to be accessible. Tenants must be able to reach the management in times of trouble, therefore tenants can call me at home. Sometimes the tenants just need somebody to talk to or somebody to put an arm around them and say, "Baby, I care. Come on, you can do better. I'll show you how."

Betty L. Thompson

Missouri State Representative

I grew up in Carr Square Village. It was way downtown, between Fifteenth and Sixteenth Streets and Cole and Carr, that area downtown. People call it the "Projects," but we called it a community.

I'm from a two-parent family. My father worked odd jobs, in and out of town. And my mother stayed home and took care of the family. There were thirteen of us, ten brothers, two sisters, and myself. We grew up in the project, we went to school, and we were just like other young people in the community. Everybody knew everybody in Carr Square Village. It was a close-knit community. People took care of each other's children. If we did something wrong, a neighbor would tell on us, and when we got home we would get a whipping. And the neighbors could discipline us. Carr Square Village was just a close-knit community where everybody knew everybody. It was a good community. We moved there in 1945, when it was new.

Because our family was so big, we moved to Pruitt-Igoe, up near Jefferson, when it opened in 1955. That was the high-rise project that everybody talks about. It was nationally known for being designed to fail. Pruitt-Igoe had high-rise buildings and no play area or rest rooms on the first floor. The elevators stopped on every other floor and little kids had to get on the elevators and go up to another floor to go home. So maybe, in a sense, it was designed to fail.

I attended school downtown. I spent two years at Vashon High School, and I graduated from Sumner High. I graduated in 1958. Tina Turner was one of my classmates. And all I knew about success, and all she knew about success, was what we learned from looking at magazines like *Better Homes and Gardens.* When I was sixteen, I had to go to work at a health center to help my family.

From being active in church and speaking in church, I became interested in public life. In high school I wanted to be a nurse, and later I wanted to be a missionary. I wanted to help others. I was active in civil rights, picketing and marching at places like Howard Johnson's and Jefferson Bank. I worked for the St. Louis Board of Elections, and I was involved with the rent strike in the projects in the sixties. But I never thought in my wildest dreams of being in politics. My daddy was always active in politics. Years ago, when we lived down in Pruitt-Igoe, he worked for a state representative named Pal Troupe. And he would have all of us out there passing out literature and working, going door to door, and all these kinds of things. But never in my wildest dream did I think that I would be in politics.

And then I was elected to the city council in University City. I was the first black female on that city council.

When people encouraged me to run for office, I realized that politics is a way that you can have a platform, that you can help your people, that you can be heard, that people will pay attention and people will understand. We need to be good examples and beacons of hope; we need to help people and lift people up. That has been the reason I went into politics. Black people have struggled down through the years. Our forebears sacrificed for us to get to where we are today. They couldn't spell education, but they knew that that's what they wanted us to have. And our young people still need so much help. So, therefore, my drive has been mostly helping African Americans. I've been accused many times of being too black. I guess that means that I do too much for my own people. But the majority of my district has always been black. So most of the people that I've helped have been black.

My oldest son has his own business. He's the construction manager for the airport, out at the East Terminal. So when you go out that way, you can look at it and smile and say, "A young black man was the construction manager for this international airport." And my other son is a detective on the police department. My daughter is a teacher and also a blackjack dealer on a boat. My youngest son is in school to be a lawyer. He loves politics, and he's my campaign manager right now. I'm running for state rep. So we have diversity in our life. My husband is retired now. He was an auditor, and he is a magician and a musician. I have been married for almost forty years. We have four children who are doing well, and we teach them to reach back into the neighborhoods and lift others up, discourage them from taking drugs, discourage them from going wrong.

I am trying to groom young people for politics. And I think that's where some of us fall short. We ignore our future. We get where we want to go, and we don't look back. We have to start grooming young people to take our places, to be leaders. Young people should try to be the best that they can be, whatever that is. Everybody's not going to be lawyers or doctors or engineers or architects. But they should be the best that they can be in whatever they do. We have to take responsibility for what our young people do and what they are. If we allow our kids to eat junk and watch junk, then we shouldn't be surprised if they turn out to be junk. We should all band together as a family and as a community to help each other. That's what life is all about.

Leonard Robinson

Assistant Director, United Auto Workers
National Community Action Program

My department handles the external politics of the UAW and many of the national community programs. We interact with the Urban League, the NAACP, the Coalition of Black Trade Unionists, the Citizens Action Coalition Program, and a number of other groups across the country. But how did I get started? Well, I went to work at Ford Motor Company in 1966, as an hourly employee putting parts on cars. And I tried to join a political caucus in the local union. Like most unions, the UAW is a highly political institution. I went to the president of the local union and asked him how I could join his caucus. And he said they didn't have any caucuses in the plant, that they ran independently through local union offices. I found that hard to believe, but rather than argue about it, I just formed my own caucus. We ran open slates and forced the other caucuses out of the closet. They didn't allow blacks to join. So I organized blacks in that plant into a caucus, the Black Rights Committee. And we made some changes at Ford. We elected local committeemen who represented the workers on the front lines.

The Ford Motor Company here was biased in their hiring practices and in their treatment of employees and promotions. There were only two black foremen when I went to work there. Through our efforts, thirteen blacks made foreman within four months. Many of them had taken the foreman's test ten years running and were always told they didn't pass. All of a sudden they passed because of the effort of our caucus.

Now I handle the external politics for the union. If anybody runs for any office, from dogcatcher to senator to president of the United States, if they're seeking the Auto Workers' support anywhere in the country, then I am the guy they see. For twenty years I covered Missouri, Kansas, Colorado, and New Mexico. When I was based in St. Louis, part of my responsibility was to lobby in Jeff City for the UAW. I was the first full-time black lobbyist, the only black lobbyist for organized labor in Missouri.

I was also the president of the Association of Black Collegians at Forest Park Community College. The junior colleges, St. Louis University, Washington University, and Fontbonne had ABC chapters. When all of the chapters came together, I headed them. We were very active here in the civil rights movement. We were more militant than some of the other organizations. We were responsible for Forest Park Community College getting its first black president. We opened up student loans to black students in a way that they had never been open before. The board of trustees of the College District made money available for student loans administered by the Black Collegians.

I also did some stuff out at the Tandy Area Council on Grand and Hebert. In the sixties the Teamsters and the Auto Workers administered a program there for the community. Around the time of the Watts riots in California, the Alliance for Labor Action put $250,000 into Watts and $50,000 into Tandy. I volunteered at Tandy in the evening when I got off work. We organized tenants in slum properties, formed tenant organizations, helped them open escrow accounts and negotiate with the owners of the property with a list of things that needed to be repaired. As the owners made the repairs we released the money until the list was clean. If they did not do that, we shut the property down and moved those families.

I came to St. Louis in 1966, and I've seen this community go backwards. A number of areas on the north side were nice areas when I came here, and look at them now. It looks like the Vietnam War. Black men and women who become successful ought to stay in these communities and set an example, show young people that you don't have to be Michael Jordan, or the kingpin drug dealer, to live a decent life. When drugs take over a black community it's because black men have abdicated their responsibility. We have not demanded enough of our local elected officials. We should be more inquisitive about how our aldermen vote, how the process works, because we're not getting anything from it. From ward to ward on the north side, you see a lack of adequate housing, a lack of black business, a lack of jobs.

The answer to the plight of black folks is a variety of things. Education is important. Jobs that my generation were able to do without an education are not available to young folks today, so they better get an education. And they have to develop a sense of community. We're going to have to stay and build these communities with our own hands. We're going to have to start to love each other, and we really don't now.

Charles Mischeaux

Vice President, Boatmen's National Bank of St. Louis; Member, St. Louis City Board
of Police Commissioners; President, St. Louis Chapter of the NAACP

I grew up in St. Louis, down on Whittier and Evans. My parents are both native St. Louisans, and I have one brother and two sisters. I went to Riddick School at the corner of Whittier and Evans, only a block from my home. All the schools were segregated at that time, but it was a good school. I went to Vashon High School for three and a half years, and then I graduated from Sumner. The teachers at Sumner did not appreciate the fact that they caught me gambling at school, so they had me transfer to Vashon.

But I have always been fascinated with money. I have worked all my life. I had a job of some sort from the time I was ten years old. I worked on a paper truck while I went to grade school. I worked on the paper truck from the time I was ten years old until I was thirteen or fourteen years old. Then I graduated to working in a grocery store. I worked at the Arrow Supermarket on the corner of Page and Prairie, right across the street from where we had moved. It was owned by two Jewish brothers. I ran the cash register, and then when I turned sixteen I drove the truck. I delivered meat to other small stores in South St. Louis. That was an experience in itself, because at that time the kids over there did not like to see an African American kid carrying the meat into their little stores. But I carried a long knife to cut the meat, so I knew I wasn't going to have a problem with them. So I worked behind the meat counter, and I worked as cashier.

I did that up until my senior year. I graduated from Vashon High School in 1954, and I left there and went into the air force. I was an air force policeman, stationed out in Las Vegas for four years. I loved it. I had never been out of St. Louis, except to Chicago, and then I hit a town as fast as Las Vegas. I worked on the town patrol, which meant I worked out of the Las Vegas Police Department, for two of those four years. I was fascinated with money and gambling, so I thought I had died and gone to heaven. After I got out of the service, I stayed in Vegas for a year, working a construction job during the day and at the Stardust Hotel at night, to save up some money.

Then I came back to St. Louis and thought I'd get a job with the St. Louis Police Department. That was 1959, and I ran into racism and politics. I had graduated from the Senior Investigating Police School in San Antonio, Texas. I had a letter of commendation I had gotten in the service, and I had a

letter from the chief of police from the Las Vegas Police Department. And I went to the St. Louis Police Department and filled out an application and everything, and they said that my weight was not what it should be for my height. I found out later that blacks did not get on the police department unless they were recommended by one of the political people at that time, like Jordan Chambers.

I started at Brentwood Bank out in Brentwood, Missouri. And eventually I moved up to the title of purchasing agent for the ABC Banks. I had an office, and I had a desk, had my name on it. I'm talking about the sixties, I guess about '63. Salesmen would stop at the receptionist's desk and want to talk to the bank's purchasing agent. She'd say, "That's Charles Mischeaux. His office is located here." And I would be sitting behind the desk doing my work, and the white salesman would come in, and he would say, "Excuse me, do you know where I could find Charles Mischeaux?" And I'm sitting there, behind the desk, with my name on that desk. They did not believe that I was the purchasing agent. Nobody else was in that office except me, sitting there with my suit and tie on, and nobody thought I was the purchasing agent for the ABC Banks.

I thought I would never be appointed to the Board of Police Commissioners because of my involvement with the NAACP. Governor Ashcroft must have felt differently, because I received a phone call from one of his staff people who asked if I was still interested in becoming a police commissioner. He said my name had come up about becoming a police commissioner. I told him I was interested, but I would have to check with the bank first, because it takes a lot of time. The bank said they would support me. They supported me when I became president of the NAACP. They said they thought it would be great for me, and be great for the city, and be great for the bank. So I told the governor's staff, yes, I was interested. I received another call a week later telling me that the governor was going to appoint me. And that was in '92.

When I was twenty-three years old I had five kids. If anyone does that, they're crazy. Young people have to stay in school. They have to try to be leaders and not succumb to peer pressure. They can only live for themselves. People should enjoy their life and try to help others on the way.

Percy Green II

Director, Minority and Women Owned Business
Certification Program, City of St. Louis

I grew up here in St. Louis, on the near south side, better known as Compton Hill. The home that I was raised in was at 3402 LaSalle. I was from a two-parent family, and my father worked at Independent Packing Company until he retired in about 1960 something. My mother was a housewife, and my father took pride in the fact that he was the breadwinner and provider. My father was a hard worker. He had a very big influence on me as far as work and the work ethic and taking pride in my work.

I have a brother and two sisters, and I am the oldest. We were all raised up in the neighborhood there, and we all finished high school at Vashon. I started in 1950 and finished in 1954.

After being out of school for some time, I received a Danforth Fellowship, and I started at St. Louis University in 1970 and finished in 1974 with a bachelor of arts degree in urban affairs. Afterwards, I went to the Washington University School of Social Work and received an M.S.W. in 1976.

I got involved in civil rights after working at McDonnell Douglas for eight years. I was doing an excellent job from all indications from my reviews, and then of course, after my involvement at the Gateway Arch, I was terminated. In 1964 I climbed the Gateway Arch to draw attention to the fact that government funds were being used to erect the Arch, yet they had no minorities involved in the construction. They didn't have any black contractors, and they had very few, if any, black employees.

I was involved with CORE early on, during the Jefferson Bank demonstration. And then, after Jefferson Bank, myself and about twenty-five of the most progressive persons who were in CORE at the time organized ACTION, a more direct action protest group. Direct action protest meant that we would initiate action upon a moment's notice. I mean, we turned protesting into an art form. We were effective because we could organize protests quickly and then dramatize why we were protesting.

One of the bigger major protests that I remember was called Stop and Think. It was a demonstration where we stalled trucks on some key arteries around McDonnell Douglas, to paralyze the production of the company, in protest of their racially discriminatory practices in employment.

Another major demonstration was the unveiling of the white Veiled Prophet in 1972, revealing that he was Tom K. Smith, a vice president at Monsanto. The unveiling was to emphasize that the Veiled Prophet Ball was a racist affair that excluded all black and most white St. Louisans, and it was always held at Kiel Auditorium, which was paid for by St. Louis taxpayers. The same fat cats who sponsored the VP Ball practiced racial discrimination in their individual firms.

I have been involved in protesting organized religion, racism in the Catholic Church, the Episcopal Church, the Lutheran Synod. We protested racism in the synagogues. We went on to protest big businesses such as McDonnell Douglas, Southwestern Bell, Laclede Gas, Union Electric. You name any of the other big companies that are important, and we were involved in some form of protest. And the thesis of our protest at that time was more and better-paying jobs for black men. We emphasized black men because the white power structure never wants to recognize black men when it comes to employment. They would rather address their employment of black women.

I think that young people need to be aware of what is happening around them. They need to develop a real thirst for knowledge. And then, of course, they need to challenge authority. You need to challenge authority to gain insight. In other words, do not accept anything just because it has been stated by an authority figure. Authority figures must earn the respect of those they are directing. And the respect will be earned when those who are being directed challenge the director. But that needs to be done in a diplomatic way. It needs to be done in a way so that both can gain from the experience.

Wayman F. Smith III

Vice President, Anheuser-Busch Companies, Inc.;
President, St. Louis City Board of Police Commissioners

I grew up in North St. Louis. We lived on Northland, close to Marcus, and then we moved to Wabada and Kingshighway when I was about fourteen. I went to all the elementary schools in that neighborhood: Washington Elementary School, Cote Brilliante Elementary School, and Cupples Elementary School. I went to Sumner High School for a year and a half, and I graduated from Soldan High School.

My mother and father are both from St. Louis. My father, Wayman F. Smith Jr., was the first black certified public accountant in the state of Missouri. He served on the St. Louis City Planning Commission and then on the St. Louis Board of Aldermen for twelve years. He was active in the Boy Scouts, and he taught at Lincoln University in Jefferson City. My mother, Edythe Smith, is a journalist. She graduated from the University of Southern California. She served as deputy director of the St. Louis Council on Human Relations. She had three children. I'm the oldest. My brother, Christopher, is a lawyer and former judge. And my sister, Robin, has been in television for around twenty-five years. I'm very proud of her. She was a journalism major like my mother.

When I graduated from Howard Law School, I went to work for Peat, Marwick, and Mitchell, one of the largest certified public accounting firms in the world. Then in 1966 I became director of conciliation for the Missouri Human Rights Commission in Jefferson City. I stayed there for two years, and I developed a specialty in civil rights law. I came back to St. Louis and opened a law practice and took over my father's business right after he died, in January of 1969. That same year Al Fleishman of Fleishman-Hillard asked me to take on Anheuser-Busch as a civil rights law client. From 1969 until 1980 I represented Anheuser-Busch as an outside lawyer, and then in 1980 I gave up my practice and became a vice president and member of the board of directors of the beer company. At the same time I was involved in public service as a judge of the St. Louis Municipal Court and from 1975 until 1987 as alderman for the Twenty-sixth Ward, Bill Clay's old ward.

I came through at a particularly interesting time. My father owned the Adams Hotel, and I met Roy Campanella there, Jackie Robinson, and Larry Doby, the first black ballplayer in the American League. I just loved to go there and meet those guys. Jackie Robinson broke into the major leagues in 1948, and the rest of those guys, Larry Doby and all of them, came in in '49 and '50. But they couldn't stay at the same hotel as the rest of their team until the public accommodations law passed in 1961.

When I was in college, I picketed for an opportunity to eat at White Castle and at Howard Johnson's on Kingshighway. But as a kid, my parents didn't take me to places where we weren't welcome. We went to White's Cafeteria, a black cafeteria that had great food. Or, if it was a special occasion, we went to Fred Harvey's in Union Station, or Fred Harvey's at the airport. My parents knew where we were accepted. And I went to the neighborhood school. The fact that it was all black didn't faze me. I'm not even sure that I recognized what segregation was all about—I mean we just didn't deal with it. I knew what my neighborhood was like, but that wasn't a bad thing. I thought it was a good thing. Sumner High School had some of the finest teachers in the whole state. I was very happy.

Then *Brown v. Board of Education* was decided in 1954, when I was fourteen years old, and when they integrated the schools I went to Soldan High School. I became involved with the National Conference of Christians and Jews at Washington University, where students came together and we got to be friends. For the most part, integration went smoothly. So when I was old enough to meet up with segregation, it was on its way out. The schools integrated in '55, public accommodations in the city integrated in '61, and all public accommodations in the country integrated in '64. There is still discrimination, but by the time I was fifteen, segregation was on its way out. Those were tumultuous times. There were the Freedom Rides, there were the bombings in Mississippi. There were the voter registration crusades in the South. And there was the March on Washington in 1963. I was there. I heard Dr. Martin Luther King give his "I Have a Dream" speech. It really was an exciting time.

I was the first black that Peat, Marwick, and Mitchell hired. And I give all the credit to those people who came before us, who really opened the doors, who fought and died and made it happen. That's why I'm impatient with people who don't vote, who don't think about the blood that was shed in order for us to have that right. Percy Green climbed the Arch and chained himself to the doors of certain businesses in order that we could have jobs. I'm one of the people who benefited from that.

Someday it will be possible for Missouri to have a black governor. A few years ago a black man, Alan Wheat, ran for the United States Senate from Missouri. I didn't think that was possible. Now I think if we have an African American who has the ability to transcend racial lines, it's possible for such an African American to become governor of Missouri.

James H. Buford

President and CEO, Urban League of Metropolitan St. Louis

When I completed college I went into sales for the Smith, Kline, and French Laboratories and for Warner-Lambert. Like most young men, I wanted to make a lot of money. After about four or five years I decided that it was financially rewarding, but that I was going nowhere vocation-wise. So I took a position with St. Louis Community College running a high school dropout education program.

Then in 1979 I moved to Washington, D.C., to work for Senator Howard Baker on his presidential campaign. When he withdrew from the race I went to work for the Republican National Committee scheduling appearances for endorsers of Ronald Reagan. I was an advance man, assigned to certain surrogates. One of the surrogates or endorsers of Reagan was Reverend Ralph Abernathy, Dr. Martin Luther King's number-two person. I coordinated the movement of Dr. Abernathy for ninety days during the Reagan campaign for the presidency. During that period, I lived with him and his daughter, hotel to hotel, as we went from city to city. I spent three or four nights a week in hotel rooms with him, listening to the stories, the inside stories, of the man who was with Dr. King on every event and who was his best friend. It gave me a lot of insight into what really happened, how things really worked, how unorganized the movement really was, but how it seemed to be so focused, and more important, what significance that movement was to black people, both then and now and in the future.

I sat there and listened to what had happened when I was in the prime of my life, when I didn't do anything about it. At the time that I was growing up, in my adolescence, when I was getting ready to enter college, graduating from high school in 1962, that was right in the middle of the civil rights movement, and it passed me by. I did not participate. And the reason that I am here, president of one of the oldest and most respected civil rights organizations, is because I swore that if ever given the opportunity, I would participate and I would make a difference. I did go to Forsyth County, Georgia, on that march when Hosea Williams was attacked. I did participate in the second march in recognition of the March on Washington. And I went to the Million Man March. Any opportunity like that that I am afforded, I am going to participate.

But the important thing is not marches, it's the movement. So I've tried to make the Urban League more aggressive. I've tried to be more visible, to speak to more issues. I cochaired the African American Jewish Dialogue. I founded the St. Louis Black Leadership Round Table. I cochaired the Civic Progress Dialogue. I'm in the coalition with the Anti-Defamation League and the Urban League. I try to act through the Urban League to create programs and to be an advocate for black people. I guess my reason for being in this line of work is Reverend Ralph Abernathy's influence on me, what he did with his life. What he contributed in the prime of his life and the assistance he gave to Dr. King was an inspiration to me. If I could do something with my life like that, I would. And I have tried to.

You must live your life so that you are comfortable with yourself. You must live your life to a standard so that, in the dark room when you have no one with you but your thoughts, you're proud of who you are as an individual, so that you've lived your life the best way you could, and you've treated others the way you would like to be treated. And whatever your vocation in life, whatever you do, give something back. Whether it be quietly, whether it be visible, whether it be political, leave a legacy. Leave a legacy so that others will say that you were a good man, or a good woman, and you did the best with what you had. As Reverend King said, "If you're a ditchdigger, dig the best ditch. If you're president, be the best president." Live your life so that whatever you've done leaves an example and a legacy for others to follow.

Prince A. Wells III

Professor of Music, Southern Illinois University–Edwardsville

I was born at Peoples Hospital in St. Louis, and I grew up in Brooklyn, Illinois. My parents grew up in Brooklyn, and so did my grandparents. I have hundreds of relatives over there. Brooklyn may have been a stop on the Underground Railroad. White people never lived there because it was just north of the stockyards and surrounded by the railroad switching yards. It was noisy and smelly. Brooklyn has always been an all-black town. It has a school district with only one school: Lovejoy School. But Lovejoy School has two buildings, an elementary school and a high school building. I went all the way through high school at Lovejoy.

I got interested in music because George Hudson was *the* music teacher in the Lovejoy School System. He had a big band that played in the thirties, forties, fifties, even into the eighties. He's in the Jazz Hall of Fame. People like Clark Terry and Ernie Wilkins, all of the big-name jazz people who came out of this area, played with him. He worked with Duke Ellington, Louis Armstrong, Count Basie. He was my grade school music teacher and my high school music teacher.

In the sixth grade we started playing instruments, and I wanted to play the trombone. But all the trombones were taken, so George gave me a trumpet. In the seventh grade I started playing in the high school band as third trumpet. There were some really good trumpet players in that band. I played through high school, and, when I graduated, I got my bachelor's degree in music education from Southern Illinois University. Then I got a job teaching at my old high school. So I taught with George Hudson. It was really great. I learned a lot from him. He was interested in the kids, and he had a tremendous amount of talent and experience.

In 1978, I went to the New England Conservatory in Boston and got a master's degree in Afro-American music and trumpet. I received a grant from the National Endowment for the Arts to spend a summer in New York, studying trumpet with Clark Terry. He is one of the musicians who had to leave St. Louis to go on to bigger and better things. There is no market for black musical talent here in St. Louis. There is no recording industry here, no really big entertainment industry. There is no upward mobility for blacks in the music industry in St. Louis.

I played trumpet for Albert King during the summer and fall of 1980. He lives in Brooklyn, and I had heard he was looking for a trumpet player to go with him to Europe. We went to England, Germany, Norway, Finland, Sweden, and Denmark. The people loved Albert. Europeans appreciate jazz and African American music, more than Americans do. That's why so many jazz musicians go to Europe.

When I came back, I thought that with my degrees and experience I could carve a niche for myself in the local music industry. I was pretty good at playing the trumpet and reading music. Places like the Muny and the Fox Theater hire musicians to sit down and read music, but for some reason they don't hire many black people. Millions of dollars are being spent in the entertainment industry in St. Louis, and blacks are pretty much excluded. When the show *The Wiz* came to town, back in 1982, they brought a few key members of the orchestra and they hired ten or fifteen local people to play in the orchestra, but they didn't hire any blacks. An all black show came to town, playing all black music, and they still wouldn't hire any blacks.

David Hines and Vernon Nashville and I did some research on the hiring of musicians in St. Louis. We went to the musicians' union and looked through the records of all the musicians hired, who they were, and how much they got paid. Over a five-year period, out of 7,318 musicians hired here in St. Louis, only 107 were black. That's less than one whole black person for one hundred whites.

Back before integration St. Louis had a white musicians' union and a black musicians' union. The black union was Local 197. In the early seventies, because of the push for integration, unions all across the country began merging. All the major cities had black unions and white unions—Kansas City, New York, Chicago, St. Louis. The St. Louis merger took place starting in 1971. And in the course of merging, over a seven-year period, the new musicians' union came up with an all-white board of directors. The black musicians' union had a building on Delmar, the building was sold, and the profits went to the new merged union, Local 2-197. After 1978 the musicians' union did nothing for blacks.

I don't think racism is the only reason the picture is so bleak for black musicians in St. Louis. There are half a million people in St. Louis, and half of them are black, and for some reason, we haven't put anything together. We take a passive attitude. But nobody else is going to do it for us.

We started the Black Music Society in 1984. We hire local talent to put on the Park Concert Series in the summer and educational programs in the schools. Our primary goal is to provide employment and artistic opportunities for black musicians and to promote black America's musical heritage.

Hazel E. Hunter

Pharmacist, Department of Nuclear Medicine,
Mallinckrodt Chemical Company; Gospel Singer

I grew up here in St. Louis, around 4200 Cook. My father is from Jackson, Mississippi; my mother is from Mexico, Missouri; and they met in St. Louis. They had ten children—seven girls and three boys. My youngest sister and my youngest brother passed. My oldest brother lives in Jackson, Mississippi. My other brother lives in Colorado. All the rest of the girls are here in St. Louis.

I attended Riddick Elementary School and then Cote Brilliante. My high school was Vashon. I lived in the Sumner area, but my brothers and sisters had attended Vashon, so I wanted to go to the same high school. I had great high school years. I was interested in science, especially chemistry. Mrs. Fitzgerald, my chemistry teacher, talked me into going into pharmacy. I loved working on experiments, math, and that kind of thing, and that's why she suggested that I go into pharmacy. I really loved the labs. I was on the quiet side. With a house full of children, you know, somebody had to be.

After high school, I went for two years to Harris-Stowe. My sister, who is two years older than I am, was at Washington University, and my father couldn't afford to send both of us to a private college at the same time. From Harris I went to the St. Louis College of Pharmacy.

When I was in pharmacy school, I did my apprenticeship at Jerry Rhodes Pharmacy. After I married I got a position at Mallinckrodt Chemical Company. They put me in the nuclear medicine division where I'm making radioactive drugs. That's where I am now. I enjoy my work. Nuclear medicine is challenging.

If I hadn't made a success in pharmacy, music was going to be my career. When I was in school, I sang at the Pleasant Green Baptist Church. I didn't take music lessons. I just sang in the choir. Then my father formed a group called the Seven Wrice Sisters, and I was the lead singer. Ronald Metcalf used to play for me. He's in New York now. He really encouraged me. He pushed me to go as far as I've gone. I enjoy singing. The Lord blessed me with a gift.

Now I sing in the New Sunnymount Baptist Church choir. We travel during the summer months when the teenagers are out of school. We've made some great trips to Detroit, Cleveland, New York. We took an eastern tour and a southern tour, too. We've gone to Tennessee and Kentucky and Atlanta. I also sing with the St. Louis in Unison Choir. It's part of the St. Louis Symphony. Robert Ray is the conductor. I have sung with him for four years. I made recordings with the symphony and with the Dello Thedford Symphonic Choir.

But performing at Carnegie Hall in New York was the experience I'll never forget. I knew Leontyne Price, Marian Anderson, and other great artists had performed at Carnegie Hall, and that just added to the feeling. When I got there, and I got up on the stage, I thought, "Wow!" The feeling was more awesome than in any other great hall or auditorium, anywhere.

Being born and raised in St. Louis was not as tough as it was in some of the southern states. But there is still a racial division in this city. For the life of me, during the twentieth century, with more being available to blacks, I don't know why we still want to be grouped up together, segregated. We should be more intertwined with each other. Race relations have improved, and they could improve more. But from my young days until now, I can see that things have improved.

We lived in University City when our children were growing up. We wanted to make sure our children got the best education. As the Jews left U. City, and went to Creve Coeur, we followed. And from Creve Coeur we went to Chesterfield, because we didn't want our children to have to be bused to get a good education. We wanted to live in a community where they would automatically get a good education.

I have three daughters, and they all sing gospel. My youngest daughter is married and lives in Detroit. My middle daughter works at Mallinckrodt, and she has two girls. My oldest daughter has two boys and works for Vitek, which is a chemical company. They didn't go into pharmacy, but they are chemists.

A deacon in my church has twin daughters, and those twins wrote a paper about my background in pharmacy. They want to do the same thing when they grow up. They just finished college, and now they're in Atlanta in pharmacy school. You never know when you might influence someone to follow in your footsteps. Sometimes your life is the only book that some people read. People should stay in school, get as much education as they can. Being African Americans, more is expected of us. In order to make it, we have to go that extra mile.

Jean Patterson Neal

Chief Executive Officer, Annie Malone
Children and Family Service Center

I grew up in Greenwood, Mississippi. We were poor, very poor. My father died before I was born, and I was raised by a single parent. My mother was a great lady. She had a limited education, but she was very intelligent. She would discuss politics when I was a kid. My mother was inspiring. She was my greatest mentor. She never put parameters on what I could do or what I could be. She never let me think in terms of segregation or racism or that I was not capable. I think that's what we need to convey to our own kids.

I have a brother, and we have a lot of foster brothers and sisters. In Mississippi there was no such thing as an Annie Malone Children's Home, so homeless children just moved in with somebody else. There were a number of children who moved in with us. It was an interesting childhood. I grew up during the Emmett Till times, during the time of segregation. We had separate schools and the whole bit. I remember teachers who were very nurturing and who gave us the best that we could have with the limited resources that they had. I remember the church was a significant part of my social life. Everybody kind of raised you in Mississippi, the principal of the school, your mother. And your pastor became your father figure if you didn't have a father.

I worked for the United Way, and Annie Malone Children and Family Service Center, formerly Annie Malone Children's Home, was one of the agencies that I worked with. I'm familiar with all of the residential agencies and family service agencies that are traditional members of the United Way and with community agencies like Grace Hill and United Neighborhood Houses. When there was an opening at Annie Malone Children and Family Services, I was encouraged to apply. In the interview they asked me what I thought about Annie Malone and what I thought I could do for Annie Malone. I knew that Annie Malone had excellent services and its tradition and history was very rich, but I felt it was not taking advantage of all the financial opportunities available. It operated very meagerly. I had been introduced to the resources that were out there by being part of the United Way, and I felt that I could lead the organization in a broader way.

My contribution to the St. Louis community and to civil rights has been that when I'm part of something, if it's predominantly white and I'm the only African American, I take it as my responsibility to ask that we open up the process to other people, so that we can benefit from diversity. My approach to civil rights has not been by demonstrating, but by challenging groups to be inclusive. I try to sensitize people to the value of being open and inclusive. So no matter what I'm a part of, if it is not an open process, then I challenge it.

I challenged one major institution regarding their promotion and equal-pay policy. Through a negotiated settlement, many policies and procedures were changed. I discovered, at that time, that individuals were afraid of the possible consequences if they supported me. But God and my family were my support system. And since then it has been gratifying to see an African American male and an African American female in leadership positions there. As a matter of fact, many African Americans have significant input in the policies of that organization now.

We need to understand our history; others need to understand our history and our contribution to this country. People need to appreciate our struggles and acknowledge our strength. We have gone to all of the wars. We have been inventors and scientists. There are a lot of things that we have done to benefit this country. We should be proud to be who we are.

I think that there has been progress in race relations, but the St. Louis community has a long way to go before we can all come to the table as equals. I don't mean that we all have to have Ph.D.s, or we all have to be rich or poor. But when there are matters of similar concern, we need to come together as equals. We're always going to see race in terms of color, but I hope it's not defining. We must not define a person simply by race, but by what they have to offer. Young people represent our hope. And what I would like to say to them is, don't let anyone tell you what you can't be or what you can't do. Be the best at whatever you want to be. We still have a long way to go.

Sherman George

Deputy Chief, St. Louis Fire Department

I was born in New Madrid, Missouri, and I came to St. Louis when I was six years old. I grew up on North Market and Taylor. We started at 4534 North Market, and then we moved across the street to 4521 North Market. I have seven brothers and four sisters. One brother is a battalion chief in the St. Louis Fire Department.

I attended Holy Ghost Catholic Grade School, which was across the street from where I lived. For high school, I attended Sumner for two years, and then I graduated from O'Fallon High School in 1962.

In high school the only thing that was on my mind was to get through school and get a job. At one time, I wanted to quit school. Of course, my mother told me that if I quit school, she was going to kill me. I remember my brothers and me sneaking out of the house on Sunday, around three or four in the morning, to sell newspapers. My mother didn't want us to do it. She was afraid of robbers and stuff like that. So we sneaked out of the house. After a while, she let us sell newspapers, and the three of us sold a lot of newspapers. A guy named Hubert had a little shack on Cora and Easton Avenue (now Martin Luther King), and he let us get our papers first, because he knew we were going to sell a lot of papers and we weren't going to come up missing any money. We sold a lot of newspapers and got a lot of Christmas presents. We thought that was great.

I lived on North Market until I was out of high school. Then we moved to Pendleton, and then I was drafted into the United States Army. After the army, I used some of my GI benefits to go to college. I went to Forest Park Community College. Instructors came down from Central Missouri State University to teach at Forest Park Community College, and I acquired my bachelor's degree through Central Missouri State University, right here in St. Louis. In 1993, I received a three-week fellowship to the Harvard University School of Government.

At one point I was the youngest fire captain in the St. Louis Fire Department. I was assigned downtown for about a year and a half, and then I transferred to Kennerly and Whittier, Engine Company No. 10. That was an outstanding position. I was in a neighborhood where I could help my people. Then in April 1985 I was assigned to the Fire Academy. In 1987 I became the first black chief instructor in the history of the St. Louis Fire Department, in charge of all training programs for the entire fire department, new recruits and all. There is a row of pictures hanging at the Fire Academy, and I'm the only black in that row of pictures, since 1857. We have had a paid fire department since 1857, and I was the first black chief instructor. I am pretty proud of that.

After that I was promoted to battalion chief and moved to District 1, which covers the Homer G. Phillips area and downtown. I requested that because I thought it was a challenge. On September 10, 1990, I was promoted to deputy fire chief. We have four deputies, and right now I'm shift commander for C shift. Stanley is commander for A shift; Schaper is commander for B shift. We are in charge of the day-to-day operations of the St. Louis Fire Department, unless the chief comes out, and then he's in charge.

It's an awesome responsibility. When one firefighter dies in a fire, sometimes three or four die. I know in Boston, one year, in a church fire they lost twelve. Usually we are working in pairs, so if something happens, I could possibly lose more than one firefighter. That's the bad thing about that. But that's my responsibility. When I go to the scene, I've got to make sure that everybody goes home. I've got to let them be aggressive to fight the fire, but at the same time I've got to decide when the building's integrity is a problem. If something happens, I've got to live with it. It takes a lot of experience and book knowledge. And you never have it all. You never have it all.

The St. Louis Fire Department has changed over the years. We have made progress in getting blacks in at the entry level and getting them promoted. However, there is always a steady fight for equality. Sometimes we're told that racism doesn't exist anymore. But I've seen the double standards that are set for blacks and whites. They still exist, and there is not a thing that I can do about it, except to say that I think it's wrong. We have some educated black men on this job, and some dedicated men. All they want is an equal opportunity. They don't need a leg up, they just need an equal chance.

My advice to young people is to be your own leader—don't let other people lead you into trouble. I grew up in a neighborhood where I knew a lot of guys who went to jail and some who got killed. I managed to make the right choices. If you think something is wrong, then it's probably wrong, so don't do it. You're not responsible for what anybody else does. But be responsible for whatever *you* do. Be your own leader. Don't be led.

Michael V. Roberts

Owner, Roberts Broadcasting Companies,
WHSL-TV, Channel 46, the Home Shopping Network

I am a third-generation St. Louisan. My parents were both educated here in the public schools. My father worked at the post office for thirty-nine years, and my mother raised us. As a side business my parents were caterers, and I can remember as a little boy doing things to help. I have a brother Steven, a brother Mark, and a sister, Lorie. I went to Cupples and Scullin Elementary Schools and Beaumont and Northwest High Schools. I graduated in 1967 and attended Central Missouri State College for a year. Then I went to St. Louis Community College at Forest Park, where I played a number of sports and was elected to the student council. I was the state champion in tennis and went to the national tennis tournament in Florida.

I went to Lindenwood College in St. Charles for my last two years of college, during the time it was changing from a women's college to include men. That was in 1969. I thought of majoring in music, because I played the trombone—I played a lot of jazz. But it didn't take me long to figure out that life as a tennis player or trombone player would not get me where I wanted to go. Lindenwood had a nice communication arts program. They owned an AM and an FM radio station, and the program provided internships, in my case at KMOX-TV. I learned about production, and I actually had my own radio show. During the late sixties I had my Afro and I was into Black Power. I was a member of ABC, the Association of Black Collegians, at Forest Park Community College, and I organized a chapter of ABC at Lindenwood.

I ended up with a Danforth Foundation Fellowship to St. Louis University Law School, and I decided to take a shot at politics. In 1981 Steve and I were operating a consulting firm and we were very active in the community, we were both on the Board of Aldermen, when the FCC established preferential treatment for minorities in the licensing of radio and television stations. Steve and I decided to apply for a license. Steve had done radio shows when he was at Clark College in Wooster, Massachusetts, so we both had experience in communications. We knew the importance of taking risks. We raised some money, and we took the shot. It took us eight years to get our license, but we finally succeeded because we were local and we were integrating ownership with management.

The Home Shopping Network was developing a network of TV stations, and they wanted to come to big cities like St. Louis. St. Louis is the eighteenth largest market in the country, and it was cities like St. Louis they wanted to have affiliations

in. So we ended up affiliated with them. They financed our station. We were at the right place at the right time.

My brother and I own the old Sears building at 1408 North Kingshighway. It is two hundred thousand square feet of offices, retail shops, and a warehouse, right in the middle of the black community. Sears built it as a department store in two sections, one in the 1920s and one in the 1930s. Sears moved out in the sixties, or middle seventies, and we bought the building in 1982. We did major renovations on it, dividing it into offices and shops, and now we have about forty or fifty tenants. We have several schools for unemployed and undereducated citizens. Here they can get their high school diplomas. They can learn hair care. They can learn carpentry. We have the NAACP office in our building, we house the Police Ethical Society, we have the Top Ladies of Distinction national corporate office. We have a men's clothing store, we have a lady's store, we have cosmetics stores, we have the Junior Achievement offices, and we have an HDC office in here. So obviously it is a diverse building. We sold some land to Aldi Incorporated, and they opened a grocery store in 1991. And we have about ten acres of land that we plan to build on eventually, expanding into a broader shopping center.

Roberts Broadcasting owns its own tower. Our tower is one hundred feet taller than any other TV station in the market. We broadcast at least ten miles further than Channel 4, Channel 5, or Channel 2. We are kicking a signal that goes out past Mount Vernon, Illinois, down to Rolla, Missouri, and up towards Hannibal, Missouri. We have this huge radius of signal that surpasses anybody else in the market, and nobody knows it. Most people think we have a little ham radio, or they think it is cable TV, or they think we are only broadcasting in North St. Louis.

Some people do not want to believe that black people can do a multimillion-dollar business in their own community. People asked, "What are you doing spending three or four million dollars in North St. Louis? You should be building in Clayton." And I said to them, "It is seldom that a politician can put his money where his mouth has been, and that is what I am doing." Why can't I put it in my own community? From my office I can see the Arch. But most influential, intelligent, black people live out in West County. We have lost the potential from our public schools. And it is our poor black kids who are suffering. I feel the one failure that I face right now is finding a way to help kids in the public schools. That is something I feel terrible about, I really do.

Steven C. Roberts

Owner, Roberts Broadcasting Companies,
WHSL-TV, Channel 46, the Home Shopping Network

I spent my first five years in the Ville. It was a nice neighborhood. There was always family around. I have two brothers and a sister, and my three cousins, my father's sister's children, lived over us. We could walk to the stores around the corner. I remember walking to the store by myself. Actually, there were two stores, a confectionery on Page and Walton and a larger supermarket at Page and Euclid. The confectionery was fairly small and black-owned. The larger store was Jewish-owned. Jewish merchants often owned stores in the black community.

We moved to a new house in 1958 in one of the first subdivisions which was not segregated. It was near Natural Bridge and Kingshighway, on San Francisco Court. It was an interesting experience to go from an all-black community to being the only blacks in a white community. We went to a new school where we didn't know anyone. The teachers and the parents were prejudiced, but our parents taught us to overlook the fact that there were people who didn't like us.

I remember, when I was about seven, we had a big yard and the kids in the neighborhood would come over to our yard to play. There were some little white boys who lived behind us in a four-family flat, and one time the father of one boy called him over to the fence. And the little boy came back to me and said, "I can't play with you because you're a nigger." I didn't know what a nigger was. So I went and asked my mother. And my mother said, "Well, he called you a bad name, and he doesn't want to play with you. You can go through life without having to associate with him anymore." And I don't remember ever playing with him again.

There was significant white flight out of our middle-class neighborhood. During first and second grade Scullin School was predominantly white. By the third grade my class was 50 percent black. Then my brother Mike and I went to Northwest High School. Northwest was another integration experience. When Mike went there, it was probably 10 percent black. He had some difficult times, because it was the first new school in northwest St. Louis. By the time I went there, the racial fights had subsided, but there was still tension. When I graduated, it was probably about 30 or 40 percent black. And two or three years later, when I came from college to recruit there, it was 90 percent black. My life's experience has been to go to a place and the white folks leave.

So that was my childhood. If the color of my skin had not been a factor, it would have been an idyllic childhood. But living in a city which was going through social change put a damper on it. However, I think it was probably a typical black childhood for the time.

Growing up, I had a lot of heroes: ministers, coaches, and people who were good neighborhood folks. I remember Robert Trace, the president of Mathews-Dickey Boys' Club. He and Mr. Mathews and Dickey Ballentine founded it together. I was on the first basketball team, the second football team, and probably the third or fourth baseball team, back when the Boys' Club was operating out of somebody's house. People like Mr. Trace and others had regular jobs and spent the other part of their lives working with young people or working as presidents of their block units. People gave unselfishly, even though they had four or five or six kids. They got out there and worked in the community.

But my parents were my biggest heroes. They taught us about the world. They did everything they could for the family, saving and scraping. My father was always there. He worked the early shift at the post office. And he played with us. He taught us sports.

I received a doctor of law, with a specialty in urban law, from Washington University Law School. During my last year of law school, I was appointed assistant chief of staff of the St. Louis Board of Aldermen. I prepared legislation and served as a staff liaison to aldermanic committees. It was fascinating. I applied what I'd learned in school as I prepared ordinances. And I worked with the mayor, the comptroller, the aldermen, all the folks I read about in the newspaper. It was fun. I stayed on the staff of the Board of Aldermen for an extra year, after I graduated, and then an alderman was appointed to another position, and the people in his ward ran me for office. I was in the right place at the right time. My brother Mike had been elected to the Board of Aldermen two years before. Imagine, two brothers on a Board of Aldermen of a major U.S. city.

I joined the National Black Caucus of Locally Elected Officials, about five thousand black mayors and council members from around the country. I discovered that problems in St. Louis were similar to problems in Newark or in San Francisco. Black communities across the country are not much different. But St. Louis has a charm about it. Even though it's a major city, people, particularly in the black community, have a connection. I think that is very special. You don't see that in other areas of the country.

Odell E. McGowan

Owner, McDonald's Restaurant Franchises

I was born right here in St. Louis. I lived at 2747 Eugenia. That was in the Mill Creek Area. But the city fathers felt a need to tear those houses down. The industrial parks, between Jefferson and Leffingwell, that's where I once lived.

My mother and father had no formal education. I think one went to the fourth grade, and one went to the fifth or sixth, but they had good common sense. I thought my childhood was great. I had nothing to compare it to. I never heard the word *ghetto* as I was growing up. I just assumed this is the way life should be. I have no regrets, growing up in that area, or in that era for that matter.

I graduated from Lincoln Grade School and went to Vashon in 1954. I graduated from Vashon in 1958. Then I attended the University of Missouri at Columbia, for about one minute and a half. My father was a steel foundry worker, and he tried to provide everything that he possibly could for us. Right after I entered the University of Missouri, my father was laid off, and I had to return to St. Louis. I came back to St. Louis and told that lie that most people tell, "I'm going to get a job, and I'm going to return." I got a job with the post office, and as I got closer to earning enough money to return to school, I saw a need for a car, a need for a stereo, and that kind of thing. So to make a long story short, I finally went back to college in the seventies.

I've had all kinds of jobs. And I always say, you shouldn't give up. I drove a bus for Bi-State for maybe nine months. I worked at Chrysler Motors, and that was an interesting job, but the commuting distance was too far, and I decided to leave. Then I joined the St. Louis City Police Department in 1966. Prior to that I tried to get a job with the Missouri Highway Patrol. At that time they had no blacks, and I was trying to become the first African American in the Highway Patrol. But I joined the St. Louis Police Department, and I had an interesting career with them. I was in the Mercantile Division of the Office of the Chief of Detectives investigating con artists, pigeon drops, and shoplifters in banks and department stores. I also flew in the traffic helicopter with Don Miller.

Then, in 1973, I went with the Treasury Department, in the Criminal Investigation Division of the IRS. I stayed with them from 1973 till 1982. That was a fun job. Every four years, we rotated into an assignment with the Secret Service, because that was our sister agency. We went with them as backup agents. I worked security for Jimmy Carter and Rosalynn Carter. As a matter of fact, I worked security for Jimmy Carter when he came to St. Louis and spoke at the University of Missouri–St. Louis. We always had it laid out, every step of the way, exactly where he would shake hands, work the crowd. If he shifted directions, we kind of panicked, because the crowd would surge forward and we would have to push them back.

I got involved with McDonald's when I was still with the Feds. I met all the big wheels from McDonald's headquarters in Oakbrook, Illinois, on Dr. Davis's boat the day before he officially opened it. Dr. Benjamin Davis, the dentist, was probably the first African American to own a McDonald's Restaurant in St. Louis. He had the riverboat restaurant down on the levee.

I started training at the McDonald's on Lindell in April of 1980. It was strictly hands-on training. I got off work at 4:30, and I reported to McDonald's around 6 P.M. I worked from six until eleven, when the store closed. I learned how to cook the burgers, check the truck, mop the floors, wash the trays, set up the shake machines, slice the onions, and clean the bathrooms. Then I attended two week-long schools here in St. Louis, a third week-long school in Nashville, Tennessee, and then I went to Hamburger U. in Oakbrook for two weeks. I met people from all over the world. It was exciting.

Then in July of 1981 or 1982, my wife and I got our first store, 4150 North Grand. Our first store was already there when we got it. Our second store at 1119 North Tucker was built from scratch. I worked on the design of that store. Then, on July 1, 1991, we got our third McDonald's, down on Hall Street, 8891 Hall Street. When we joined McDonald's only three blacks owned McDonald's: Ben Davis, Jamie Rivers, and Jim Perry. Dwight Flowers and Judson McClaren came in when we did. We six were the only black owners until around 1990. McDonald's has a lot of restrictions, but it is an opportunity to be an entrepreneur.

To be a real entrepreneur you have to care about the community, you have to have an interest in the community. Being successful is not just coming into the community and selling. At our McDonald's stores we work with our employees, help them with their homework. We've had some real success stories from our staff: two brothers who started with us in 1982 are with the St. Louis Fire Department, there's an engineer, a police officer, a guy with the Highway Patrol, a woman who's getting a degree in psychology, and another woman with the St. Louis Public Schools who is getting a Ph.D. You have to have a commitment to the community. You have to want to give something back.

Doris Moore Glenn

Educator, Harris-Stowe State College;
Vice President, William L. Clay Scholarship Fund

I grew up in St. Louis, in the Ville. I attended Marshall Elementary School, Sumner High School, and Stowe Teachers College, which later became part of Harris-Stowe Teachers College. My father was a steelworker, and he owned a couple of cabs. That helped us maintain a fairly decent standard of living. My mother worked for a year or two at the small-arms plant on Goodfellow, during the war. That's the only time I remember her working. It wasn't because we didn't need the money. But that was a different era. Women who had children just didn't work.

I remember going to the Woolworth's ten-cent store on Sixth and Washington as a child. They had the best hotdogs in the world. They had a counter for whites and a separate counter for African Americans. The white people had seats at their counter, and the black people stood. One day my mother said, "We are not going to do this anymore. No, we are not buying another hotdog in here." I remember crying. But it stood out in my mind, and I wanted to do something about the situation. That is why, as a young adult, I became involved with Bill Clay and the picket of White Castle, marching on the picket line with my baby in my arms. Eventually, we were able to get jobs for African Americans at White Castle. Now it's taken for granted that we could always do that. The jobs were not that great, but we should have had the opportunity to have them all along.

I got the best preparation that I could have had by going to Stowe Teachers College. Stowe not only prepared us to teach, but it developed us culturally. It prepared us to live in a civilized world. The teachers were all African Americans who had degrees from prestigious white institutions. But African Americans could not get good jobs in St. Louis, so they ended up teaching. Those teachers were outstanding. They took young people from very simple families and polished them. They taught us how to speak, how to dress. We even had a teacher who insisted that young ladies sit with their knees together. Those teachers were wonderful human beings. Stowe was a fabulous place, and it produced outstanding black teachers.

I graduated from Harris-Stowe and started teaching at Hempstead Elementary School in 1959. It was a challenging experience because the school was badly overcrowded. My first classroom had fifty-three third graders. I learned to control fifty-three third graders in a basement classroom. And

that's how I got into teaching. The next year I taught first grade. The following year I taught seventh- and eighth-grade social studies. I taught a lot of black history, because I wanted to give back to the community what had been given to me. Can you imagine all of that in less than three years? It was quite an experience. I think that experience is what made me a good teacher. Early in my career I was named Outstanding Young Educator.

I went from Hempstead to Harris-Stowe. And I supervised student teachers for the next ten years. I also got master's degrees in urban education and special education.

Then Congressman Clay became chairman of the Post Office and Civil Service Committee in Washington, D.C., and he made me an offer I couldn't refuse. So I moved to Washington to become the deputy staff director for the Committee on Post Offices and Civil Service. When the Republicans abolished that committee, I became a senior legislative associate for the Committee on Education and Labor. Congressman Clay was the ranking member on Education and Labor. I actually developed and wrote legislation. It was probably the most challenging and worthwhile job I ever had. For two years I worked on the bill for senior citizens. Through our work we were able to save many of the programs for senior citizens, such as Meals on Wheels. I know I got a great deal more from that job than I gave. As I walked the halls of Congress all I could think of was, "Maddie and Willie's daughter is walking the marble halls of Congress." I get goosebumps just thinking of it. To be intimately involved with the historical things that I had taught all my life—that was an experience.

African Americans have made great strides. We definitely have a black middle class. But at the same time, we have developed an underclass. That is tragic, and unless we do something about it, that underclass will destroy all of us. That is what we must focus on now. We must help young people achieve what blacks my age have accomplished. That is why I'm so passionate about the William L. Clay Scholarship Fund. I was at the meeting when that scholarship fund began. Now I am the vice president, and it is the passion of my life. We are helping young people who otherwise would not have an opportunity to go to college.

Young people need to set goals. They need to work hard to get to where they want to be. It's up to each one of them to make the best they can of their lives.

Donald M. Suggs

Oral Surgeon; Publisher, *St. Louis American*

I grew up in East Chicago, Indiana, a blue-collar community that lies between Gary, Indiana, and Chicago. My father was born in Terre Haute, Indiana, and my mother was born in Mississippi. My father was a steelworker. Although he only went through the fourth grade, he was an intellectually curious person. My mother went through the eighth grade. I went to public schools and to Indiana University, where I earned a bachelor's degree and a dental degree in 1957. When I left there I had the opportunity to go to graduate school in Philadelphia or to a hospital program in New York City, but I came to St. Louis because I wanted to come to Homer G. Phillips Hospital. I was interested in coming to an all-black institution.

I came to Homer Phillips Hospital in 1959. I was the first black to matriculate as a graduate student at the Washington University School of Dentistry. Then I went into the air force and served as chief of oral surgery at Dover Air Force Base Hospital in Delaware. I came back to St. Louis to teach at Washington University, but when I arrived at Washington University, the dental school decided they didn't want a black person on the faculty. I took a job at Homer Phillips Hospital as an anesthetist to feed my family and started my private practice in oral surgery. In the early years I also worked as an anesthetist in the operating rooms at Homer Phillips, Peoples Hospital, and St. Mary's Infirmary and taught at St. Louis University Dental School. That was in 1962.

I have always been interested in newspapers. I'm a newspaper junkie. My father was an enthusiastic reader of newspapers and there were a number of newspapers available in the Chicago area. In addition to intellectual stimulation, my family gave me a strong sense of social conscience. They taught me that I had an obligation to try to make a contribution to society. That led me to be active in the civil rights movement, and my interest in politics developed after that. I was looking for a way to pursue that interest when an opportunity arose for me to get involved with the *St. Louis American* newspaper. I became a part owner of the *American* in 1981, and in 1986 I bought majority control of the company and became publisher.

The mission of the black press had long been to inform the black community and to serve as an advocate for integration. Before the Supreme Court decision in the early fifties, white newspapers paid very little attention to black businesses, black events, black personalities, black institutions. After that time they steadily increased coverage of the black community and hired a number of blacks in the newsroom. Actually they have

employed many of the more talented black journalists since that time. And now with people depending increasingly on television for news coverage, the newspaper industry has changed considerably. For the black weekly to thrive, we have to find a way to satisfy our readers in this new age of increased coverage of black issues in the white media and the advent of television. Since I became publisher, a goal of the *St. Louis American* has been to be interesting, informative, and entertaining enough to have a large enough readership to attract advertisers.

After I had been publisher for about two years, the paper was not growing as fast as I wanted, so we became a free-distribution newspaper. The *Post-Dispatch* is the only general-interest newspaper in St. Louis that charges. All of the other major newspapers are distributed free. That arrangement enables them to reach more people and thus be more attractive to advertisers.

The dominant print medium in St. Louis is the *Post-Dispatch,* and after that comes formidable competition from some of the forty-plus newspapers of the Suburban Newspapers chain, the *North Side Journal,* the *North County Journal,* the *Clayton Citizen,* the *Central West End Journal.* All these papers claim a large amount of black readership. They are highly organized and have been very successful. The *Riverfront Times* has 20 percent of its circulation among black readers. The rest of our competition comes from other black weeklies. Black radio is also an important competitor, because when advertisers are trying to speak directly to blacks, they are accustomed to reaching them through black radio.

The *St. Louis American* holds a community awards banquet each year, an event we call "A Salute to Excellence." The proceeds from that dinner go to scholarships. In 1988, on the sixtieth anniversary of the newspaper, that awards banquet attracted about six hundred people. Since then banquet attendance has grown to attract over two thousand people. The banquet has featured some of the nation's most prominent speakers.

I was raised by my parents to believe that you ought to be educated first and then undertake meaningful work that makes a contribution to the community. I have tried to instill that in my children. I am grateful to my parents and to the people of this community who have supported me in my endeavors and made it possible for me to have the resources to afford my children broad exposure and varied experiences. I hope my children will return some of that, through public service, to the community.

Patricia and Fredrick McKissack

Authors; Recipients of the Newbery Honor Book Award,
the Caldecott Honor Book Award, and the Coretta Scott King Award

Pat: I lived for a while here in St. Louis; then I moved to Nashville with my mother. In the summers I was back and forth between Nashville and St. Louis. I started at Turner School in Meacham Park, a typical all-black school. It was overcrowded, underfunded, and had no equipment. But, you know, we made it. As kids, we just grabbed ahold of what was there and made the most of it. Consequently, we learned about adversity at a young age, not realizing that we were learning to overcome it. I was one of the first kids to integrate Robinson School in Kirkwood. It was difficult to go from an all-black school to an all-white school. I was the only black child in my sixth-grade class, and that was traumatic. School is much more than just learning. It is also the sense of community, the sense of belonging, playing in the band, singing in the choir. I tried out for cheerleader, and I didn't make it. When you want to be a cheerleader or a writer or a singer, it's subjective. You're never quite good enough. You almost make it, but you never do.

Fred: I was born in Nashville, Tennessee, and that's where I went to school. Nashville was the segregated South. My extended family lived all together on one street. Across from me lived my grandfather and grandmother. On the other side of me was my great-uncle Calvin. Right next door to me was my father's brother. And two doors down from me was Uncle Samuel. My father is an architect. He is still living. His father, my grandfather, was the first registered black architect in the state of Tennessee. He built three thousand buildings throughout the South. My grandmother was an early graduate of Fisk University, and she taught music. This was my neighborhood. I always thought that my father was the most brilliant architect in America. But segregation just overwhelmed my family. If you were a black architect in those days, your didn't design public buildings or become an architect for a large corporation. The only jobs open were the small churches built in the black communities.

Pat: When I graduated from high school in 1961, Fred was coming out of the marine corps, so we entered college at the same time. And that's when the civil rights movement just mushroomed.

Fred: Of course, the civil rights movement was not one day, or not one month. It goes on and on. When the sit-ins started in Nashville, George Parker, a friend who lived four doors up the street, was arrested and put in jail. People began to gather at the First Baptist Church, and my friend Horace Jones and I went too. My first sit-in was at Woolworth's. I did not get arrested, but I will never forget a shotgun being pointed at me at Woolworth's. I will never forget the long marches down to the sits-ins, and then going back to the church to sing songs and wonder at all that was happening.

Pat: My best friend was Carolyn Hardy. Her brother John was on the Freedom Bus in Anniston, Alabama, and he was beaten horribly. John was someone that I knew. He wouldn't harm a flea. He was funny. He's an actor now. The horror that someone would beat someone I knew, for no reason other than hatred, brought the civil rights movement to my front door. When it happened to John, I remember seeing his mom cry. Mrs. Hardy went to work that day, and her boss said to her that she ought to tell her son to stop being involved in this movement. Mrs. Hardy pulled herself tall that day. She told him that she was going to tell her son that she was proud of him, that she was glad he did it, and if she had two or three other sons to commit to the movement she would. And she walked off and left that job.

Fred: Talk of racism takes up much of the time in the black community. Pat and I believe that the way to end it is to shine a light in every corner of it. From Africa across on those boats to the Caribbean, from the Caribbean up to South Carolina to the years in the tobacco fields and cotton fields and sugarcane fields, shine a light on it. A lot of times you don't like what comes out. Few blacks like the idea that in West Africa blacks helped put blacks on those ships. Pat and I believe that if we are going to help end racism, we must accept the truth, and shine a light on it. That is our mission. That is why we write books.

Pat: We want to help those babies who are coming along to be honest and to understand what happened in the past. We do not write only for black children. We write for all children. We want children to learn our stories and our heroes. We are people who have overcome some of the worst possible situations in life. We are survivors.

Freeman Bosley Jr.

Attorney; Mayor, City of St. Louis

I grew up in North St. Louis. Initially I lived at 4824 Luduc, off of Marcus Avenue. I went to Cupples School until I was in the second grade. Then my family moved to the north side, around Fairground Park, to a street called Palm, and I went to Farragut Grade School. And I have lived here ever since. I bought a house two doors from where I grew up, and I live here now with my wife and daughter.

I have one sister, Pamela, who is a year younger than I am. My father was an electronics engineer. He worked at places like Carson Union May Stern when I was little, and then he went into business for himself. He owned Bosley Radio and TV. He had a record shop for a while. He worked for Union Electric, and then for McDonnell Aircraft. And then he ran for public office, and he has been an alderman ever since. My mother was an administrative secretary for Southwestern Bell Telephone and then worked for the U.S. government at ATCOM, out on Goodfellow. She retired about six years ago. She enjoys retirement.

I really enjoyed my childhood. I was a cutup. I liked to hang out with the kids in the neighborhood and spend as much time doing as little homework as possible. I got in trouble a lot. My family had high standards, and I always knew that there was a price to pay for going beyond the limits. My mother let us know what the limits were, and she helped me become a more disciplined person. My grandfather was also a big influence in my life. He taught me to love to recite poetry and give speeches. He was always quick with a poem or a refrain or a story. We tell a lot of stories in this family.

My family got involved in politics around 1970. When we moved into this neighborhood in 1964, it was a neighborhood in transition. The neighborhood was probably 60 percent white and 40 percent black. By the 1970s it was probably 30 percent white and 70 percent black. So we began to think about the political transition, as well.

In 1972 our block unit decided to support Melvin Halston and Geneva Rome for committeeman and committeewoman. I organized all the kids I grew up with who still lived in the neighborhood. We passed out literature and gave out bumper stickers and things like that. Halston and Rome were elected by a landslide in August 1972, and we celebrated. We expected them to support my father for alderman in 1973, but they

double-crossed my father. He had to run against the ward organization. That was our first experience with the political double cross. But my father came back and won the committeemanship in 1974. And then in 1977 he was elected alderman. My dad was elected and reelected, and in 1985 he ran for mayor.

The St. Louis Public Schools are very dear to my heart. I went to Central High School, and then I went to St. Louis University and received undergraduate degrees in political science and urban affairs in 1976. Then I graduated from St. Louis University School of Law. When I graduated from law school in 1979, I went to work for Legal Services, and I came in contact with the office of the circuit clerk. I was disappointed in the way that office was run, the access to the files, and the services that were provided there. I decided I could run for that office, and I could make a difference. It was time to get involved in politics again. I was elected clerk of the Circuit Court in 1982 and reelected in 1984 and in 1986. In 1986 I became the chairman of the City Democratic Committee, and then in 1993 I ran for mayor.

I am very proud of the fact that while I was mayor I was able to pass a three-eighths-cent sales tax, which adds $13 million to the general revenue fund each year, and then I passed a one-half-cent sales tax, which generates $17.5 million for capital improvements each year. Previous mayors had tried for years to pass a tax levy to keep St. Louis from going bankrupt. I built up the city's surplus substantially in three years.

The civil rights movement played a major role in my development and in the development of all black people. Civil rights made it possible for me to go to St. Louis University and St. Louis University Law School, to be elected clerk of the Circuit Court, and to be the first African American mayor of this community. We elected Bill Clay the first African American congressman from Missouri, back in 1968. We elected an African American comptroller, an African American Circuit Court clerk, and then we elected the first African American mayor. We have made great strides.

St. Louis is a racially polarized community. And we can do better. We need to do more than just go to work every day and do our jobs. We must see what else we can do to improve the quality of life in this community. St. Louis is a great city. I love it. I have dedicated my life to it, and I will continue to do that.

George Sams

Musician; Educator; Consultant

I grew up in a couple of places, but I spent my formative years here, in St. Louis. My father was in the military, and we were what are referred to as "army brats." We migrated to St. Louis because this is my mother's home. I started second grade at Turner School, which is now known as Turner Middle School.

I started playing a horn before I got to high school. I played the bugle in the American Woodmen Drum and Bugle Corps, which was sponsored by the Tom Powell Post of the American Legion. By the time I got to Sumner High School I had set my sights on music, and there was a natural transition to the trumpet. I played the trumpet in the band at Sumner, and then when I was transferred to Beaumont High School I did not join the band, but I continued to play the trumpet with little basement and garage bands. I worked in little blues clubs in East St. Louis at night. It gave my mother fits, so I had to sneak over there. During my high school years I was running around with a lot of the professional musicians here in the city, people like Jerome Harris, the percussionist; Oliver Lake; Julius Hemphill; Willie Thompson; Bobby Danzer; and a trumpet player who had a great impact on me, Rozwell Darby.

At age nineteen I went on the road with the band, and then I stayed gone. I was a professional trumpet player, and I was fortunate to always keep my own band. At the time that my sails were getting wind in them, I was not willing to sit and wait for someone to call and offer me some work. I was lucky. I got some recordings made, and promoters in Europe liked them. So I did some European tours. I lived in Europe for a year after an extended tour over there. I did tours through the States, too, with people like Andrew Hill. For a while I had an apartment in New York and a house in California.

I taught in the music department of a college in San Francisco for six years, and I also counseled the music students about their careers, while I pursued my other love as a performing musician. I saw a deficit in the industry, a lack of people who could actually help further a young career. And I just saw a niche for myself. So I began consulting with artists about developing a press package, making demo tapes, touring, finding funding. I mean, the whole nine yards. Since that time, my consulting has mushroomed into working with organizations, long-range planning, board development, and things along those lines. I work as a consultant for the National Jazz Service Organization in Washington, D.C. I hope the NJSO will be addressing a lot of the deficits that still plague jazz artists, such as health benefits, retirement, touring, relations with record companies, and those kinds of issues.

Jazz was originally backseat music. You know, it was black folk stuff. It was even called jack-ass music, actually spelled J-A-S-S. But now that jazz has been adopted by other cultures and now that second-class music is made by all these first-class citizens, it has gravitated from the small clubs into the concert halls. And now that jazz is on the stage, they allow black artists to perform in the concert halls, so they can speak the truth about its origin.

Jazz is an infusion of the African Americans: the African coming to this country and utilizing the European, Western music philosophy, adapting it, and developing what we know as jazz. It has influenced just about every element of music on this planet. But there is still the question of who's going to control it. Who's going to make the money? The record companies? Who owns the record companies? Who owns the distribution?

It's interesting, but we are celebrated all over Europe. They love black people in Europe. They like originality. They would rather hear it from the source. They don't want a copy, a clone—they want the source. They pride themselves on embracing the American jazz artist. They treat us like Leonard Slatkin was treated at the symphony.

Congress has declared jazz a national treasure. But a lot of the cultural organizations that are the first to take advantage of that status are Eurocentrically controlled. So now it is up to the artists. Even though Louis Armstrong is dead, and Duke Ellington is dead, we must continue to keep the flame alive. It's about preservation now. Jazz is Made in America. Check that out now. Made in America, an American industry. Jazz and blues are Made in America.

Look at things for what they are. Do you hear me? Respect the source. Respect yourself. Love yourself. Stretch your mind, not your hair. You know what I'm saying? Love your hair. Love your skin tone. I mean, the Supreme Being don't make no mistakes.

Kathryn E. Nelson

Educator; Program Director, Danforth Foundation

Great things get done when people don't recognize their limits, when they recognize their goals and head for them lickety-split, without looking back. And when they get there they say, "Gee, wonder how I got here." That's the way you discover what you can do. Any fool can be successful if they have enough backing and enough support.

I went to high school at Booker Washington, in Memphis. There were so many kids in those classes, I marvel when I think about what those teachers tried to do at that school. In the first place the method of managing kids' behavior was to put the fear of God into them. But on the other hand, there were caring people who worked with you. Mrs. Ingram looked at me one day and said, "You know, you're going places one of these days." And when I graduated I got three scholarships. I got one to Talladega, but I couldn't afford the train fare to Talladega. I got one to Henderson Business College, but I could only type thirty-five words a minute after all those typing lessons. And then there was a seventy-five-dollar scholarship to LeMoyne-Owen College in Memphis. Now, tuition was one hundred dollars for the year at LeMoyne-Owen, so I had to hock my watch.

I asked my mama one day, "Why is it we have to sit in the back of the bus? What did we do? What is the matter with us?" And my mama turned to me, and she said, "Baby, there are some people in this world who don't feel like they are worth anything unless they are looking down on somebody. And we have to feel sorry for them. If they knew what a wonderful person you were, they would be dying to sit next to you." Now, I knew I wasn't a wonderful person because I got in trouble too much. But I also knew what Mama thought of me, and that I dare not be anything else, because that is what she saw when she looked at me. I see people in the grocery store calling their children some of the worst names and things. Now what do those children get reflected out of their parents' eyes? Every child that is born has wonderful stuff inside of them. It's like a flame. You have to fan it and poof it. Our only hope is making wonderful things happen with our children; otherwise, we have no future.

Big Mama, my great-grandmother, was my inspiration. When I was a little girl, she said to me, "It ain't going to be easy for you. Let me tell you what you do. When the door cracks you put your toe in, and then you put your knee in, and your hip in, and the next thing they know, you'll be sitting in there with them making decisions."

I have worked with Navajo Indians, with children and families in Haiti, with children and families in Memphis, with children and families here. Most recently I was at the Danforth Foundation, working with children and families across the country. One of my programs was Leadership St. Louis, and then it became the Leadership Center. I worked with Confluence St. Louis, and I worked with the World of Difference.

I helped the Confluence Task Force that wrote the *Report on Racial Polarization in St. Louis.* You know, there was a time when people didn't want to deal with race in this town. They acted like it didn't exist. But we made it part of the agenda. If we make a bridge over folks, the way they did in the past, we lose some of our better minds, some of our better-educated people. We've had a hemorrhage here, in St. Louis. Folks go to universities. Do they come back here? They go elsewhere. Bright kids, sharp kids, well-educated kids, they have opportunities elsewhere.

When I was growing up there was a drunk guy in our neighborhood, and we called him Mr. Baby Boo. And one day Mr. Baby Boo was drunk and carrying on, and we were laughing at him, and Big Mama stopped us cold, and she said, "You respect other people not because of who they are, but because of who you are." The whole task of being somebody worth being is in our own hands. It's not in the hands of the white folks. It's not in the hands of the folks who pay a small salary. It's not in the hands of the folks who discourage us. It's in our hands. And that is what I want kids to know, that they can make a difference in their own lives. Life is out there for the taking.